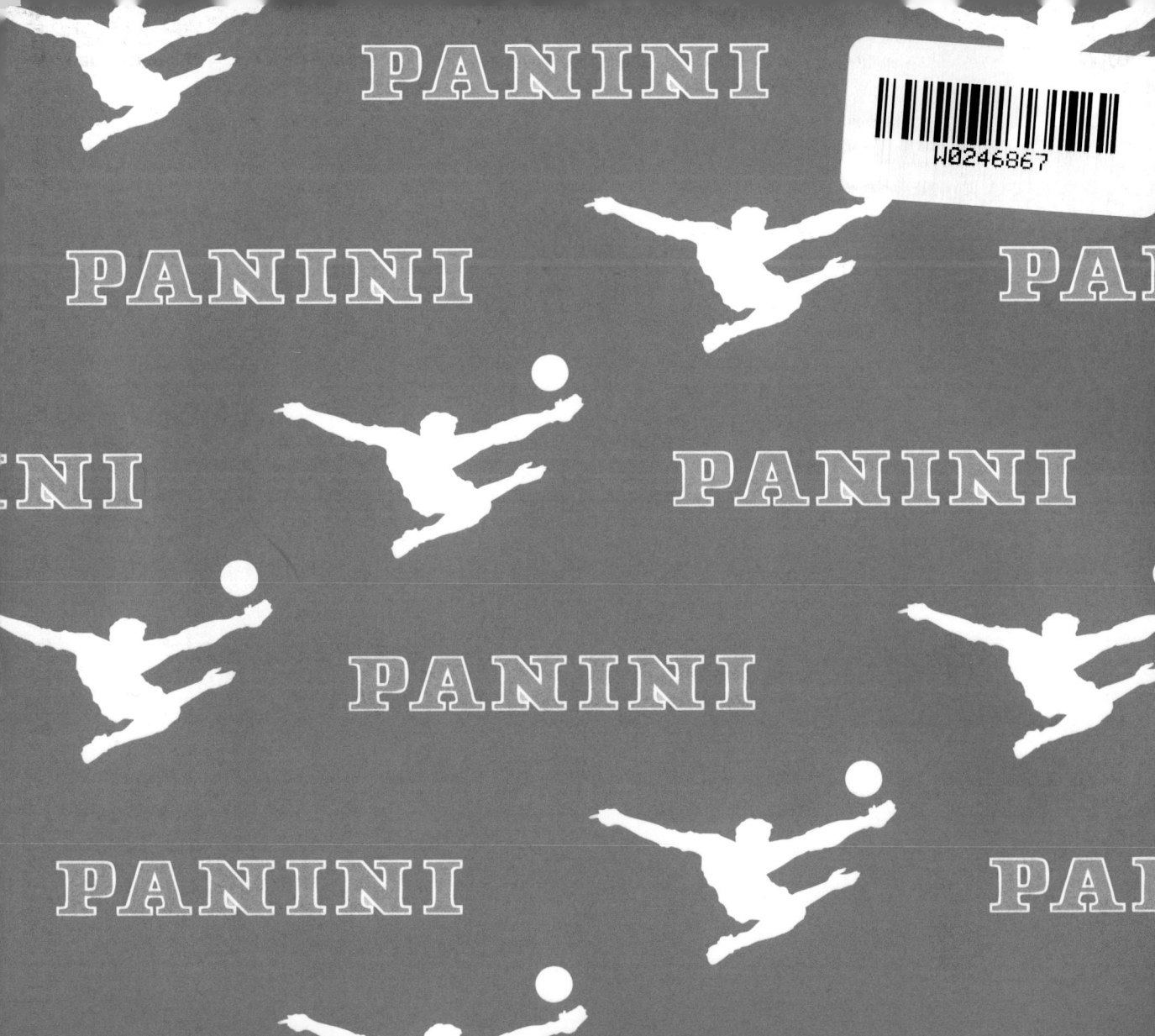

PANINI LEGENDS

The checklists for the main Panini Legends profiles featured in this book contain a minimum of domestic leagues, World Cups and international continental tournament Panini album appearances (such as the Euros and Copa América) for playing careers up to May 2024. Examples of other stickers are referenced where space allows. Some numbers may differ depending on an album's version if there have been multiple releases – but we generally have opted for the standard album issue number. This book only covers appearances in Panini sticker form.

BLOOMSBURY SPORT

Bloomsbury Publishing Plc
50 Bedford Square, London, WC1B 3DP, UK
29 Earlsfort Terrace, Dublin 2, Ireland

First published in Great Britain 2024

A catalogue record for this book is available from the British Library

Library of Congress Cataloguing-in-Publication data has been applied for

ISBN: HB: 978-1-3994-1233-9; eBook: 978-1-3994-1232-2

2 4 6 8 10 9 7 5 3 1

Typeset by D.R. ink

Printed and bound in China by C&C Offset Printing Co

MIX
Paper | Supporting responsible forestry
FSC® C008047
www.fsc.org

To find out more about our authors and books visit www.bloomsbury.com and sign up for our newsletters

www.paninigroup.com

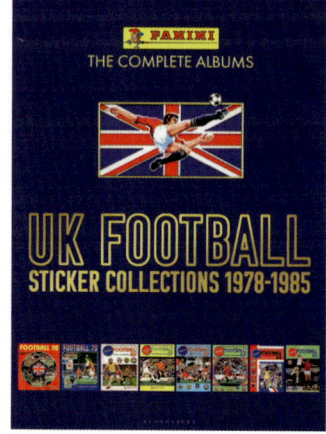
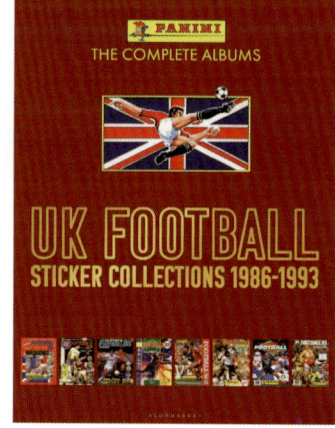
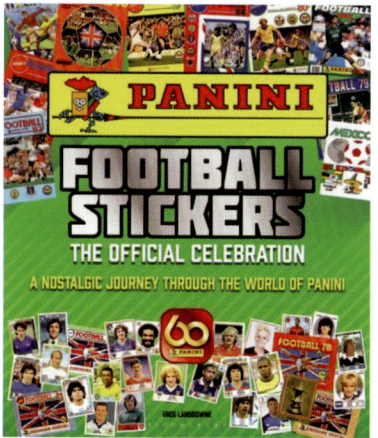

Also available from Bloomsbury

PANINI LEGENDS

A Celebration of the World's Greatest Football Stickers

Greg Lansdowne

BLOOMSBURY SPORT

LONDON · OXFORD · NEW YORK · NEW DELHI · SYDNEY

CONTENTS

INTRODUCTION

Since its humble beginnings with the *Calciatori* album of 1961–62, Panini have celebrated many thousands of professional footballers in card and sticker form, and it is just over 80 of those who are recognised in *Panini Legends*.

There are few better ways to reflect upon a footballer's career than through their Panini sticker history and remembering their transfer movement, the often garish kits they donned and changing hairstyles. For some readers it will also evoke memories of specific Panini sticker designs, and of desperately needing – and sometimes never getting – certain images.

When putting this book together, we felt it was important to reflect the extensive Panini sticker content that now spans more than six decades and countless releases all around the world. While lots of the pictures depicting the biggest names will be familiar to many, of course, those greats appear in Panini albums that only a comparative few have ever clapped their eyes upon. It is fascinating, too, to look back on the players who starred in competitions, but didn't have stickers to commemorate those performances, and those who were part of collections for tournaments in which they never participated.

Then there are the players who would need a book to themselves to showcase all their Panini stickers. Dino Zoff's first *Calciatori* appearance came in 1963–64 and the Italian goalkeeper was still going strong when he lifted the World Cup in 1982. Italy has by far the longest run of domestic league albums, so it is appropriate that many of those with the longest consecutive runs of sticker appearances are

Italians: Gianluigi Buffon, Paolo Maldini and Francesco Totti lead the way and all feature in this book.

As Panini acquired Colecciones ESTE in the 2000s, there is also a 50-year back catalogue of stickers to draw upon for Spanish football. Meanwhile, Panini's unbroken runs of domestic football albums in Belgium and France go back as far as 1972–73 and 1975–76 respectively. Panini's pool of players has also grown hugely year by year and decade upon decade thanks to new countries and new leagues being given the sticker album treatment. From the men's and women's World Cups and Euros to the African Cup of Nations, Copa América and beyond, the global presence expands all the time.

Then there are those individuals whose careers took in numerous countries, and the clubs within them. The eye-catching collages of their shirts of varying hues and designs contrast starkly with the one-club players. Trevor Francis, Ray Wilkins and Jürgen Klinsmann rank among the most-travelled entrants in *Panini Legends*.

Historical sections in albums have traditionally helped to educate collectors about a time when Panini didn't exist, certainly not outside its Italian homeland, and as a result heroes of long ago, such as Alfredo Di Stéfano, Ferenc Puskás and Sir Stanley Matthews, have all featured on Panini stickers, just not frequently enough to merit selection for *Panini Legends*. However, players from every men's World Cup-winning team since the first Panini collection for Mexico 70 make the cut, along with stars of all four women's World Cups since the first release of Germany 2011.

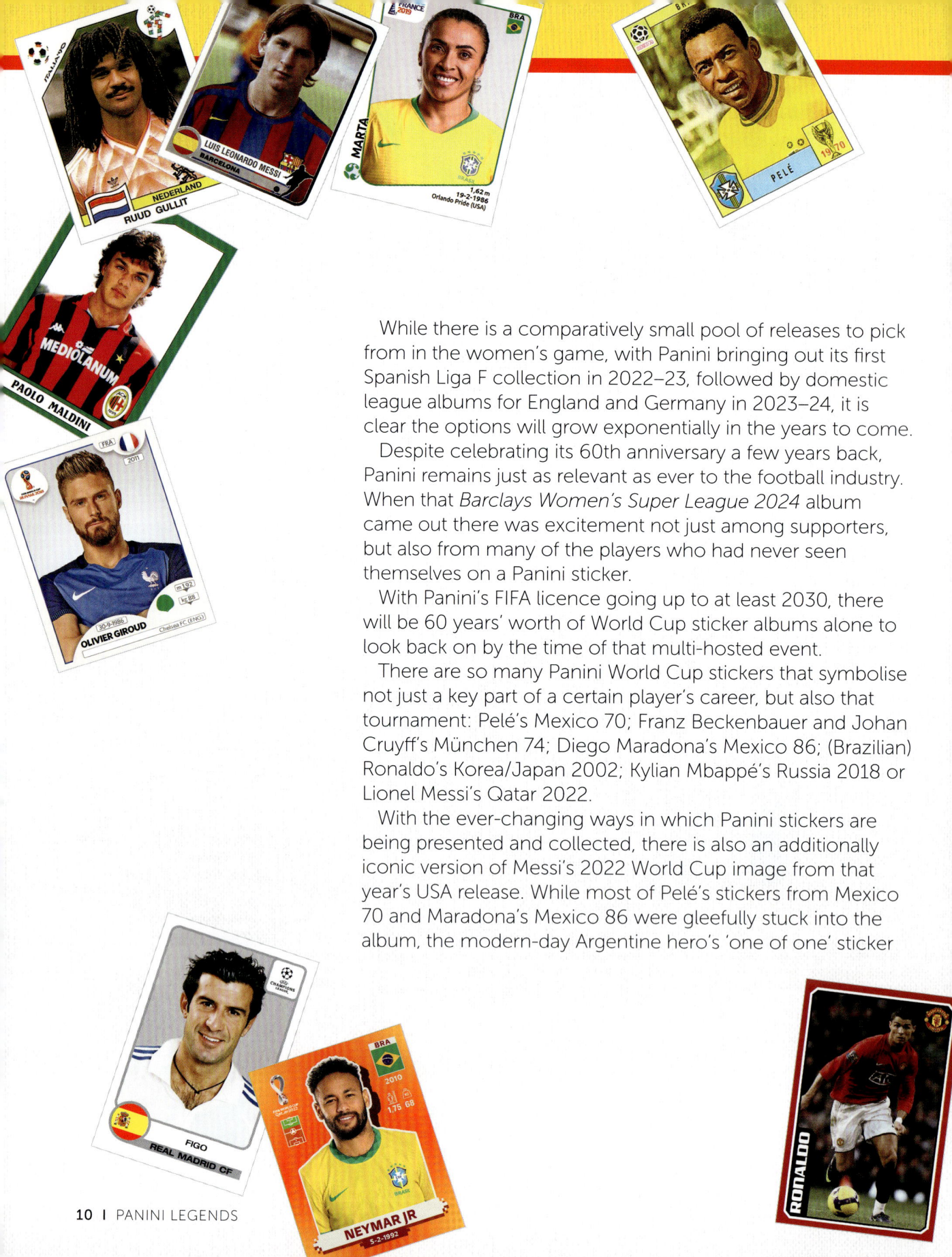

While there is a comparatively small pool of releases to pick from in the women's game, with Panini bringing out its first Spanish Liga F collection in 2022–23, followed by domestic league albums for England and Germany in 2023–24, it is clear the options will grow exponentially in the years to come.

Despite celebrating its 60th anniversary a few years back, Panini remains just as relevant as ever to the football industry. When that *Barclays Women's Super League 2024* album came out there was excitement not just among supporters, but also from many of the players who had never seen themselves on a Panini sticker.

With Panini's FIFA licence going up to at least 2030, there will be 60 years' worth of World Cup sticker albums alone to look back on by the time of that multi-hosted event.

There are so many Panini World Cup stickers that symbolise not just a key part of a certain player's career, but also that tournament: Pelé's Mexico 70; Franz Beckenbauer and Johan Cruyff's München 74; Diego Maradona's Mexico 86; (Brazilian) Ronaldo's Korea/Japan 2002; Kylian Mbappé's Russia 2018 or Lionel Messi's Qatar 2022.

With the ever-changing ways in which Panini stickers are being presented and collected, there is also an additionally iconic version of Messi's 2022 World Cup image from that year's USA release. While most of Pelé's stickers from Mexico 70 and Maradona's Mexico 86 were gleefully stuck into the album, the modern-day Argentine hero's 'one of one' sticker

will never have its backing removed, and was instead sold on by the original holder for an auction sale price of US $140,000 (£115,000).

There are many ways to appreciate Panini stickers, but all are tied up with the way football unites the world. Collectors and investors alike will enjoy this book, it will rekindle happy days of filling in albums while also providing a host of ideas to those keen on picking up rookie and/or rare stickers to boost their coffers. The stories of many football greats haven't begun yet, but when they do you can be sure Panini will be at the forefront of charting their progress. For now, we give you the stars of the moment and yesteryear in all their rectangular-shaped glory.

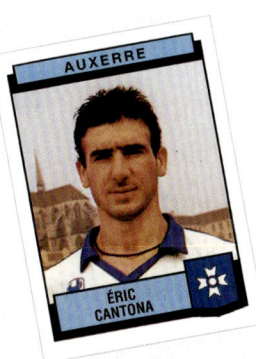

HOW TO COLLECT

Collecting Panini stickers has evolved in recent years and writing about it even five years ago would have been quite different. What has long been familiar to those who participate in the hobby in North America was alien to a large proportion of football card and sticker collectors in Europe, right up until the pandemic of 2020. For a start, although it was a phenomenon that had been creeping in for a while, Panini stickers were still generally being stuck in an album rather than kept loose.

Spring forward a few years and Panini have reacted to this trend by creating parallel stickers of increasing rarity and therefore increasing value. That means the inveterate sticker fan gets their 'base' version to put in an album, while the investors pursue the shorter print run varieties. The first Panini World Cup album to introduce this phenomenon was Qatar 2022, with the USA version of the collection upping the stakes by producing 'one of one' stickers for each player. The unique Son Heung-min sticker was stuck into an album, as intended, while Lionel Messi's US $140,000 (£115,000) sticker, once opened and located, was subsequently sold at auction.

That sum, while impressive, comes nowhere near to the most expensive Panini sticker to date, however. Examples of Cristiano Ronaldo's and Messi's first-ever Panini stickers (at Sporting Lisbon and Barcelona respectively) have both gone considerably higher, although way out in front is Diego Maradona's *Calciatori 1979–80*. There are many factors in truly hitting paydirt on a Panini sticker (or, indeed, any football card or sticker). It has to be rare, of one of the game's all-time greats, and preferably the first, or at least an early, release that is in top condition. Maradona's sticker ticked all those boxes, including being accorded a 'Gem Mint 10' quality rating from a grading company (PSA in this case). As multiple versions of the sticker have since come to light, the $555,960 price accrued at the early April 2021 Goldin auction may well turn out to be the high water-mark for that particular image, though.

Generally speaking, Messi, Cristiano Ronaldo, Pelé and Maradona are the kings of the football collectables at this juncture, but Pelé also has a host of options before you get to his first Panini cards in the *Calciatori* and *Campioni dello Sport* albums of the 1960s. Among the chasing pack are a couple of current-day players who still have plenty more to add to their legends: Kylian Mbappé and Erling Haaland.

The curious case of Haaland's rookie sticker from the Austrian *Fussball 19–20* is relayed in his profile later in this book, while Mbappé's first appearance, in *Foot 2016–17*, also fetches remarkably huge sums for a recent sticker printed in such huge quantities. Few would have had the foresight at the time to hunt out Mbappé's first-ever sticker, produced during his final season at Monaco, and, more importantly, not stick it in the album.

By contrast, Haaland's first Panini appearance, for Red Bull Salzburg, was the perfect storm for a new age of collectors. The Norwegian's goalscoring feats were so impressive during the first half of the season that he earned a winter move to Borussia Dortmund, for whom his early form was even more spectacular. Just a couple of months into his time in Germany, people around the world were heading into a covid-enforced lockdown. Many sports enthusiasts in North America had a lot of extra time to assess their collecting habits, including looking into the value of the soccer market.

For decades, one of the key interests among US sports collectors has been the rookie concept, whereby a player's first or first-season cards (and they generally are cards rather than stickers) are particularly sought after. Should that player's career begin to rise, those early releases become increasingly popular, ideally with a high grade (a condition rating out of 10) attached to it. While the first collectables of some of the all-time greats were already starting to rise by then, an opportunity to pick up Haaland's first release on the cheap was too good to resist. If he turned out to be a one-season

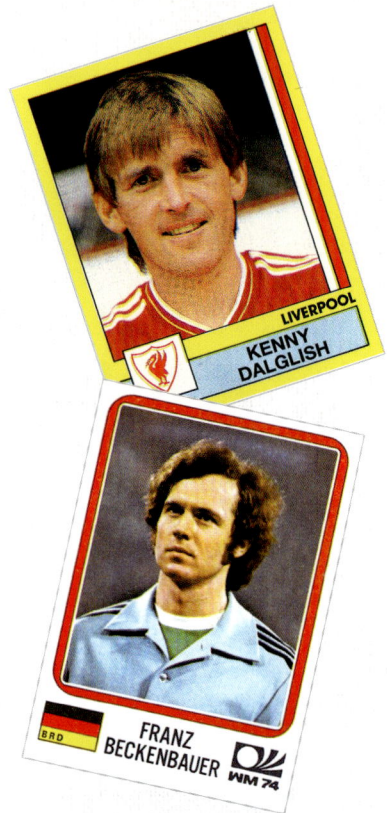

wonder there was little lost, but things have panned out pretty well so far for both player and holders of his rookie sticker.

Women's football has been hugely popular in the USA for decades, so that country has also helped to swell the interest in women's football collectables. As with the men's World Cup for Mexico 70, the first women's World Cup sticker album, for the 2011 tournament, will always be among the most iconic collections. That Germany 2011 album is even more significant than its male counterpart because there had never been a standalone release for the women's game. As a result, every player in the album was either a rookie sticker or, at the very least, one of their earliest collectables.

Prices for some of the greats of women's football, such as Marta, Alex Morgan and Megan Rapinoe, are steadily rising in a sector that should experience sizeable growth in the years ahead. As an anomaly for recent sticker albums, there are also approximately another 30 stickers that accrue higher than normal sums from that album, because they appear to have been printed in shorter numbers.

In general, the stickers for that album were all printed in smaller quantities than would generally be the case for a major tournament and were only available in host country Germany, because they were seen as a test run for the viability of women's football stickers. A reprint was required just a few weeks after the initial release date, so the demand was clear. Every women's World Cup has had a Panini sticker album since and then, from 2017, came the album for the Euro competition, the Spanish Liga F from 2022–23, and then the English and German domestic leagues from 2023–24. With Barclays Women's Super League stickers flying off the shelves, and collectors now firmly on top of their rookie game, it is unlikely any of the Panini newcomers in that album will ever be in short supply.

One of the biggest changes in the football sticker collecting landscape in recent times has been the growth of the community. While people have been collecting on social media and dedicated websites such as LastSticker and SwapStick for many years, as well as purchasing their needs via online auction sites and Panini's missing stickers service, the scope for face-to-face contact with fellow collectors tended to disappear once the school playground was left behind. Prior to the pandemic there were no large-scale card shows in the UK or Europe and there was a certain sense of FOMO among UK/European collectors: North America seemed to have a surfeit of card shows, many of which have been running for decades. No such lack of opportunity for collectors to meet up exists now, though, as thousands of enthusiasts flock to meets throughout the UK and in continental Europe and many spent their lockdown wisely, building up social media profiles and forging relationships with peers.

Other traits adopted from across the pond have been the emergence of the first UK grading companies and dedicated sports card stores. It may seem small fry compared to what has existed in the USA since the 1980s, but these are early days in this new phase of collecting in other regions.

During the '80s in the UK a football collectables enthusiast was largely restricted to a Panini sticker album covering the English and Scottish leagues, as well as a World Cup or Euro collection in alternate years. It seems like slim pickings, and it was, but most collectors of that era still view it as a golden age.

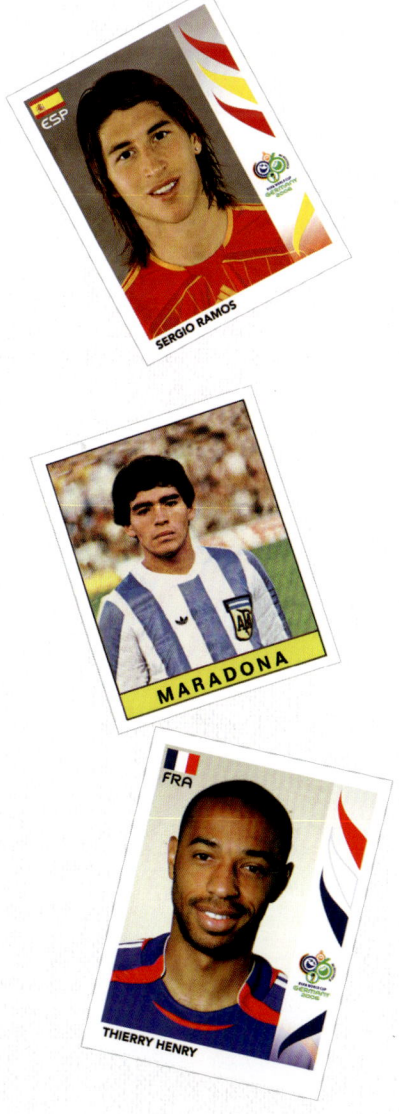

However, just taking the English game as an example, there are now Premier League and BWSL sticker albums, plus a series of card releases over the course of the season. Add in various products for international tournaments and the easier access to order collectables from overseas and it can be a 365-days-a-year hobby.

There remains a hardy group of sticker addicts intent on filling every space in their album, eagerly swapping to completion via online and in-person means. A growing bunch are keener on building up personal collections of favourite players, in unstuck form, as well as researching other stickers that can be graded, encased in a slab and moved on at a profit. Big-money examples of many of the stickers in this book have been sold on auction sites and major auction houses, with US companies such as Goldin and PWCC upping their game ahead of the 2026 World Cup in their homeland.

The presence of football stickers and cards in supermarkets and other outlets is commonplace and access to advice and information for collectors young and old has never been so readily available. There has rarely been a better time to be a Panini sticker collector.

DIEGO MARADONA

Diego Armando
MARADONA
F.C. BARCELONA

Panini Futbol 83

F.C. BARCELONA

Diego Armando
MARADONA

Panini Futbol 84

A sensational and sometimes controversial player, Diego Maradona earned his place in the football pantheon through his wonderful dribbling, goalscoring and set-piece skills. Such was his status, he has so far made more than 50 Panini album appearances. He was a star by the time he joined Boca Juniors in 1981, immediately helping them win the league in his native Argentina. After one season, he ventured to Europe with Barcelona, where he appeared in the La Liga albums. However, it was at his next club, Napoli, where his legend grew.

The Lanús-born genius inspired the club to their first Scudetto in 1987, repeating the feat in 1990 and scoring in the two-legged 1989 UEFA Cup final triumph over VFB Stuttgart. During this period he made seven consecutive Panini *Calciatori* appearances. To honour his 2020 death, Napoli renamed their ground Stadio Diego Armando Maradona. His club playing career ended back in Argentina with Newell's Old Boys and Boca Juniors for a second time.

Maradona was given the nickname *El Pibe de Oro* — 'The Golden Boy' — a nickname that carried throughout his football career.

ARGENTINA

DIEGO ARMANDO MARADONA

Mexico 86

Diego Maradona led Argentina to victory in the Mexico 86 World Cup. He scored 34 goals in 91 games for *La Albiceleste*.

MARADONA

Calciatori 1979-80

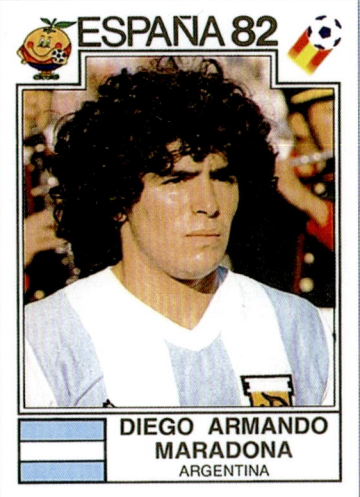

ESPAÑA 82

DIEGO ARMANDO
MARADONA

ARGENTINA

España 82

ITALIA '90

ARGENTINA

DIEGO ARMANDO MARADONA

Italia '90

USA 94

ARGENTINA

DIEGO ARMANDO
MARADONA

USA '94

Maradona appeared in Panini collections representing Boca Juniors, Barcelona, Napoli, Sevilla and Argentina.

Liga 82–83 (Colecciones ESTE)

Liga 83–84 (Colecciones ESTE)

Maradona played in four consecutive World Cup finals tournaments between 1982 and 1994. His performances in the 1986 tournament are legendary: taking the lead role in Argentina's triumph, winning the Golden Ball for best player and scoring two of the greatest ever World Cup goals against England and Belgium.

In January 2021, his rookie Panini sticker, which appeared in the *Calciatori 1979–80* album, was sold at auction for £470,000, while his rookie World Cup sticker from Panini's *España 82* is also highly sought after.

Calciatori 1984–85

Calciatori 1985–86

DIEGO ARMANDO MARADONA

napoli

NAPOLI

DIEGO ARMANDO MARADONA

Calciatori 1986–87

Napoli

DIEGO ARMANDO MARADONA (1)

Calciatori 1987–88

NAPOLI

DIEGO ARMANDO MARADONA

Calciatori 1988–89

NAPOLI

DIEGO ARMANDO MARADONA

Calciatori 1990–91

SEVILLA C.F.

Diego Armando MARADONA

Panini Futbol 93–94

Playing Career

Argentinos Juniors (1976–1981); Boca Juniors (1981–1982); Barcelona (1982–1984); Napoli (1984–1991); Sevilla (1992–1993); Newell's Old Boys (1993–1994); Boca Juniors (1995–1997) and Argentina (1977–1994)

Panini Album Rookie Appearances

First club album appearance: Calciatori 1979–80 (Italy) (312); First World Cup album appearance: *España 82* (176)

Selected Panini Appearances

Calciatori 1979–80 (Italy) (312); *Sport Superstars Euro Football 82* (230); *España 82* (176); *Liga 82–83* (Colecciones ESTE) (Spain) (F6); *Panini Futbol 83* (Spain) (50, 405); *Football 83* (Switzerland) (433); *Liga 83–84* (Colecciones ESTE) (Spain) (18); *Panini Futbol 84* (Spain) (54); *Calciatori 1984–85* (Italy) (203); *Football 85* (UK) (249); *Calciatori 1985–86* (Italy) (176)); *Mexico 86* (84); *Calciatori 1986–87* (Italy) (209); *Football 87* (UK) (287, 291); *Fussball 87* (Germany) (390); *Calciatori 1987–88* (Italy) (180); *Football 88* (UK) (283, 383); *Calciatori 1988–89* (Italy) (232); *Football Egypt 1988–89* (343); *Calciatori 1989–90* (Italy) (260); *Italia '90* (128); *Calciatori 1990–91* (Italy) (241); *Liga 92–93* (Colecciones ESTE) (Spain) (326); *Panini Futbol 93–94* (Spain) (255); *USA '94* (257); *Panini Supergol 2000* (Israel) (398); *Xentenario Boca 1905–2005* (Argentina) (31; 168–185); *Russia 2018* (676); *FIFA 365 2019* (441); *Calciatori 2021* (Top Team Panini 60 – X18); *Panini Fútbol Argentino 2021* (Maradona special feature – 4–8); *CONMEBOL Copa América 2021* (LE1–4)

KENNY DALGLISH

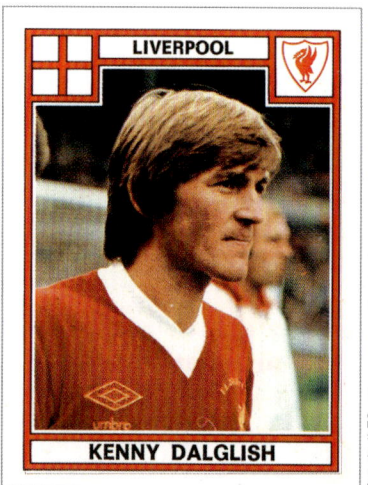

Football 78

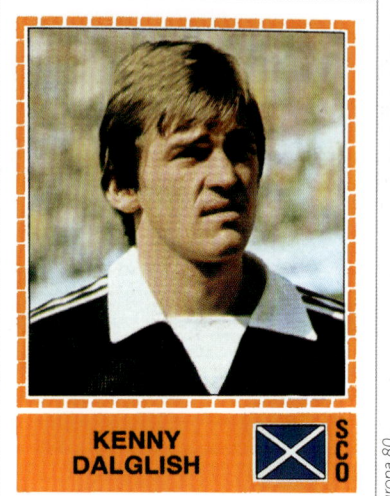

Europa 80

'King Kenny' was the darling of Celtic and Liverpool fans, providing goals and craft during periods of great success for both clubs.

The Scot's first sticker appearance was as a Celtic player in Panini's debut album release in the UK – *Euro Football* in 1977 – but that summer, with four Scottish league titles and four Scottish Cups to his name, Dalglish moved to Merseyside to replace Kevin Keegan at Liverpool. That meant the striker was able to claim a place in the first Panini UK domestic sticker album, his image in *Football 78* taken just ahead of his Charity Shield debut appearance against Manchester United at Wembley.

As a player, Dalglish won six Division One titles, an FA Cup, four League Cups and three European Cups. The last of those league successes and solitary FA Cup were won in his first campaign as player-manager in 1985-86. That dual success was commemorated in a special *Liverpool at the double* section of *Football 87*, in which Dalglish featured prominently. Dalglish added two more Division One titles and an FA Cup between 1988 and 1990 – by which time his playing days were all but over.

After stepping down in 1991, Dalglish returned to the Anfield hot seat 20 years later, adding yet another League Cup to his trophy haul. In between, he managed Blackburn to the Premier League crown and Celtic to the League Cup.

Dalglish's international career lasted from 1971 to 1986, taking in four Panini World Cup sticker album appearances for Scotland, the first of those for *München 74* under the abbreviated first name of 'Ken'.

Münchén 74

KEN DALGLISH
SCO
WM 74

Kenny Dalglish played 102 times for Scotland and starred in four Panini World Cup albums.

Playing Career
Celtic (1969–77); Liverpool (1977–1990) and Scotland (1971–1986)

Panini Album Rookie Appearances
First club album appearance: Euro Football (1976–77) (255)
First World Cup album appearance: *München 74* (209)

Selected Panini Appearances
München 74 (209); *Euro Football (1976–77)* (255); *Football 78 (UK)* (208); *Euro Football 78* (230 A); *Argentina 78* (326); *Football 79 (UK)* (208); *Euro Football 79* (8, 14, 15, 19, 20–23, 87); *Football 80 (UK)* (201); *Calciatori 1979–80 (Italy)* (311); *Europa 80* (246); *Football 81 (UK)* (178); *Football 82 (UK)* (136); *Sport Superstars Euro Football 82 (UK)* (145); *España 82* (413); *Football 83* (132); *Football 84 (UK)* (2, 131, 380); *Football 85 (UK)* (132); *Football 86 (UK)* (136); *Mexico 86* (341); *Football 87 (UK)* (1, 119, 270–272); *Football 88 (UK)* (108); *Football 89 (UK)* (104); *Football 90 (UK)* (126); *The All-Time Greats 1920–1990 (UK)* (58); *Football 1991 (UK)* (147 – as manager); *Celtic FC 1999–2000* (114, 142–144, 155–156)

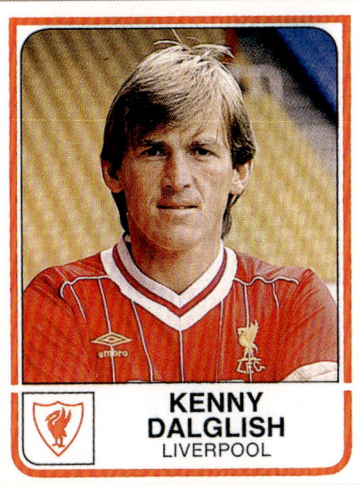

KENNY DALGLISH
LIVERPOOL

Football 84

ARGENTINA 78

KENNY DALGLISH

SCO

Argentina 78

SCOTLAND

KENNY DALGLISH

Mexico 86

GARY LINEKER

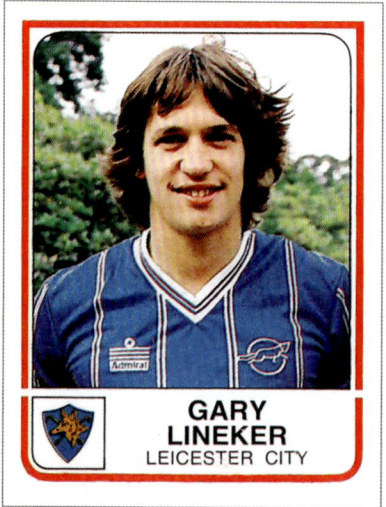

Football 84

Football 85

Born in Leicester, Gary Lineker rose to prominence playing for his hometown club. As the Foxes spent some of the first half of the 1980s in Division Two, it wasn't until *Football 84* that Lineker was afforded his first individual Panini sticker, but he is instantly recognisable, despite looking somewhat less groomed than he does today.

Two years later he was in the Everton section of *Football 86*, followed by his first England sticker a few months later for *Mexico 86*. That World Cup alerted fans around the world to his deadliness in front of goal and he slotted home six times to finish as the tournament's leading scorer. Barcelona, managed by fellow Englishman Terry Venables, snapped him up later in the summer, resulting in Lineker featuring in the *Brits Abroad* section of *Football 87*, and he also made first appearances in the Panini and Colecciones ESTE Spanish league albums (*Futbol 87* and *Liga 86/87*).

Lineker went on to win the Copa del Rey and European Cup Winners' Cup during his three years in Spain, before he returned to England to take his place in the Tottenham pages of *Football 90*. The highlight of three prolific years at White Hart Lane was the 1991 FA Cup victory and he ended his playing days in Japan with Nagoya Grampus Eight. His England career finished at Euro 92, having previously added another Panini World Cup sticker in *Italia '90* and scoring four of his 48 international goals in that tournament.

Gary Lineker made his first Panini sticker appearance. in *Football 84*

ENGLAND

GARY LINEKER

Mexico 86

ENGLAND

GARY LINEKER

Italia '90

EVERTON

GARY
LINEKER

Football 86

TOTTENHAM HOTSPUR

GARY LINEKER

Football 90

LINEKER
FUTBOL CLUB BARCELONA

Liga 88–89 (Colecciones ESTE)

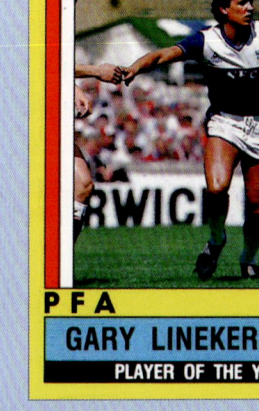

P F A
GARY LINEKER
PLAYER OF THE YEAR

Football 87

Playing Career
Leicester City (1978–1985); Everton (1985–1986); Barcelona (1986–1989); Tottenham Hotspur (1989–1992); Nagoya Grampus Eight (1992–1994) and England (1984–1992)

Panini Album Rookie Appearances
First club album appearance: *Football 84* (UK) (115) First World Cup album appearance: *Mexico 86* (415)

Selected Panini Appearances
Football 84 (UK) (115); *Football 85* (UK) (116); *Football 86* (UK) (100); *Mexico 86* (415); *Panini Futbol 87* (Spain) (51); *Football 87* (UK) (2, 448); *Fussball 87* (Germany) (417); *Football 87* (France) (453); *Supersport* (UK) (1987) (70, 238); *Panini Futbol 88* (Spain) (57); *Football 88* (UK) (386, 447); *Calciatori 1987–88* (Italy) (556); *Euro 88* (177); *Panini Futbol 89* (Spain) (52); *Football 90* (UK) (288); *Italia '90* (399); *The All-Time Greats 1920–1990* (UK) (79); *Football 1991* (UK) (331, 527, 530, 531); *Soccer's Super Sevens* (UK) (1991–92) (139) *English Football 1992* (238); *Euro '92* (110); *One England* (2023) (212)

KEVIN KEEGAN

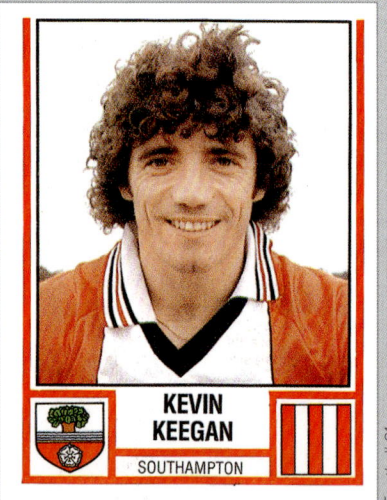

Football 81

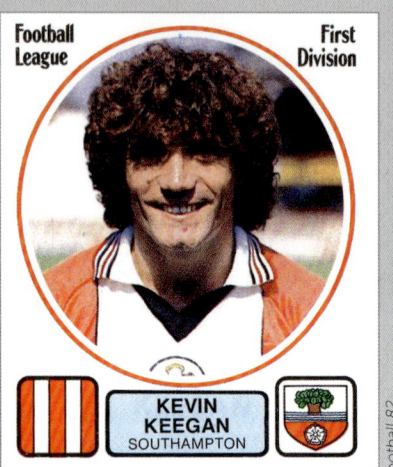

Football 82

England's outstanding player of the 1970s, Kevin Keegan inspired clubs to success almost everywhere he went, making more than 20 Panini appearances during his playing career. After his formative days with Scunthorpe United in Division Four, he was signed by Liverpool manager Bill Shankly in 1971 at the age of 20. It wasn't long before the effervescent forward established himself in attack, forming a partnership with John Toshack which would serve the club well for many years.

Keegan's early Panini appearances came in the Top Sellers albums before his first 'official' sticker featured in the Stars of Europe section in the Italian *Calciatori 1975–76* album, where he was pictured in an England shirt (he played for his national side between 1972 and 1982). In 1977, though, he was shown in a Liverpool jersey in the *Euro Football* album. This was during his last season at Anfield, which he left having won three league titles, one FA Cup, one European Cup and two UEFA Cups.

Keegan then opted to take his talents abroad – a path few Englishmen had chosen at that point – where his reputation reached even greater heights. During his three years with Hamburger SV, he helped them win the league title in 1979 and reach the European Cup Final in 1980. That period also saw Keegan win the Ballon d'Or, in 1978 and 1979. His time in West Germany coincided with Panini's first domestic releases in the country, and Keegan appeared in action shots in both *Fussball Bundesliga '79* and *Fussball 80*.

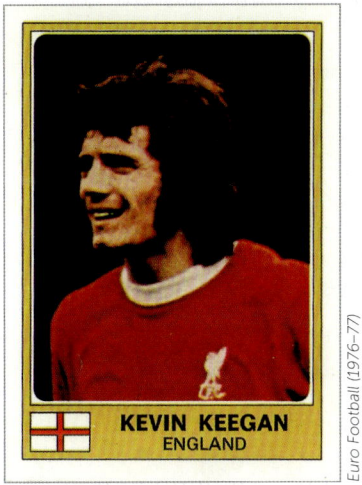

Euro Football (1976–77)

KEVIN KEEGAN
ENGLAND

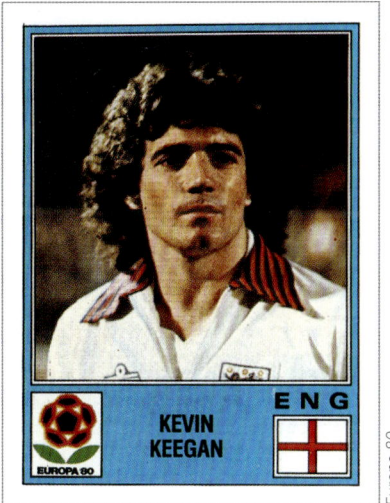

Europa 80

ENG

KEVIN
KEEGAN

Argentina 78

ENG

KEVIN
KEEGAN

España 82

ESPAÑA 82

KEVIN
KEEGAN
ENGLAND

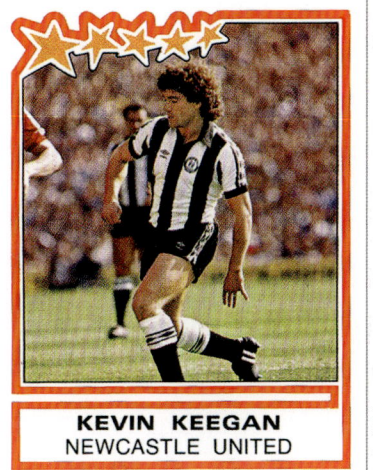

Football 84

KEVIN KEEGAN
NEWCASTLE UNITED

Playing Career
Scunthorpe United (1968–1971); Liverpool (1971–1977); Hamburger SV (1977–1980); Southampton (1980–1982); Newcastle United (1982–1984); Blacktown City (1985) and England (1972–1982)

Panini Album Rookie Appearances
First club album appearance: Football 73 (UK) (Top Sellers/Panini) (177)
First World Cup album appearance: Argentina 78 (360)

Selected Panini Appearances
Football 73 (UK) (Top Sellers/Panini) (177); Fotboll 73 (Sweden) (Williams Förlags/Panini) (233); Football 74 (UK) (Top Sellers/Panini) (171); Football 75 (UK) (Top Sellers/Panini) (162); Football 76 (UK) (Top Sellers/Panini) (177); Calciatori 1975–76 (Italy) (629); Football 77 (UK) (Top Sellers/Panini) (147); Euro Football (1976–77) (68); Argentina 78 (360); Fussball Bundesliga '79 (Germany) (191); Fussball 80 (Germany) (166); Calciatori 1979–80 (Italy) (306); Europa 80 (125); Football 81 (UK) (270); Football 82 (UK) (224); España 82 (250); Football 84 (UK) (390); Football 85 (UK) (391) The All–Time Greats 1920–1990 (UK) (54); One England (2023) (167)

Next it was back to England and he featured in Southampton colours in *Football 81* and *Football 82* before making Panini's Second Division All-Star Team in *Football 84* for Newcastle United, still sporting his trademark collar-length bubble perm. He helped the club win promotion in his final season before retirement, and the most celebrated period of his subsequent managerial career was also at Newcastle: during his first spell there in charge, his flamboyant side won the hearts of millions, although it ultimately missed out on major silverware.

DAVID BECKHAM

The Official PFA Collection '97

Champions League 1999/2000

The master of the set piece, David Beckham was a mainstay of a golden era for Manchester United besides representing England with distinction for well over a decade. He made in excess of 20 Panini sticker appearances across World Cup, Euro, domestic and Champions League albums. Beckham was one of several younger players to establish himself in the United side during the 1995–96 season. The Red Devils clinched the Premier League title on the final day and went on to complete the double as Beckham's corner was fired home in the FA Cup final against Liverpool by Eric Cantona. However, it was during the 1996–97 season that Beckham truly rose to prominence, a campaign in which he also made his first Panini appearance, in *The Official PFA Collection '97*. A spectacular goal on the opening day, struck from the halfway line against Wimbledon, was followed up the following month by the first of his 115 England caps.

Beckham's involvement in United's historic treble of the Premier League, FA Cup and Champions League earned him second place in the 1999 Ballon d'Or and FIFA World Player of the Year. A first Panini England sticker then followed in Euro 2000, preceding three consecutive World Cup album appearances, the first of which was for the *Korea/Japan 2002* album. Although part of England's squad for France 98, he missed out on a sticker in the World Cup album.

A move to Real Madrid in 2003–04 made him a regular fixture in the Colecciones ESTE albums before he switched to the MLS with LA Galaxy in 2007. Loan spells with AC Milan and a last hurrah at Paris Saint-Germain then spread his Panini portfolio still further, before retirement in May 2013.

MANCHESTER UNITED FC

DAVID
BECKHAM

Champions League 2000/2001

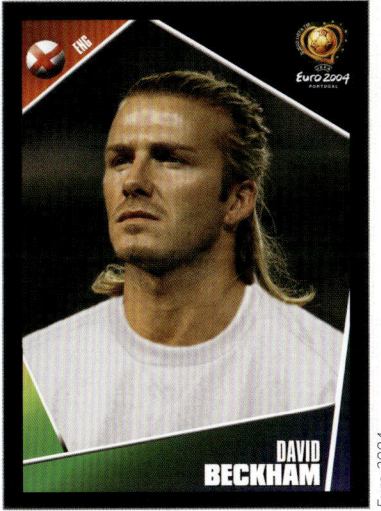

DAVID
BECKHAM

Euro 2004

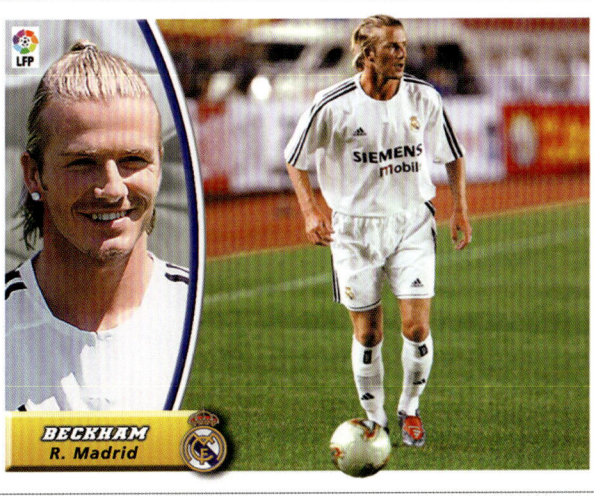

BECKHAM
R. Madrid

Liga 2003–2004 (Colecciones ESTE)

Playing Career

Manchester United (1992–2003); Preston North End (loan) (1995); Real Madrid (2003–2007); LA Galaxy (2007–2012); AC Milan (loan) (2009 and 2010); Paris Saint-Germain (2013) and England (1996–2009)

Panini Album
Rookie Appearances

First club album appearance: *The Official PFA Collection '97* (England) (22)
First World Cup album appearance: *Korea/Japan 2002* (430)

Selected Panini Appearances

The Official PFA Collection '97 (England) (22); *Superplayers 98* (England) (23, AA, BB, P3); *Champions League 1999/2000* (129); *Euro 2000* (85); *Champions League 2000/2001* (258); *Champions League 2001/2002* (179); *Korea/Japan 2002* (430); *Liga 2003–2004* (Colecciones ESTE) (Spain) (220, 221); *Panini Superliga de Estrellas 2003–2004* (Spain) 23, 215); *Euro 2004* (124); *Liga 2004–2005* (Colecciones ESTE) (Spain) (240); *Fussball 04–05* (Germany) (498); *Liga 2005–2006* (Colecciones ESTE) (Spain) (258); *Germany 2006* (103); *Liga 2006–2007* (Colecciones ESTE) (Spain) (320); *Calciatori 2008–09* (Italy) (A72); *Calciatori 2009–10* (Italy) (a51); *South Africa 2010* (190); *London 2012 Olympics* (257); *Foot 2012–13* (France) (M31); *Premier League 2022* (England) (336)

ENG   DAVID BECKHAM

South Africa 2010

MILAN

DAVID BECKHAM

Leytonstone (Gran Bretagna), 2-5-1975
CENTROCAMPISTA - m 1,83, kg 76.
Nazionale: Inghilterra (115 presenze, 17 reti)

Calciatori 2009–10

PARIS SAINT-GERMAIN

32   DAVID BECKHAM
Leytonstone (ENG)
1,83 75 |02|05|1975| M ENG

Foot 2012-13

PAUL GASCOIGNE

ENGLAND
PAUL GASCOIGNE

Italia '90

ENGLAND
PAUL GASCOIGNE

European Football Championship England '96.

Of all the rookie stickers in Panini UK football albums between *Football 78* and *Football '93*, there is one that has captured the imagination of collectors more than any other – that of Paul Gascoigne. He featured in *Football 87* having become a regular in the Newcastle United side the previous season, but after one more year wearing the black and white stripes, he opted to move to Tottenham Hotspur by the time of *Football 89*.

His England debut came early in that 1988–89 season and, although his place in the starting line-up was only confirmed a few weeks before the tournament began, it led to a sticker in the *Italia '90* album. His World Cup performances then secured him a place in the hearts of a nation and it seemed assured that he would stride the international stage for at least the next decade.

Gascoigne's 1990 World Cup Panini sticker is a must-have among fans of the midfielder, evoking memories of a fledgling talent soon to have the world at his feet. However, while semi-final defeat to West Germany meant there was to be no fairytale ending, a star had been born. The following domestic campaign saw the Geordie dominate Tottenham's march to the FA Cup final, capped by a stunning free-kick in the semi-final win over double-chasing Arsenal. An injury sustained when he tackled Nottingham Forest's Gary Charles in the final ruled him out of the entire 1991–92 season, though he still made Panini's English *Football 1992* album. However, as soon as he got his boots back on he was on his way to Lazio.

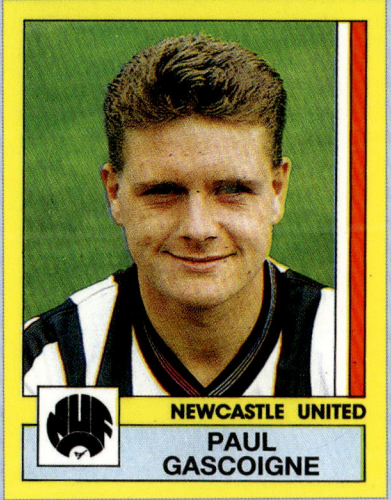
Football 87

PAUL GASCOIGNE
NEWCASTLE UNITED

TOTTENHAM HOTSPUR

PAUL GASCOIGNE

Football 89

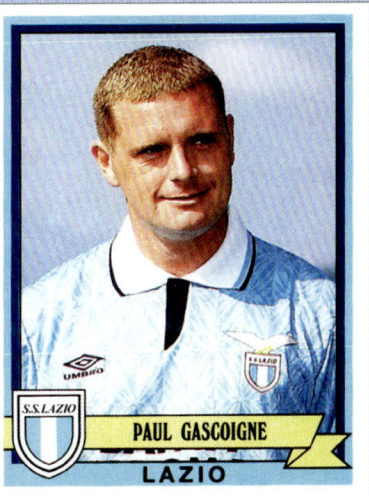
PAUL GASCOIGNE
LAZIO

Calciatori 1992–93

PAUL GASCOIGNE
LAZIO

Calciatori 1993–94

Playing Career

Newcastle United (1985–1988); Tottenham Hotspur (1988–1992); Lazio (1992–1995); Rangers (1995–1998); Middlesbrough (1998–2000); Everton (2000–2002); Burnley (2002); Gansu Tianma (2003); Boston United (2004) and England (1988–1998)

Panini Album Rookie Appearances

First club album appearance: Football 87 (UK) (190)
First World Cup album appearance: Italia '90 (394)

Selected Panini Appearances

Football 87 (UK) (190); Football 88 (UK) (159); Football 89 (UK) (2, 268); Football 90 (UK) (283); Italia '90 (394); The All-Time Greats 1920–1990 (UK) (80); Football 1991 (UK) (324, 524, 527); Soccer's Super Sevens (UK) (1991–92) (138); English Football 1992 (236); Euro '92 (103); Calciatori 1992–93 (Italy) (17, 204); Calciatori 1993–94 (Italy) (151); Scottish Premier Division 96 (296); England '96 (22, 80–84); European Football Championship England '96 (45); Scottish Premier Division 97 (286, 298); Scottish Premier Division '98 (316, 334, 335); European Football Stars (1998) (64); Rangers FC 1999–2000 (163, 164); Rangers FC 2000–2001 (168)

His time in Italy saw him make two *Calciatori* appearances, but injuries meant a transfer to Glasgow, where he signed for Rangers, in the summer of 1995. Panini were by then producing standalone Scottish football albums, expanding Gascoigne's sticker career still further. Somewhat ironically, one of the stand-out moments of Euro 96 was his unforgettable manoeuvre and volley against Scotland, and, fittingly, the final view of Gascoigne's infectious grin in a Panini international tournament album can be found in *European Football Championship England '96*.

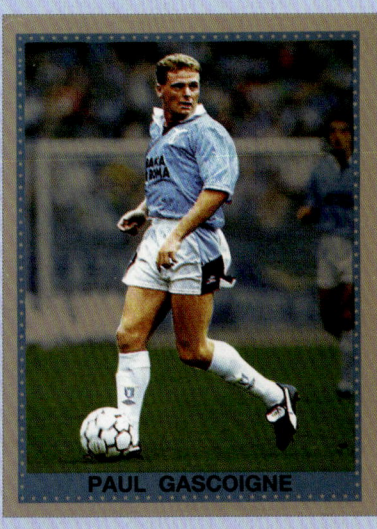
PAUL GASCOIGNE

Calciatori 1992–93

GARETH BALE

Euro 2016

Qatar 2022

Having agonisingly missed out on qualification for major tournaments in the 1980s and 1990s, Wales reached the promised land a couple of decades later — thanks to the brilliance of Gareth Bale. At times unstoppable for his opposing full-back, the wide player scored seven goals in qualifying as Wales reached Euro 2016. Making it to the finals of their first big competition in 58 years resulted in Panini bringing out a dedicated *We're Going To France* album, in which a sizeable number of stickers were assigned to the Welsh talisman.

It was then almost inevitable that Bale's left foot – from a trademark free-kick – would be responsible for his nation's first goal in a major tournament since 1958. He even went on to score twice more as the Red Dragons made it all the way to the semi-finals. Another Panini Euro album followed with the delayed Euro 2020 competition and the nation's first full Panini World Cup album appearance (although they had made a special non-qualifier appearance in *Argentina 78*) arrived with the *Qatar 2022* release.

Bale's first Panini appearance had come in card form in the 2007 Championship collection, while he was playing at Southampton. Converting from a full-back to a winger following a move to Tottenham, his only Panini sticker during his first spell in north London was in the *Champions League 2010–2011* album. Nonetheless, his own superlative form – reaching its apogee with 21 Premier League goals in 2012–13 – resulted in a move to Real Madrid, where he became a Panini sticker fixture. His medal tally in Spain was

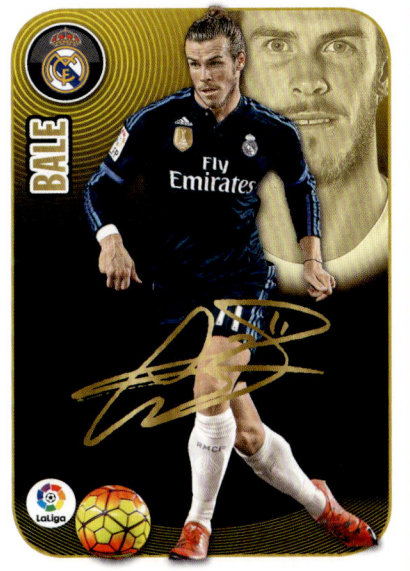

Liga 2016–17 (Colecciones ESTE) (Serie Oro)

Liga 2013–14 (Colecciones ESTE)

Liga 2020–21 (Colecciones ESTE)

Playing Career
Southampton (2006–2007);
Tottenham Hotspur (2007–2013);
Real Madrid (2013–2022); Tottenham
Hotspur (loan) (2020–2021); Los
Angeles FC (2022–2023) and Wales
(2006–2022)

Panini Album
Rookie Appearances
First club album appearance:
Champions League 2010–2011 (42)
First World Cup album appearance:
Qatar 2022 (WAL17)

Selected Panini Appearances
Champions League 2010–2011 (42);
London 2012 Olympics (260); *Liga
2013–14* (Colecciones ESTE) (Spain)
(740); *Champions League 2013–2014*
(88); *Liga 2014–15* (Colecciones ESTE)
(Spain) (403); *Champions League 2014–
2015* (117); *Liga 2015–16* (Colecciones
ESTE) (Spain) (377); *Wales: We're Going
to France* (2016) (35, 149–154, 194); *Euro
2016* (195, 201, CC-G); *Liga 2016–17*
(Colecciones ESTE) (Spain) (415);
FIFA 365 2017 (84, 106); *Liga 2017–18*
(Colecciones ESTE) (Spain) (474, 642);
Liga 2018–19 (Colecciones ESTE) (Spain)
(446); *Liga 2019–20* (Colecciones ESTE)
(Spain) (415); *Euro 2020 Preview Edition*
(International) (WAL6); *Liga 2020–21*
(Colecciones ESTE) (Spain) (383); *Euro
2020 Tournament Edition* (97, 116);
Premier League 2021 (England) (349,
547); *Liga 2021–22* (Colecciones ESTE)
(Spain) (396); *FIFA 365 2022* (131); *Qatar
2022* (WAL17)

vast and he scored three goals while playing in four winning
Champions League finals, including a spectacular bicycle
kick against Liverpool in 2018.

In 2020–21, a loan spell back at Spurs finally brought
him his first Panini Premier League sticker, before he
returned to Madrid and was an unused sub in the final
as his teammates won yet another Champions League.
A handful of games in the MLS preceded Bale's final
professional games at the 2022 World Cup, which was a
fitting stage for one of his generation's leading players to
take a curtain call.

JOHAN CRUYFF

Liga 1975/76 (Colecciones ESTE)

One man stood out among the Dutch masters of the 1970s Total Football era: Johan Cruyff's command of a football set him apart as one of the greatest to have ever played the game. The Amsterdam-born playmaker established himself in the Ajax team as a precocious teenager, scoring 16 goals in just 19 league games during the 1965–66 season, to more than play his part in the club's title success.

Honours flowed thereafter, culminating in three consecutive European Cup final wins between 1971 and 1973. The last of those triumphs coincided with Cruyff making his first Panini sticker appearance, in the World Stars section of Panini Belgium's debut album – *Football 1972–73*.

It was also around this period when Cruyff won the Ballon d'Or three times in the space of four seasons. His third, in 1974, came at the height of his powers when his only Panini World Cup album appearance – in *München 74* – preceded his Player of the Tournament star turn. While the Netherlands may have been pipped in the final by West Germany, it was undoubtedly the Dutch who stole the hearts of viewers around the world. He famously won a penalty in the first minute of the final, his mazy dribble leaving two opponents trailing in his wake, and this was also the tournament when the 'Cruyff turn' was first seen on a global stage.

NED JOHAN CRUYFF

WM 74

Cruyff made his Panini World Cup debut in *München 74*.
This would be his only appearance as a participating player.

112 · CALCIO
JOHAN CRUYFF

CRUYFF / F.C. BARCELONA

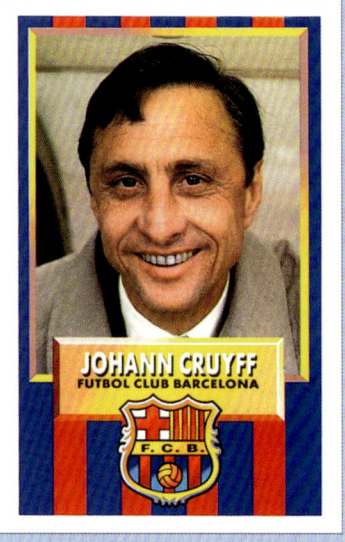

JOHANN CRUYFF
FUTBOL CLUB BARCELONA

Liga 93–94 (Colecciones ESTE)

JOHANN CRUYFF
Fútbol C. Barcelona

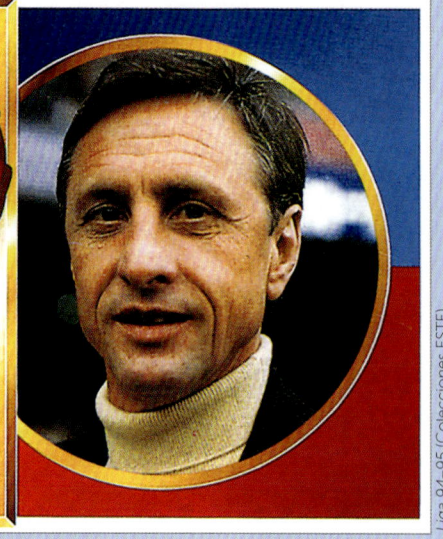

Liga 94–95 (Colecciones ESTE)

JOHANN CRUYFF
FUTBOL C. BARCELONA

Liga 91–92 (Colecciones ESTE)

JOHANN CRUYFF
FUTBOL CLUB BARCELONA

Liga 92–93 (Colecciones ESTE)

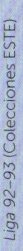

JOHANN CRUYFF
FUTBOL CLUB BARCELONA

Liga 89–90 (Colecciones ESTE)

Cruyff had gone into the finals on the back of helping Barcelona to their first La Liga in 14 years, during his first season at the club. Trophies were harder to come by during the rest of his stay in Catalonia – albeit signing off with a Copa del Rey in 1978 – but when he returned as manager, it was a joyous period for any Barça fan. The man synonymous with the number 14 shirt as a player featured as a jacket-wearing manager in eight consecutive Colecciones ESTE albums between 1988–89 and 1995–96, during a reign in which he won 11 trophies, including four league titles and the club's first-ever European Cup.

Liga 88–89 (Colecciones ESTE)

Cruyff featured in eight consecutive Colecciones ESTE albums as Barcelona coach. He won 11 trophies, including four league titles and the club's first-ever European Cup.

Liga 95–96 (Colecciones ESTE)

Playing Career

Ajax (1964–1973); Barcelona (1973–1978); Los Angeles Aztecs (1979); Washington Diplomats (1980 and 1981); Levante (1981); Ajax (1981–1983); Feyenoord (1983–1984) and Netherlands (1966–1977)

Panini Album Rookie Appearances

First club album appearance: Football 1972–73 (Belgium) (344) First World Cup album appearance: *München 74* (246)

Selected Panini Appearances

As player: *Football 1972–73 (Belgium)* (344); *Fotboll 1973 (Sweden) (Williams Förlags/Panini)* (237); *Campioni dello Sport (Italy) 1973–74* (112); *München 74* (246); *Liga 1974/75 (Colecciones ESTE) (Spain)* (BA14); *Liga 1975/76 (Colecciones ESTE) (Spain)* (BA14); *Futbol 75/76 (Spain) (Ediciones Vulcano/Panini)* (56); *Calciatori 1975–76 (Italy)* (617); *Football 76 (France)* (358); *Euro Football (1976–77)* (193); *Futbol 76/77 (Spain) (Ediciones Vulcano/Panini)* (56); *Liga 1976/77 (Colecciones ESTE) (Spain)* (BA14); *Liga 1977/78 (Colecciones ESTE) (Spain)* (113); *Euro Football 78* (182 A); *Liga 80–81 (Colecciones ESTE) (Spain)* (AA21); *Football 90 (UK)* (316) As manager: *Liga 88–89 (Colecciones ESTE) (Spain)* (2); *Panini Futbol 89 (Spain)* (40); *Liga 89–90 (Colecciones ESTE) (Spain)* (2); *Liga 90–91 (Colecciones ESTE) (Spain)* (2); *Liga 91–92 (Colecciones ESTE) (Spain)* (23); *Liga 92–93 (Colecciones ESTE) (Spain)* (20); *Liga 93–94 (Colecciones ESTE) (Spain)* (31); *Liga 94–95 (Colecciones ESTE) (Spain)* (39); *Liga 95–96 (Colecciones ESTE) (Spain)* (28)

MEGAN RAPINOE

France 2019

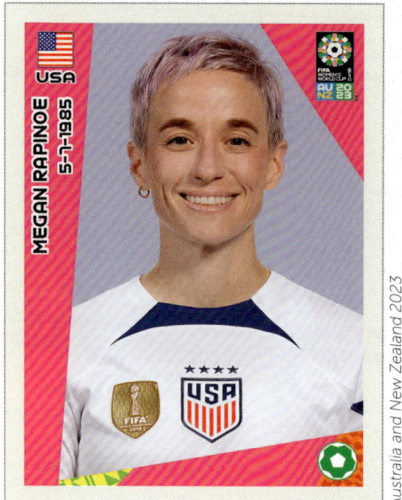

Australia and New Zealand 2023

Megan Rapinoe appeared in the first four Panini Women's World Cup sticker albums, coinciding with a period in which she was one of the world's leading players. After coming to prominence in college soccer she was selected as second pick – behind fellow USA great Amy Rodriguez – in the draft for the inaugural season of Women's Professional Soccer (WPS) in 2009.

Rapinoe was already a fixture of the USA squad by this time, having made her debut in 2006, but injuries had ruled her out of both the 2007 World Cup and 2008 Olympics. That meant her World Cup entrance corresponded with Panini bringing out the first-ever Women's World Cup sticker collection – for Germany 2011. Her bequiffed look certainly made for an eye-catching sticker, but it was her game-changing dynamism on the field that truly captured the attention in that competition, even though Japan beat the US in the final, 3-1 on penalties, following the game ending 2-2 after extra-time.

Revenge was swift, however, as USA defeated Japan in the 2012 Olympics final, with Rapinoe again excelling with goals and assists at key moments in the tournament. A first World Cup winner's medal was then secured against Japan in 2015 when the USA romped to a 5-2 victory in the Vancouver final.

Rapinoe's personal crowning glory came in France at the 2019 World Cup when she scored her country's first goal in the final victory over the Netherlands, as well as winning the Golden Boot as top scorer and Golden Ball as Player of the Tournament. Her efforts resulted in multiple appearances

Megan Rapinoe

Germany 2011

Rapinoe appeared in the first Women's World Cup album. Released for Germany 2011, the collection was a huge success.

Playing Career
Portland Pilots (USA college career) (2005–2008); Chicago Red Stars (2009–2010); Philadelphia Independence (2011); magicJack (2011); Sydney FC (2011); Seattle Sounders (2012); Lyon (2013–2014); Seattle Reign (2013–2023) and USA (2006–2023)

Panini Album Rookie Appearances
First club album appearance: FIFA 365 2020 (8, 412, 413, 414) First World Cup album appearance: *Germany 2011* (192)

Selected Panini Appearances
Germany 2011 (192); Canada 2015 (264); France 2019 (419); FIFA 365 2020 (8, 412, 413, 414); FIFA 365 2021 (407); Australia and New Zealand 2023 (293, 321)

in the Panini *FIFA 365 2020* album, including a shot of her penalty against the Dutch. There was time for one more Panini World Cup sticker, in 2023 – opting to bow out with a shock of pink hair – but no fairytale ending when USA lost to Sweden on penalties in the round of 16.

BEYOND GREATNESS™
MEGAN RAPINOE

Australia and New Zealand 2023

FINAL
USA-Netherlands 2-0

FIFA 365 2020

KARIM BENZEMA

Foot 2007

Foot 2008

French striker Karim Benzema has collected nearly as many winner's medals as Panini sticker appearances since making his professional debut at just 17 years and one month old. While the prolific scorer is best-known for his 14 seasons with Real Madrid, he had already been part of four successive title-winning campaigns at Lyon by the age of 20. After six Ligue 1 games in his breakthrough season, greater opportunities in 2005–06 convinced Panini to give him his rookie sticker in *Foot 2007*.

Fifty-four goals in all competitions during his last two seasons in France persuaded Real Madrid that Benzema was the man to lead the club's attack into a new era, alongside fellow new signing Cristiano Ronaldo. By the time their Madrid careers ended they were the two highest goalscorers in the club's history, Benzema's 354 strikes putting him in second place.

The first of Benzema's five Champions League wins came in the seventh of his eight consecutive Panini competition album appearances – 2013–14. Highlighting his overall value to the team beyond the plentiful goals, Benzema was one of the leading assist-makers during that season's tournament. His subsequent Champions League successes were all commemorated in the Panini *FIFA 365* albums, the first collection being released in 2015–16, the season of his second triumph.

However, with several other star names among his teammates, it took until *FIFA 365 2023* for Benzema to finally make the cover, a just reward for the incredible feats that won him the 2022 Ballon d'Or. His 44 goals in 46 games made him as responsible as any Madrid player for winning

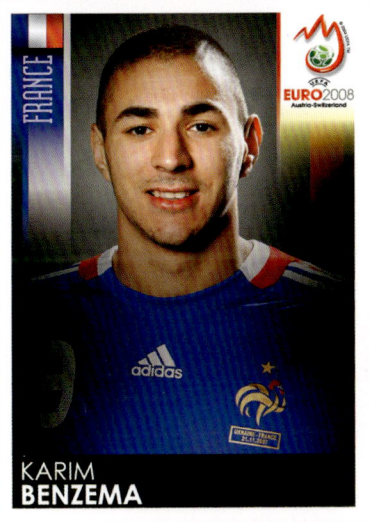

FRANCE

EURO 2008
Austria–Switzerland

KARIM
BENZEMA

Euro 2008

BENZEMA

LaLiga Santander

Fly Emirates

TOP
BOMBERS

Liga 2018–19 (Colecciones ESTE)

FIFA WORLD CUP
Brasil

Real Madrid CF (ESP)

19-12-1987 | 1,87 m | 79 kg

KARIM BENZEMA

Brasil 2014

KARIM **BENZEMA**

Lyon (Francia)

1987 1.83M 73KG

LaLiga Santander

Fly Emirates

Liga 2020–21 (Colecciones ESTE)

Playing Career
Lyon (2004–2009); Real Madrid (2009–2023); Al-Ittihad (2023–) and France (2007–2022)

Panini Album Rookie Appearances
First club album appearance: *Foot 2007* (France) (180)
First World Cup album appearance: *South Africa 2010* (104)

Selected Panini Appearances
Foot 2007 (France) (180); *Foot 2008* (France) (204, 208); *Euro 2008* (354); *Foot 2009* (France) (229, 234); *Liga 09–10* (Colecciones ESTE) (Spain) (234); *South Africa 2010* (104); *Liga 2010–2011* (Colecciones ESTE) (Spain) (290); *Liga 2011–12* (Colecciones ESTE) (Spain) (262); *Euro 2012* (480, 483/204 in Dutch Edition); *Liga 2012–13* (Colecciones ESTE) (Spain) (322); *Liga 2013–14* (Colecciones ESTE) (Spain) (381); *Brasil 2014* (392); *Liga 2014–15* (Colecciones ESTE) (Spain) (407); *Liga 2015–16* (Colecciones ESTE) (Spain) (380); *Liga 2016–17* (Colecciones ESTE) (Spain) (420, 644); *Liga 2017–18* (Colecciones ESTE) (Spain) (478); *Liga 2018–19* (Colecciones ESTE) (Spain) (450, 645); *Liga 2019–20* (Colecciones ESTE) (Spain) (419, B13); *Liga 2020–21* (Colecciones ESTE) (Spain) (392); *Euro 2020 Tournament Edition* (590x – Update); *Liga 2021–22* (Colecciones ESTE) (Spain) (373, 393); *Liga 2022–23* (Colecciones ESTE) (Spain) (360, 618, 623, T12); *Qatar 2022* (FRA16)

the 2021–22 Champions League, La Liga, Club World Cup, UEFA Super Cup and Supercopa de España. It also took until the 2022–23 season for Benzema to make the front of the Colecciones ESTE Spanish *Liga* album, a collection in which his achievements of the previous year earned him four stickers.

Benzema made three Panini World Cup appearances and was part of the France section for Panini's Qatar 2022 album, although injury would ultimately rule him out and he announced his retirement from international football shortly after his nation's final defeat by Argentina. Three Panini Euro album stickers did coincide with the same number of squad selections, though, on the way to a final haul of 37 goals for Les Bleus.

ZLATAN IBRAHIMOVIĆ

ZLATAN IBRAHIMOVIC

SVERIGE

2002 FIFA WORLD CUP

Korea/Japan 2002

M·F·F

MAXI

ZLATAN IBRAHIMOVIC

Fotboll 2000

Panini have only ever put their name to seven domestic football sticker albums in Sweden, so it was serendipitous that the most recent coincided with Zlatan Ibrahimović's rise to prominence in his homeland. The album compilers had even more foresight in adding two clubs outside the top flight (Allsvenskan), including Malmö, for whom a teenage Ibrahimović scored 12 goals in the Superettan (second tier) to earn promotion. Compared to his generally more hirsute subsequent Panini history, the precocious striker was a close-cropped sight in *Fotboll 2000*.

Just two years after his Panini bow, Ibrahimović made a meteoric rise to a first World Cup sticker album appearance in *Korea/Japan 2002*. The imposing attacker's image stood out in a collection of players looking straight into the camera. Always the maverick, Ibrahimović opted to be captured staring into the distance – perhaps contemplating the upward mobility quickly awaiting him in the domestic game.

He took the leap to the Dutch *Voetbal* album during his time at Ajax, though there was only one release during his stay there, and from 2004–05 he was elevated to the prestigious *Calciatori* productions. Proving himself to be quite the asset, the Swede won the Serie A title five years in a row during his time with Juventus and Internazionale, although Juventus were subsequently stripped of their 2004–05 and 2005–06 titles over a referee-influencing scandal.

JUVENTUS

ZLATAN IBRAHIMOVIC

The brilliantly talented Swede won the Serie A title five years in a row during his time with Juventus and Internazionale.

Calciatori 2004–2005

Zlatan IBRAHIMOVIĆ
SWE | Malmö | 3-10-1981

Calciatori 2019–2020

MILAN

ZLATAN IBRAHIMOVIC
Malmö (Svezia)
3 10 1981

Calciatori 2011–2012

ZLATAN IBRAHIMOVIC

Calciatori 2008–09

Zlatan IBRAHIMOVIĆ
SWE
MALMO
3-10-1981

Calciatori 2022–2023

ZLATAN IBRAHIMOVIC

Calciatori 2006–07

ZLATAN IBRAHIMOVIĆ

SWE 2001 1,95 m / 95 kg
Paris Saint-Germain (FRA) 3-10-1981

Euro 2016

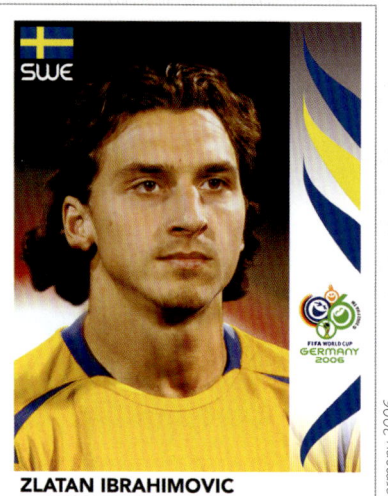

ZLATAN IBRAHIMOVIC

Germany 2006

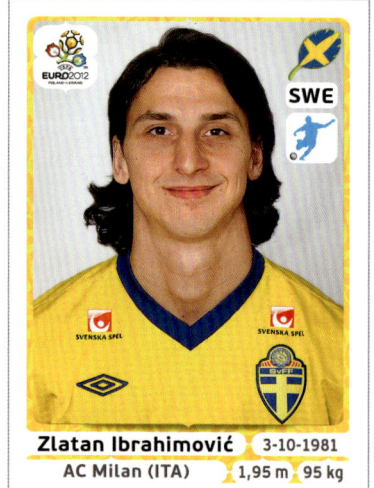

Zlatan Ibrahimović 3-10-1981
AC Milan (ITA) 1,95 m / 95 kg

Euro 2012

After one trophy-laden season at Barcelona, it was back to Italy for one more Serie A title with AC Milan before four Ligue 1 titles and four Panini *Foot* album appearances in a row with Paris Saint-Germain. Though he was by now approaching his mid-30s, there was still time for Ibrahimović to prove age is only a number by adding well over a hundred more goals to his tally in spells with Manchester United, LA Galaxy and AC Milan.

Sweden failed to qualify for the 2010 and 2014 World Cup finals and retirement from international football in 2016 precluded him from the 2018 Russian-held tournament, meaning Ibrahimović was restricted to two Panini World Cup stickers. Four additional Euro stickers, a record 62 goals for his country and a stellar club career nonetheless ensures that a version of that first Malmö sticker in good condition is very sought after.

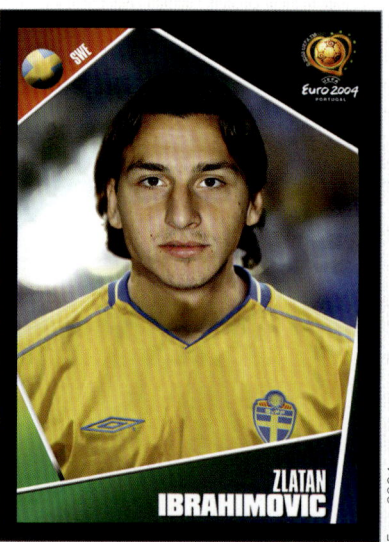

ZLATAN IBRAHIMOVIC

Euro 2004

Ibrahimović appeared in two World Cup and four Euro Championship collections. He scored 62 goals in 122 appearances for Sweden, making him one of the country's greatest players.

ZLATAN IBRAHIMOVIC

Euro 2008

ZLATAN IBRAHIMOVIĆ
SWE | Malmö, 3-10-1981

Calciatori 2021–2022

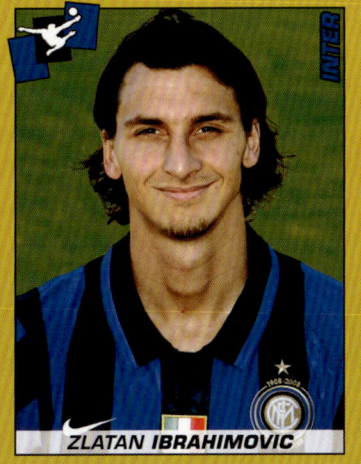

Calciatori 07–08

Calciatori 2005–06

ZLATAN IBRAHIMOVIC

Calciatori 2010–2011

ZLATAN IBRAHIMOVIĆ
Malmö (SWE)
03 10 1981

Foot 2012–13

Playing Career

Malmö FF (1999–2001); Ajax (2001–2004); Juventus (2004–2006); Internazionale (2006–2009); Barcelona (2009–2011); AC Milan (loan) (2010–2011); AC Milan (2011–2012); Paris Saint-Germain (2012–2016); Manchester United (2016–2018); LA Galaxy (2018–2019); AC Milan (2020–2023) and Sweden (2001–2023)

Panini Album Rookie Appearances

First club album appearance: Fotboll 2000 (Sweden) (253)
First World Cup album appearance: Korea/Japan 2002 (456)

Selected Panini Appearances

Fotboll 2000 (Sweden) (253); Korea/Japan 2002 (456); Voetbal 04 (Netherlands) (39); Euro 2004 (197); Calciatori 2004–2005 (Italy) (190); Calciatori 2005–06 (Italy) (165); Champions of Europe 1955–2005 (176); Germany 2006 (166); Calciatori 2006–07 (Italy) (174); Calciatori 07–08 (Italy) (165, 702, T9); Euro 2008 (406, 521); Calciatori 2008–09 (Italy) (191, V8, X10); Liga 09–10 (Colecciones ESTE) (Spain) (644); Liga 2010–2011 (Colecciones ESTE) (Spain) (110); Calciatori 2010–11 (Italy) (335); Calciatori 2011–2012 (Italy) (312, V2, V9, V11); Euro 2012 (451, 454); Foot 2012–13 (France) (291); Foot 2013–14 (France) (332); Foot 2014–15 (France) (384); Foot 2015–16 (France) (358); Euro 2016 (543, 567); Calciatori 2019–2020 (Italy) (M28); Calciatori 2021 (Italy) (343, C3); Calciatori 2021–2022 (Italy) (285); Road to FIFA World Cup Qatar 2022 (538); Calciatori 2022–2023 (Italy) (296)

ERIC CANTONA

ERIC
CANTONA
AUXERRE

Football 87

FRANCE

ERIC
CANTONA

Euro '92

Eric Cantona's grand tour of Ligue 1 during the first half of his playing career makes for a neat encapsulation of his inability to ever truly feel at home in French football. In all he made seven Panini appearances for four different clubs (as well as two additional loan spells elsewhere). At first a nomad, Manchester would eventually become Cantona's home.

After making his first Panini appearance as a teenager with Auxerre in *Football 86*, the mercurial striker spent a further two seasons in Burgundy ahead of a big-money move to Marseille. Despite featuring in the white shirt of Marseille in *Foot 89*, the forward had fallen out with the club by the time most collectors were unwrapping his sticker, and had been sent on loan to Bordeaux. A further loan took place for the whole of the 1989–90 season, resulting in a shirt of the same hue, but this time for Montpellier.

There he was embroiled in more controversy, but Cantona did contribute to the team winning the French Cup. This persuaded his mother club to give him another chance and, back at Marseille for *Foot 91*, he helped them win the league, albeit not being a regular. They then decided to cut their losses and sell him to Nîmes, for whom he donned the red shirt in *Foot 92*, but that turned out to be another brief stay because he was banned after throwing the ball at a referee.

A change of country was considered the best way for Cantona to get his career back on track, with Leeds signing him, initially on loan, in January 1992. Although he scored only three goals in 15 appearances, the Frenchman still played a significant role in the Yorkshire club winning the Division One title. With Panini's *Football '93* displaying only 12 players from each of the newly founded Premier League

AUXERRE

ERIC CANTONA

Football 86

FRANCE

ERIC CANTONA

European Football Championship England '96

MARSEILLE

ÉRIC CANTONA

Foot 89

Marseille

Panasonic

ÉRIC CANTONA

Foot 91

Playing Career

Auxerre (1983–1988); Martigues (loan) (1985–1986); Marseille (1988–1991); Bordeaux (loan) (1989); Montpellier (loan) (1989–1990); Nîmes (1991–1992); Leeds United (1992); Manchester United (1992–1997) and France (1987–1995)

Panini Album Rookie Appearances

First club album appearance: Foot 86 (France) (25)
First World Cup album appearance: N/A

Selected Panini Appearances

Football 86 (France) (25); *Football 87* (France) (14); *Football 88* (France) (12); *Foot 89* (France) (138); *Foot 90* (France) (194); *Foot 91* (France) (102); *Foot 92* (France) (199); *Euro '92* (61); *Panini Futbol 92–93* (Spain) (189); *Superplayers '96* (England) (171); *Supercalcio 1995–96* (Italy) (188) *European Football Championship England '96* (191) *The Official PFA Collection '97* (England) (49); *Türkiye 1. Futbol Ligi 1996–1997* (246); *Manchester United 2006–07* (O); *Manchester United 2009–10* (124)

club squads, Cantona then missed out to Rod Wallace for a spot in the following season's album. However, perhaps the Panini selectors had an inkling Cantona wouldn't last the season: he moved to Manchester United in late November.

Just as he'd done the previous year at Leeds, Cantona helped galvanise his new side's league challenge over the second half of the season. The Red Devils had waited 26 years for a top-flight title, but the France international managed it in a matter of months. Cantona would stroll magisterially around Old Trafford over the next four seasons and three more Premier League titles were won in that time.

Cantona appeared in the *European Football Championship England '96* album but never made the final France squad.

eric cantona
MAN UTD

The Official PFA Collection '97

RUUD GULLIT

HAARLEM

RUUD GULLIT

Voetbal 80

RUUD GULLIT
FEYENOORD

Voetbal 85

Ruud Gullit began Panini sticker life in *Voetbal 80,* his rookie sticker showing him without his trademark dreadlocks. He was 16 that season when he made his debut for Haarlem, but his team was relegated at the end of the 1979–80 campaign. Panini's second-tier coverage was strong during that period, however, so Gullit still appeared in the following *Voetbal 81* album, sharing his sticker with English full-back Keith Masefield. That 1980–81 season saw Haarlem immediately bounce back into the top flight, with Gullit voted best player.

There was no stopping Gullit once he moved to Feyenoord in 1982, though, and he won Dutch Footballer of the Year in his second season in Rotterdam, a season in which a side that also featured Johan Cruyff won the league and cup double. Gullit's achievements were rewarded with a cover photo on the *Voetbal 85* album. By now sporting dreadlocks, he was seen tussling for the ball with Manchester United's Gordon McQueen in a pre-season friendly in August 1984.

Gullit moved on to PSV Eindhoven in 1985, once again winning the Dutch Footballer of the Year in his first season. After helping the club to two successive league titles, he then joined AC Milan, where he won three Serie A titles and two European Cups among his many honours. As an individual, Gullit won the Ballon d'Or in 1987. Panini acknowledged the player's status by featuring him on the covers of the Italian and Spanish versions of the *Supersport* album (in AC Milan and Oranje kit respectively). He was also among the constellation of stars chosen for the front of the *Calciatori* 1987–88 album, beside other big names such as Diego Maradona, Marco van Basten and Rudi Völler.

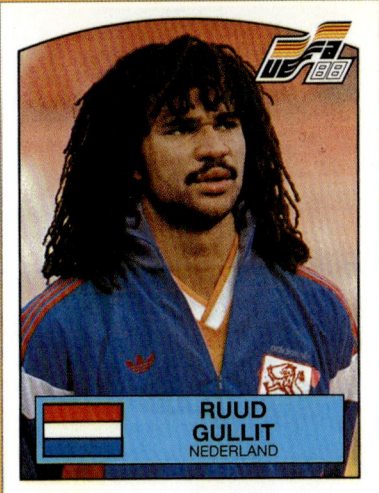

Euro 88

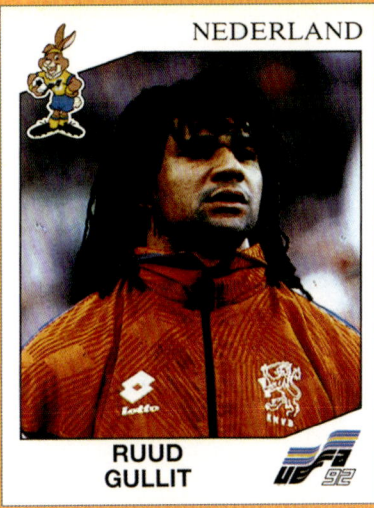

Euro '92

USA '94

Italia '90

Gullit won the Ballon d'Or in 1987. Panini acknowledged the player's status by featuring him on the covers of the Italian and Spanish versions of the *Supersport* album.

Calciatori 1987–88

RUUD GULLIT

MILAN

RUUD GULLIT

Calciatori 1988–89

MILAN

RUUD GULLIT

Calciatori 1989–90

Gullit's crowning glory on national duty came at the end of that first season in Italy, which coincided with the first of his four Panini international tournament stickers. The Netherlands defeated the Soviet Union 2-0 in the Euro 88 final with Gullit heading in the opening goal. After appearing in *Italia '90* and *Euro '92*, Gullit was given a further Panini sticker in the *USA '94* album, but did not participate after a fall-out with coach Dick Advocaat.

A better relationship was forged with Sven-Göran Eriksson at Sampdoria, the club he went to after AC Milan, and he captained the side to a Coppa Italia during his two seasons there. Chelsea manager Glenn Hoddle brought him to England in the summer of 1995 and he made his final two Panini appearances for the west London club. The second of those – in *The Official PFA Collection '97* – came when he had replaced England-bound Hoddle as boss, winning the FA Cup in his only full season in charge.

MILAN

RUUD GULLIT

Calciatori 1990–91

MILAN

RUUD GULLIT

Calciatori 1991–92

Calciatori 1993-94

RUUD
GULLIT

SAMPDORIA

SAMPDORIA

RUUD
GULLIT

Calciatori 1994-95

ruud gullit
CHELSEA

The Official PFA Collection '97

Playing Career
HFC Haarlem (1979–1982); Feyenoord (1982–1985); PSV Eindhoven (1985–1987); AC Milan (1987–1994); Sampdoria (loan) (1993–1994); Sampdoria (1994–1995); Chelsea (1995–1998) and Netherlands (1981–1994)

Panini Album Rookie Appearances
First club album appearance: *Voetbal 80* (Netherlands) (115) First World Cup album appearance: *Italia '90* (416)

Selected Panini Appearances
Voetbal 80 (Netherlands) (115); *Voetbal 81* (Netherlands) (384); *Voetbal 82* (Netherlands) (144); *Voetbal 83* (Netherlands) (71); *Voetbal 84* (Netherlands) (101); *Voetbal 85* (Netherlands) (89); *Voetbal 86* (Netherlands) (244); *Voetbal 87* (Netherlands) (218); *Fussball 87* (Germany) (413); *Supersport* (UK) (1987) (55); *Calciatori 1987–88* (Italy) (161); *Voetbal 88* (Netherlands) (33); *Football 88* (UK) (380); *Euro 88* (227); *Calciatori 1988–89* (Italy) (212); *Voetbal 89* (Netherlands) (1, 2, 354, 361); *Foot 89* (France) (379); *Calciatori 1989–90* (Italy) (241); *Voetbal 90* (Netherlands) (329); *Italia '90* (416); *Calciatori 1990–91* (Italy) (222); *Voetbal '91* (Netherlands) (337); *Calciatori 1991–92* (Italy) (221, 360); *Voetbal '92* (Netherlands) (245); *Euro '92* (132); *Calciatori 1992–93* (Italy) (221); *Panini Futbol 92-93* (Spain) (192); *Calciatori 1993–94* (Italy) (292); *USA '94* (427); *Calciatori 1994–95* (Italy) (326); *Supercalcio 1994–1995* (Italy) (146); *Superplayers '96* (England) (65); *The Official PFA Collection '97* (England) (105, J); *Euro 2012* (Dutch special edition) (82, 110, 177)

GEORGE
WEAH

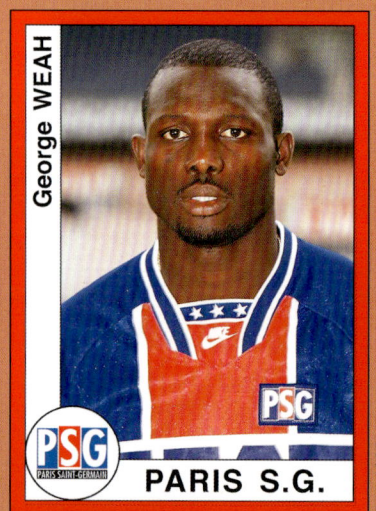

Foot 1995

Foot 93

Beginning professional life in his Liberian homeland and Cameroon, when George Weah was brought to Monaco by Arsène Wenger in 1988, he began a decade of considerable individual and team success in Europe. The forward made his first Panini appearance in the *Foot 90* album, alongside Monaco teammates who included Glenn Hoddle and Emmanuel Petit. However, such was Weah's impact that by the 1991–92 season he was featured on the cover of *Foot 92*, Chris Waddle and Jean-Pierre Papin among those sharing the honour with him.

At times unplayable, Weah spearheaded Monaco to the Coupe de France in 1991 and the final of the Cup Winners' Cup the following year, before moving on to Paris Saint-Germain. His first appearance for the club, in a predominantly white shirt, came in *Foot 93* and he won the first of two Coupes de France with the Parisians at the end of that season. The following campaign saw Weah appear in *Foot 1994* resplendent in a red and blue ensemble as PSG rang the sartorial changes. That season was another triumph on the pitch, too, because PSG won Ligue 1. Weah followed that up by finishing as leading scorer in the 1994–95 season as *Foot 1995* saw PSG once again redesign their strip, with blue now taking on a greater role.

At the end of that year Weah was an AC Milan player and earned the Ballon d'Or, as well as the FIFA World Player of the Year award. He appeared on the cover of *Calciatori 1995–96* after just a handful of appearances for the Rossoneri. A first Serie A title was duly won at the close of his first season and

Foot 92

Africa '96

Foot 1994

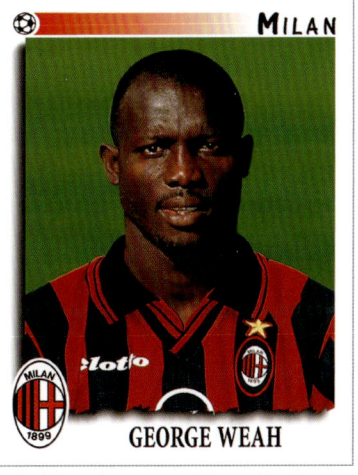

Calciatori 1997–98

Calciatori 1996–97

Playing Career
Young Survivors (1981–1984); Bong Range United (1984–1985); Mighty Barrolle (1985–1986); Invincible Eleven (1986–1987); Tonnerre Yaoundé (1987–1988); Monaco (1988–1992); Paris Saint-Germain (1992–1995); AC Milan (1995–2000); Chelsea (loan) (2000); Manchester City (2000); Marseille (2000–2001); Al Jazira (2001–2003) and Liberia (1986–2018)

Panini Album Rookie Appearances
First club album appearance: Foot 90 (France) (176)
First World Cup album appearance: N/A

Selected Panini Appearances
Foot 90 (France) (176); *Foot 91* (France) (126); *Foot 92* (France) (143); *Foot 93* (France) (193); *Foot 1994* (France) (230); *Foot 1995* (France) (246); *Calciatori 1995–96* (Italy) (167); *Supercalcio 95–96* (Italy) (135); *Africa '96* (186); *Calciatori 1996–97* (Italy) (183); *Supercalcio 96–97* (Italy) (185); *Türkiye 1. Futbol Ligi 1996–1997* (257); *Los Mejores Equipos de Europa 1997* (168); *African All-Star* (1997) (95); *Calciatori 1997–98* (Italy) (227); *Supercalcio 97–98* (Italy) (184); *Los mejores Equipos de Europa 1997–98* (167); *Calciatori 1998–99* (Italy) (205, 437); *Super Football 99* (156); *Calciatori 2000* (Italy) (215); *Supercalcio 2000* (Italy) (144); *Champions League 1999–2000* (305)

another was added in 1999. Weah's Panini days came to an end the following season, his last at AC Milan, before short stays at Chelsea, Manchester City and Marseille, and two years at Al-Jazira, heralded the conclusion of a stellar career. The sharpshooter was also part of Panini's first-ever African Cup of Nations album in 1996 – *Africa '96* – and he graced the cover of the limited-release *African All-Star* album a year later, too. Both are now hard to find.

LOTHAR MATTHÄUS

Fussball 82

Fussball '94

While most young hopefuls went largely under the radar at the time of their Panini 'rookie' appearance, Lothar Matthäus started as he intended to go on over the next two decades. Rather than just settle for a standard *Fussball 81* rookie sticker in the Borussia Mönchengladbach spread (he had made his debut for the club the previous season), the midfield powerhouse was also depicted in shiny form: although still a teenager, Matthäus had made his full debut at Europa 80 and was part of a special *Sondersticker Nationalspieler* section, an extra 24 stickers depicting the West Germany international players in foil.

Although he did play in the 1982 World Cup finals, Matthäus missed the cut for the 16 West Germans picked for the Panini *España 82* album, but he appeared in the Panini *Euro 84* collection, the first of seven major tournament albums. This included his great achievement at Italia 90 where, a relentless presence in midfield, he captained West Germany to the World Cup – scoring four goals along the way – and ended the year by winning the Ballon d'Or.

Matthäus had four silverware-laden seasons at Bayern Munich ahead of moving to Internazionale in 1988. A Serie A title, in his first season in Italy, plus a UEFA Cup were the highlights of his four years in Milan, much of which was spent alongside compatriots Andreas Brehme and Jürgen Klinsmann. He returned to a by-now unified Germany in the summer of 1992, adding a further four Bundesliga titles with Bayern Munich, making it seven in total.

LOTHAR MATTHÄUS — BRD

Euro 84

DEUTSCHLAND-BRD

LOTHAR MATTHÄUS

Mexico 86

DEUTSCHLAND-BRD

LOTHAR MATTHÄUS

Italia '90

INTER

LOTHAR MATTHÄUS

Calciatori 1990–91

Playing Career
1. FC Herzogenaurach (1978–1979); Borussia Mönchengladbach (1979–1984); Bayern Munich (1984–1988); Internazionale (1988–1992); Bayern Munich (1992–2000); MetroStars (2000); 1. FC Herzogenaurach (2018) and West Germany/Germany (1980–2000)

Panini Album Rookie Appearances
First club album appearance: *Fussball 81* (Germany) (320, R16)
First World Cup album appearance: *Mexico 86* (302)

Selected Panini Appearances
Fussball 81 (Germany) (320, R16); *Fussball 82* (Germany) (280); *Fussball 83* (Germany) (309); *Fussball 84* (Germany) (446); *Euro 84* (148); *Fussball 85* (Germany) (272); *Fussball 86* (Germany) (231); *Mexico 86* (302); *Fussball 87* (Germany) (263, 377); *Fussball 88* (Germany) (243); *Euro 88* (65); *Calciatori 1988–89* (Italy) (132); *Calciatori 1989–90* (Italy) (165); *Italia '90* (259); *Calciatori 1990–91* (Italy) (146); *Calciatori 1991–92* (Italy) (163, 366); *Euro '92* (207); *Fussball 93* (Germany) (220); *Fussball '94* (Germany) (31); *USA '94* (175); *Fussball '95* (Germany) (12); *Fussball 96* (Germany) (148); *Fussball 97* (Germany) (34); *Fussball 98* (Germany) (8, 15); *Fussball 99* (Germany) (3, 33, 39); *Fussball 2000* (Germany) (6, 17); *Champions League 1999/2000* (227); *Euro 2000* (9); *Österreichische Fußball-Bundesliga 2006–2007* (Austria) (39 – as manager)

Injury ruled him out of Euro 92 (although not the Panini album) but he appeared in USA 94, skippering his nation once more. While he played at the France 98 World Cup, he was a late replacement and didn't appear in the album. However, he did feature in the *Euro 2000* album, where he made his final three Germany appearances at the age of 39, as well as Panini's first-ever *Champions League* album in the season just gone. The serial winner then spent the next decade as a much-travelled coach, with his achievements including a sticker in the Austrian domestic football album of 2006–07, a season in which he led Red Bull Salzburg to the title.

MICHAEL LAUDRUP

Calciatori 1984–85

MICHAEL
LAUDRUP

Michael
LAUDRUP
F.C. BARCELONA

Panini Futbol 92–93

As well as being the most explosive element of the 'Danish Dynamite' side of the 1980s, Michael Laudrup secured his place as Denmark's greatest player of all time by winning major trophies with four of Europe's most iconic clubs. Since there has never been a Panini sticker collection for the Danish league, Laudrup's early years at KB and Brondby were left unchronicled. Juventus then signed the stylish playmaker when he was still a teenager, but his first two *Calciatori* appearances came for Lazio, where he was on loan, because the Turin club already had two foreign players and that was the maximum number allowed at the time. The emerging Dane finally donned the black and white stripes in *Calciatori 1985–86*, winning the Serie A title in his first campaign.

At the end of that season came the first of two memorable World Cup tournaments for the attacking maestro. Panini's images for their *Mexico 86* album needed to be sourced well in advance, so an earlier Hummel-produced kit was seen underneath Laudrup's tracksuit top, rather than the famous 'half and half' shirts worn for Denmark's World Cup adventure. Fortunately Denmark also made it to Euro 88, so what many consider to be one of the greatest shirts of all time was donned by Laudrup and co in that Panini album.

Laudrup joined Barcelona the following year to begin a spellbinding five-year period at the club as a vital cog in Johan Cruyff's 'Dream Team', the side that won four successive La Liga titles between 1991 and 1994, as well as the club's first European Cup in 1992. However, the Dane's relationship with Cruyff fell apart when he was left out of the 1994 Champions League final, leading to a move to deadly rivals Real Madrid that

DANMARK

MICHAEL LAUDRUP

Mexico 86

MICHAEL LAUDRUP
LAZIO

Calciatori 1983–84

Juventus

MICHAEL LAUDRUP

Calciatori 1987–88

ARISTON

MICHAEL LAUDRUP

juventus

Calciatori 1985–86

Playing Career
KB (1981); Brøndby (1982–1983); Lazio (1983–1985); Juventus (1985–1989); Barcelona (1989–1994); Real Madrid (1994–1996); Vissel Kobe (1996–1997); Ajax (1997–1998) and Denmark (1982–1998)

Panini Album Rookie Appearances
First club album appearance: Calciatori 1983–84 (Italy) (136) First World Cup album appearance: *Mexico 86* (361)

Selected Panini Appearances
Calciatori 1983–84 (Italy) (136); *Euro 84* (77); *Calciatori 1984–85* (Italy) (165); *Football 85* (UK) (262); *Calciatori 1985–86* (Italy) (125); *Supercalcio 1985–86* (Italy) (156); *Mexico 86* (361); *Calciatori 1986–87* (Italy) (174); *Calciatori 1987–88* (Italy) (145); *Euro 88* (123); *Calciatori 1988–89* (Italy) (153); *Liga 89–90* (Colecciones ESTE) (Spain) (420); *Liga 90–91* (Colecciones ESTE) (Spain) (20); *Liga 91–92* (Colecciones ESTE) (Spain) (38); *Liga 92–93* (Colecciones ESTE) (Spain) (33); *Panini Futbol 92–93* (Spain) (165); *Panini Futbol 93–94* (Spain); *Panini Liga '94–'95* (Spain) (198); *Panini Liga 95–96* (Spain) (237); *European Football Championship England '96* (287); *Voetbal 98* (Netherlands) (96, 109); *France 98* (224)

MICHAEL LAUDRUP
DANMARK

Euro 88

summer. In the first of two seasons in the capital, Laudrup was a star turn as Real ended Barça's long run of La Liga dominance.

After a spell in Japan, Laudrup returned for both a shiny and standard sticker as part of Ajax's double-winning team in *Voetbal 98*. His last playing sticker came in *France 98*, where he bowed out on a high as part of the FIFA All-Star Team as Denmark reached the quarter-finals. After hanging up his boots, Laudrup enjoyed a widely travelled managerial career, including a sticker in Colecciones ESTE Spanish *Liga 2010–2011* during his only full season with Mallorca.

RONALDO

Ronaldo Luís Nazário de Lima, regarded as one of Brazil's greatest players, arrived at PSV Eindhoven from Cruzeiro in the summer of 1994, at the age of 17. His arrival came shortly after making his country's World Cup squad, although he didn't feature in any of Brazil's matches on their way to winning the trophy. His first campaign in the Netherlands served notice of what was to follow over the next decade and more, as he scored 30 Eredivisie goals and displayed the pace, power and dribbling skills that would leave defenders trailing in his wake.

A move to one of the bigger European leagues was inevitable, with Barcelona winning the battle for his services in July 1996. Panini's Spanish *Liga* and the Colecciones ESTE albums of 1996–97 capture the Brazilian during a season that many consider to be his peak and in which he scored 47 goals in 49 games and helped the club win the Cup Winners' Cup. Ronaldo's stay at Camp Nou was short-lived, however, and after one season he moved to Internazionale for another world record fee, where, in a successful first campaign, he scored 25 league goals and won the 1998 UEFA Cup final.

Voetbal 95

Voetbal 96

France 98

BRASIL

RONALDO

2002 FIFA WORLD CUP

Korea/Japan 2002

INTER

RONALDO

Calciatori 1997–98

INTER

RONALDO

Calciatori 1998–99

BRA

RONALDO

Germany 2006

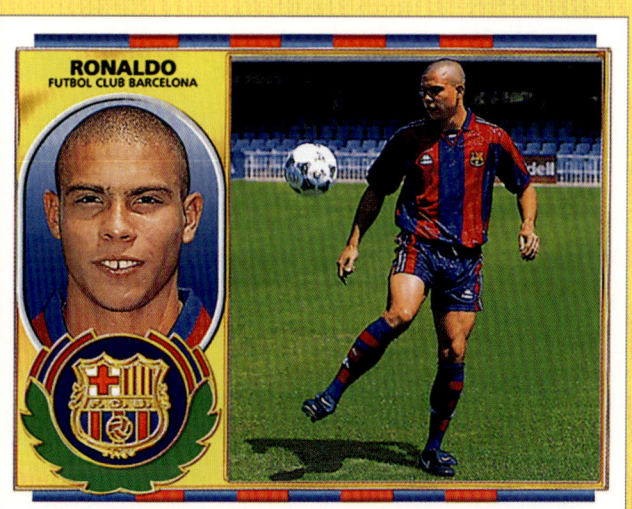

RONALDO
FUTBOL CLUB BARCELONA

Liga 96–97 (Colecciones ESTE)

Liga 02–03 (Colecciones ESTE)

Liga 2003–2004 (Colecciones ESTE)

Liga 2004–2005 (Colecciones ESTE)

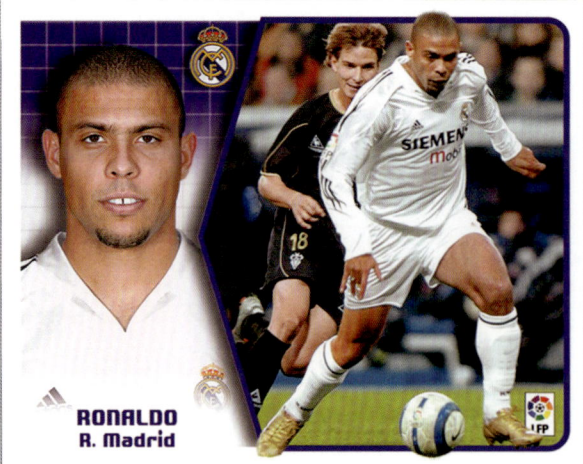

Liga 2005–2006 (Colecciones ESTE)

Liga 2006–2007 (Colecciones ESTE)

Calciatori 2006-07

Calciatori 07-08

Playing Career
Cruzeiro (1993–1994); PSV Eindhoven (1994–1996); Barcelona (1996–1997); Internazionale (1997–2002); Real Madrid (2002–2007); AC Milan (2007–2008); Corinthians (2009–2011) and Brazil (1994–2011)

Panini Album Rookie Appearances
First club album appearance: _Voetbal 95_ (Netherlands) (78, 91)
First World Cup album appearance: _France 98_ (28)

Selected Panini Appearances
Voetbal 95 (Netherlands) (78, 91); _Voetbal 96_ (Netherlands) (75, 90, 411); _Supercalcio 95–96_ (Italy) (196); _Liga 96-97_ (Colecciones ESTE) (Spain) (51); _Panini Liga 96/97_ (Spain) (393); _Calciatori 1997–98_ (Italy) (144, 408); _Liga 97–98_ (Colecciones ESTE) (Spain) (51); _Supercalcio 1997–98_ (Italy) (165); _Foot 98_ (France) (432); _France 98_ (28); _Calciatori 1998–99_ (Italy) (134, 432); _Euro Super Clubs 1999_ (143); _Calciatori 1999–2000_ (Italy) (118, 469); _Supercalcio 1999–2000_ (Italy) (153); _Calciatori 2001–02_ (Italy) (141); _Korea/Japan 2002_ (184); _Liga 02-03_ (Colecciones ESTE) (Spain) (520, 521); _Panini Superliga de Estrellas 2002–2003_ (Spain) (39, 199); _Liga 2003–2004_ (Colecciones ESTE) (Spain) (230); _Panini Superliga de Estrellas 2003–2004_ (Spain) (43, 222); _Liga 2004–2005_ (Colecciones ESTE) (Spain) (248); _Liga 2005–2006_ (Colecciones ESTE) (Spain) (264); _Germany 2006_ (396); _Liga 2006–2007_ (Colecciones ESTE) (Spain) (325); _Calciatori 2006–07_ (Italy) (A72); _Calciatori 07–08_ (Italy) (263); _Champions League 2007–2008_ (25); _CONMEBOL Copa América Brasil 2019_ (350, 351); _FIFA 365 2024_ (433)

This was the perfect preparation for Ronaldo's second World Cup finals – and the first in which he would feature. Indeed, France 98 was the first of three consecutive Panini World Cup appearances for his nation's talisman, with the 2002 World Cup providing the triumph he was denied four years previously. Eight goals, including two in the final victory over Germany, won him the Golden Shoe (subsequently renamed Golden Boot) as top scorer and by the end of the year he was carrying home his second Ballon d'Or.

By now a Real Madrid player, Ronaldo enjoyed a domestic football renaissance with Los Blancos, winning La Liga in his first season and Supercopa de España in his second season. _Il Fenomeno_ eventually called time on his Real career after 82 league goals in 127 games. He then signed for AC Milan, and a move back to his Brazilian homeland brought further honours in his first season with Corinthians.

Ronaldo has starred in Panini albums released for the Dutch, Spanish and Italian domestic leagues.

DIDIER DROGBA

DIDIER DROGBA

CIV

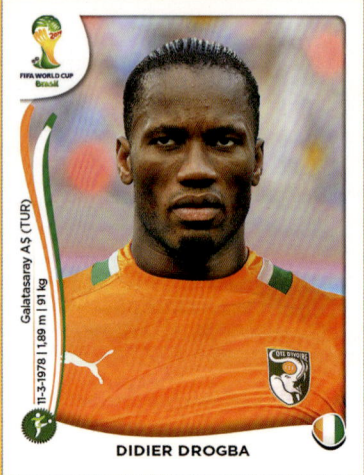

DIDIER DROGBA

Born in Ivory Coast, Drogba moved to France at the age of five. He found his feet first in the French Second Division with Le Mans and it wasn't until the latter stages of the 2001–02 season that he was finally elevated to the top flight, signing for Guingamp. By no means prolific at this stage of his career, the forward earned a belated first Panini sticker in the *Foot 2003* album – the 24-year-old was one of two alternatives to fill the number 67 slot in the album (along with Guingamp teammate Cédric Bardon), as space was at a premium in this collection. At this time he cut a relatively slender figure compared to the powerhouse striker that would terrorise Premier League defences in the decade ahead.

After impressing with 17 league goals in his only full season with Guingamp, Drogba moved to Marseille the following summer and it was there he caught the attention of would-be suitors from around Europe. Drogba's performances earned him the Players' Player of the Year award while his goals were decisive in Marseille reaching the UEFA Cup final, where they lost 2-0 to Valencia. That would turn out to be a rare final loss for Drogba: his move to José Mourinho's Chelsea in 2004 ushered in a period of unprecedented success for the Blues, with the Ivorian often the matchwinner.

His first two seasons at Stamford Bridge ended with a Premier League title, augmented in his first campaign by a League Cup victory. With no Champions League album in 2004–05, Drogba began a run of 10 successive Panini appearances in the showpiece competition release a year later. The west London club went deep into the latter stages on numerous occasions, including two finals in 2007–08 and 2011–12. The second of those was Drogba's crowning glory

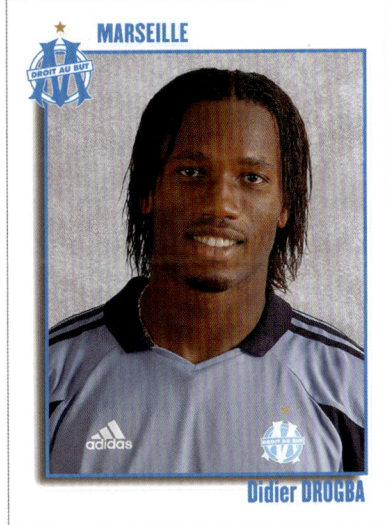

Foot 2004

Germany 2006

Champions of Europe 1955–2005

Playing Career

Le Mans (1998–2002); Guingamp (2002–2003); Marseille (2003–2004); Chelsea (2004–2012); Shanghai Shenhua (2012–2013); Galatasaray (2013–2014); Chelsea (2014–2015); Montreal Impact (2015–2016); Phoenix Rising (2017–2018) and Ivory Coast (2002–2014)

Panini Album Rookie Appearances

First club album appearance:
Foot 2003 (France) (67a)
First World Cup album appearance:
Germany 2006 (205)

Selected Panini Appearances

Foot 2003 (France) (67a); Foot 2004 (France) (186); SuperFoot 2004 (France) (154); SuperFoot 2004–2005 (France) (170); Champions of Europe 1955–2005 (142); Germany 2006 (205); Foot 2007 (France) (21); Champions League 2006–2007 (105); Champions League 2007–2008 (142); Africa Cup 2008 (114); Champions League 2008–2009 (244); Champions League 2009–2010 (225); Africa Cup 2010 (248); South Africa 2010 (542); Champions League 2010–2011 (361); Champions League 2011–2012 (292); Spor Toto Süper Lig 2012–2013 (Turkey) (U6); Champions League 2012–2013 (5); Champions League 2013–2014 (127, 309); Brasil 2014 (240, P16); Champions League 2014–2015 (506); Premier League 2023 (England) (334)

when he headed a late equaliser against Bayern Munich and then side-footed the clinching penalty in the shoot-out.

Drogba left for China that summer, but he remained a presence in the Panini *Champions League 2012–2013* album, featuring in part of a section that commemorated the holders. As it transpired, the commanding attacker did end up playing in the Champions League quarter-final that season – for Galatasaray – after cutting short his stay in China, and he featured as one of six update stickers in the Panini *Spor Toto Süper Lig 2012–2013*.

On the international front, Drogba led Ivory Coast to their first World Cup in 2006, and appeared in three successive Panini World Cup albums.

MARTA

MARTA
FC Rosengård (SWE)
19-2-1986 1,62 M BRA

Canada 2015

BRA
MARTA
1,62 m
19-2-1986
Orlando Pride (USA)

France 2019

Brazilian striker Marta is one of the first superstars of the modern women's game and appeared in each of the first four Panini Women's World Cup sticker albums. Having made her full international debut at the age of 17, Marta Vieira da Silva went to Sweden two years later and her rise to the pinnacle of the game was rapid. At Umeå IK she averaged more than a goal a game, winning the league four times in a row, as well as the UEFA Women's Cup in 2004. Marta's first FIFA World Player of the Year award came two years later, the first of five in succession.

Once the inaugural season of Women's Professional Soccer (WPS) was announced for 2009, it was inevitable Marta would be lured to the USA. Her first season was a triumph: she finished as top scorer and Los Angeles Sol won the regular season title. A move to FC Gold Pride in 2010 saw her win almost every accolade going on her team's way to topping the league standings and then winning the championship final.

Marta's final year in the WPS – this time with Western New York Flash – was another huge success before she became part of Panini history later in 2011. Having inspired Brazil to the final of the 2007 Women's World Cup, a beaming Marta was one of the must-haves in Panini's first-ever album for the tournament – *Germany 2011*. Appearing again in the 2015 World Cup follow-up in Canada, one of her nation's leading sports stars also figured prominently in Panini's *Team Brasil Rio 2016 Olympics* special release album – an event at which Brazil heartbreakingly lost on penalties to Sweden in the semi-final.

Germany 2011

Australia and New Zealand 2023

By the time of her third Panini World Cup appearance in 2019, Marta was in record-breaking mood again, becoming the first player, male or female, to score in five successive World Cup finals tournaments. Injury restricted Marta's impact during her fourth consecutive Panini World Cup album appearance in 2023.

Marta has appeared in four consecutive Panini World Cup albums, and is the first player, male or female, to score in five successive World Cup finals tournaments.

Playing Career
Vasco da Gama (2000–2002); Santa Cruz (2002–2004); Umeå IK (2004–2008); Los Angeles Sol (2009); Santos (loan) (2009–2010); Gold Pride (2010); Santos (2011); Western New York Flash (2011); Tyresö FF (2012–2014); FC Rosengård (2014–2017); Orlando Pride (2017–) and Brazil (2002–2024)

Panini Album Rookie appearances
First club album appearance: N/A
First World Cup album appearance: *Germany 2011* (272)

Selected Panini Appearances
Germany 2011 (272); *Canada 2015* (345); *Team Brasil Rio 2016 Olympics* (27, 28, 127, 128); *France 2019* (232); *Australia and New Zealand 2023* (285, 299, 427)

ROMÁRIO

ROMARIO DE SOUZA FARIA

Voetbal 89

ROMARIO DE SOUZA FARIA

Voetbal 90

Still scoring with regularity into his 40s, Romário was one of the deadliest finishers of his era. The penalty-box predator caught the attention of European suitors while at Vasco da Gama, scoring at a phenomenal rate from an early age. A move to the Netherlands earned Romário his first Panini appearance in *Voetbal 89*, a season in which he scored 26 goals in 34 games to help PSV Eindhoven win a domestic double.

Romário featured in four more Panini *Voetbal* albums in red and white, picking up two more Eredivisie titles and another domestic cup. The Brazilian can be seen in an aerial challenge on the front of *Voetbal '92*, as well as in an extra sticker at the end of the album as the joint 1990–91 Eredivisie top scorer alongside Ajax's Dennis Bergkamp, who was given an additional image, too.

After Romário's 128 goals in 149 games for Eindhoven, Barcelona manager Johan Cruyff decided to add a further dimension to his all-conquering Barcelona 'Dream Team'. The Rio-born attacker was only at Camp Nou for one full season, but his 30 league goals in 33 appearances in that campaign secured his place in the club's annals.

At the end of that La Liga title-winning season there was even greater glory to come in the second of his Panini World Cup album appearances. The goal-poacher struck five times on the way to Brazil triumphing at USA 94, and scoring a penalty in the shoot-out final win against Italy. Two seasons of Spanish league sticker album appearances for Barcelona were followed by two more during a less successful spell at Valencia later in the 1990s, intersected by a prolific year back in Brazil with Flamengo. Romário made his third successive Panini World Cup album for France 98, only for injury to rule him out.

Italia '90

USA '94

Playing Career
Vasco da Gama (1985–1988);
PSV Eindhoven (1988–1993);
Barcelona (1993–1995);
Flamengo (1995–1996); Valencia
(1996–1997); Flamengo (loan)
(1997); Flamengo (1998–1999);
Vasco da Gama (2000–2002);
Fluminense (2002–2004); Al
Sadd (loan) (2003); Vasco da
Gama (2005–2006); Miami FC
(2006); Adelaide United (loan)
(2006); Vasco da Gama (2007);
America–RJ (2009) and Brazil
(1987–2005)

**Panini Album
Rookie Appearances**
First club album appearance:
Voetbal 89 (Netherlands) (152)
First World Cup album
appearance: *Italia '90* (208)

**Selected Panini
Appearances**
Voetbal 89 (Netherlands) (152);
Voetbal 90 (Netherlands) (159);
Italia '90 (208); *Voetbal '91*
(Netherlands) (145); *Voetbal
'92* (Netherlands) (110, 270);
Voetbal '93 (Netherlands) (1, 19);
Panini Liga 93–94 (Spain) (372);
Liga 93–94 (Colecciones ESTE)
(Spain) (40); *USA '94* (107); *Panini
Liga 94–95* (Spain) (69); *Liga
94–95* (Colecciones ESTE) (Spain)
(47); *Supercalcio 94–95* (Italy)
(219); *Supercalcio 95–96* (Italy)
(195); *Liga 96–97* (Colecciones
ESTE) Spain) (UF23); *Panini Liga
96/97* (Spain) (403); *Liga 97–98*
(Colecciones ESTE) (Spain) (510);
Panini Liga 97/98 (Spain) (138);
France 98 (29); *Road to FIFA World
Cup 2002* (136); *PSV Droomalbum
2017–2018* (Netherlands) (133)

Even though he was 36 by the time of the next World Cup, his astonishing scoring rate back in his homeland for Vasco da Gama – the second of four spells at the club – put him in contention for Korea/Japan and earned him a place in Panini's *Road to FIFA World Cup 2002*. Brazil manager Luiz Felipe Scolari opted not to select the veteran, though, but he was given a farewell international appearance in 2005, scoring in a friendly against Guatemala to finish with 70 caps and 55 goals.

ROMARIO Fútbol C. Barcelona

Liga 93–94 (Colecciones ESTE)

ROMARIO
BRASIL

France 98

CRISTIANO RONALDO

Futebol 2002–2003

Germany 2006

If collectors of *Futebol 2002–2003* had known the impact the young Sporting Lisbon prospect on number 306 would have over the next two decades, a good many more stickers would have endured in mint condition. At the height of its popularity, Cristiano Ronaldo's rookie achieved an auction price in excess of $100,000!

The Madeira-born player's rapid elevation meant he played only one season of senior football in his homeland before joining Manchester United in August 2003. A decade of Panini Champions League album appearances began with the *Champions of Europe 1955–2005* release for the 2005–06 campaign. His first Champions League winner's medal came in 2007–08, he won the first of his Ballon d'Or titles in 2008, and by the end of the 2008–09 season he completed a hat-trick of Premier League successes.

Having won the lot at Old Trafford, he moved to Spain. Arriving too late to be incorporated into the Real Madrid section of the 2009–10 release, he was celebrated later in the album as one of the *Últimos Fichajes* (latest signings). The 2011–12 season brought the first of two La Liga titles, while the first of four Champions League triumphs with Los Blancos arrived in 2013–14. Ronaldo won the Ballon d'Or four more times between 2013 and 2017, scoring at a phenomenal rate that would see him end his Bernabéu career with 451 goals in 438 games.

POR
2003
Real Madrid CF (ESP)
1,85 m
80 kg
5-2-1985

CRISTIANO RONALDO

Euro 2016

Between 2013 and 2017, Cristiano Ronaldo won the Ballon d'Or four times and led his nation Portugal to Euro glory in 2016.

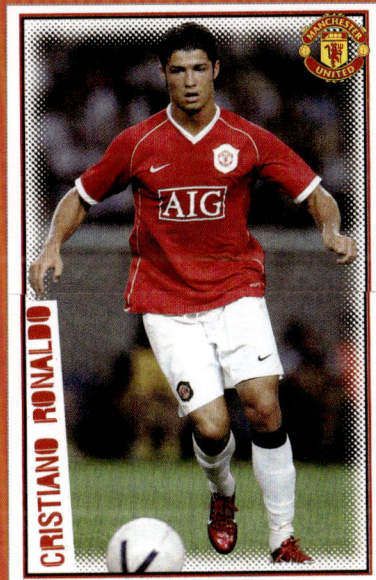

Manchester United 2006/07

Manchester United 2007/2008

CRISTIANO RONALDO
POR | Funchal | 5-2-1985

Calciatori 2019–2020

CRISTIANO RONALDO
POR | Funchal, 5-2-1985

Calciatori 2021

CRISTIANO RONALDO

Cristiano Ronaldo dos Santos Aveiro
Funchal (Portugal)
05.02.1985 / 1.84 M. / 75 KG.
Manchester United (09-10) / INT

Liga 2017–18 (Colecciones ESTE)

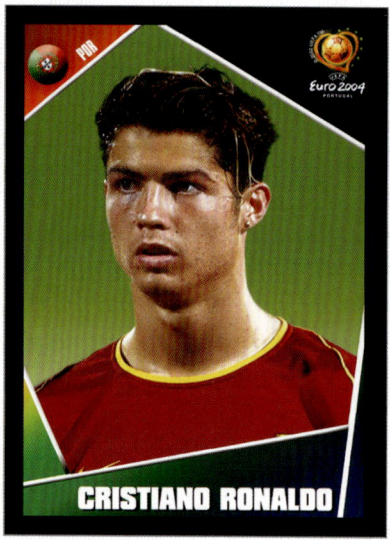

CRISTIANO RONALDO

Euro 2004

CRISTIANO RONALDO

Euro 2008

CRISTIANO RONALDO

Brasil 2014

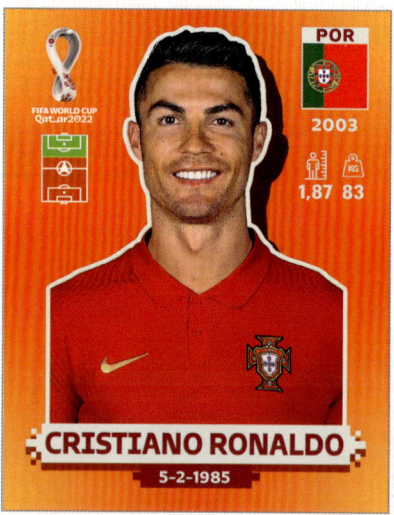

CRISTIANO RONALDO
5-2-1985

Qatar 2022

Cristiano Ronaldo has been a regular fixture in Panini albums since his first appearance during the 2002—03 season.

Liga 2012–13 (Colecciones ESTE)

Liga 2014–15 (Colecciones ESTE)

Ronaldo's strike rate during three seasons in Serie A with Juventus was only marginally inferior and he made the cover of his *Calciatori* bow in 2018–19, with four stickers inside, including a shot of his first goal in the black and white (against Sassuolo) in the *Film del Campionato* update to chronicle the story of the season. Two league titles and a Coppa Italia were the highlights of his three campaigns with Juve, before he departed early in the 2021–22 season for a return to Manchester United – and the cover of Panini's *Premier League 2022* album.

Playing Career
Sporting Lisbon (2002–2003); Manchester United (2003–2009); Real Madrid (2009–2018); Juventus (2018–2021); Manchester United (2021–2022); Al Nassr (2023–) and Portugal (2003–)

Panini Album Rookie Appearances
First club album appearance: Futebol 2002–2003 (Portugal) (306) First World Cup album appearance: *Germany 2006* (298)

Selected Panini Appearances
Futebol 2002–2003 (Portugal) (306); *Euro 2004* (23); *Champions of Europe 1955–2005* (228); *Germany 2006* (298); *Champions League 2007–2008* (243); *Euro 2008* (120, 509); *Liga 09–10* (Colecciones ESTE) (Spain) (632, 691, 724); *South Africa 2010* (559); *Liga 2010–2011* (Colecciones ESTE) (Spain) (289); *Liga 2011–12* (Colecciones ESTE) (Spain) (260); *Euro 2012* (277, 280, P6 in Platinum Edition/31, 206 in Dutch Edition); *Liga 2012–13* (Colecciones ESTE) (Spain) (323, 604); *Liga 2013–14* (Colecciones ESTE) (Spain) (380, 787); *Champions League 2013–2014* (90, 322); *Brasil 2014* (523); *Liga 2014–15* (Colecciones ESTE) (Spain) (406); *Liga 2015–16* (Colecciones ESTE) (Spain) (379); *Euro 2016* (596, 597); *Liga 2016–17* (Colecciones ESTE) (Spain) (419, 645); *Liga 2017–18* (Colecciones ESTE) (Spain) (497, 644); *Russia 2018* (118, MP6); *Calciatori 2018–2019* (Italy) (280, 281, C1, C8); *Liga 18–19* (Colecciones ESTE) (Spain) (449, 647, 817); *Calciatori 2019–2020* (Italy) (259, 263, 790, 807); *Euro 2020 Preview Edition* (POR6); *Calciatori 2021* (Italy) (290, X20 – Top Team Panini 60); *Euro 2020 Tournament Edition* (657, 676); *Liga 2021–22* (Colecciones ESTE) (Spain) (616); *Premier League 2022* ((England) (423, 432); *Qatar 2022* (POR17, CR – Extra Sticker); *Premier League 2023* (England) (450, 461)

RAY WILKINS

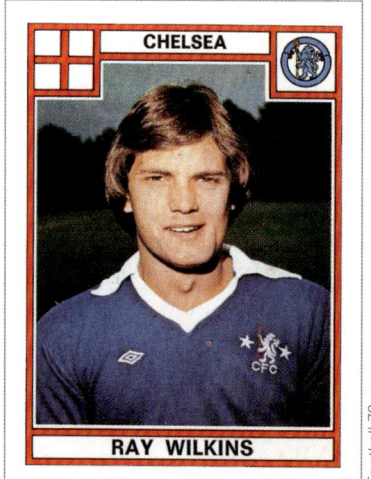

Football 78

Football 79

One of the few players to appear in Panini's first UK domestic album, *Football 78*, and the last in its initial run, *Football '93*, creative midfielder Ray Wilkins dipped out of the British game for spells in Italy and France, but that failed to halt a run of 16 consecutive seasons featuring in Panini collections around Europe.

Wilkins began his career at Chelsea and the 1975–76 campaign saw him given the captaincy, even though he hadn't quite turned 19 – a position he would hold until his departure to Manchester United in 1979. He won the FA Cup with United in 1983 before joining AC Milan in 1984.

Three seasons at the San Siro were followed by a short spell at Paris Saint-Germain, where he appeared in the French Panini *Football 88* album. He then had periods at Rangers, Queens Park Rangers and Crystal Palace.

The cultured passer won 84 caps for England, appearing in Panini form in *Europa 80* and *Mexico 86*, but missing the cut for *España 82*, despite ultimately playing every game.

Ray Wilkins had a run of 16 consecutive seasons in Panini collections. He appeared in the British, Italian and French albums as well as in the *Europa 80* and *Mexico 86* tournament collections.

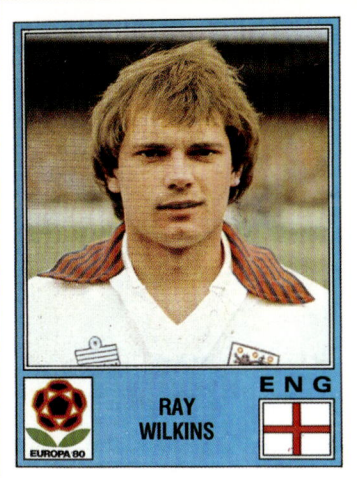

RAY WILKINS

E N G

Europa 80

ENGLAND

RAY WILKINS

Mexico 86

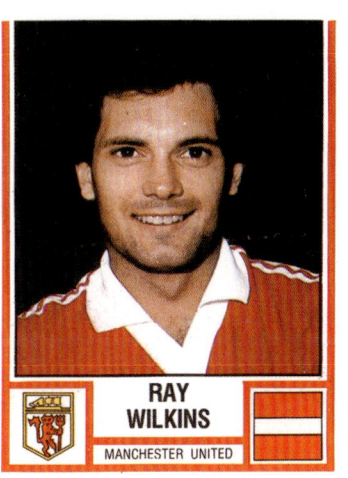

RAY WILKINS

MANCHESTER UNITED

Football 81

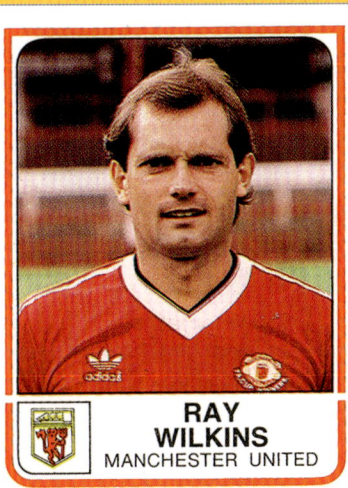

RAY WILKINS

MANCHESTER UNITED

Football 84

RAYMOND WILKINS

milan

Calciatori 1985–86

MILAN

RAYMOND WILKINS

Calciatori 1986–87

PARIS S.G.

RAY WILKINS

Football 88

Playing Career
Chelsea (1973–1979); Manchester United (1979–1984); AC Milan (1984–1987); Paris Saint-Germain (1987); Rangers (1987–1989); Queens Park Rangers (1989–1994); Crystal Palace (1994); Queens Park Rangers (1994–1996); Wycombe Wanderers (1996); Hibernian (1996–1997); Millwall (1997); Leyton Orient (1997) and England (1976–1986)

Panini Album Rookie Appearances
First club album appearance: Football 76 (UK) (Top Sellers/Panini) (81)
First World Cup album appearance: *Mexico 86* (410)

Selected Panini Appearances
Football '76 (UK) (Top Sellers/Panini) (81); *Football 78* (UK) (85); *Euro Football 78* (78b); *Football 79* (UK) (103); *Football 80* (UK) (232); *Europa 80* (122); *Football 81* (UK) (205); *Football 82* (UK) (162); *Football 83* (UK) (173); *Football 84* (UK) (161); *Calciatori 1984–85* (Italy) (180); *Calciatori 1985–86* (Italy) (156); *Mexico 86* (410); *Supercalcio 1985–86* (Italy) (136); *Calciatori 1986–87* (Italy) (188); *Football 87* (UK) (453); *Football 88* (France) (299); *Football 89* (UK) (451); *Football 90* (UK) (449); *Football 1991* (UK) (256); *Soccer's Super Sevens* (1991–92) (109); *English Football 1992* (181); *Football '93* (England) (198); *Superplayers '96* (England) (237 – as player-manager)

ROBERT LEWANDOWSKI

Ekstraklasa 08–09

Russia 2018

Free-scoring Robert Lewandowski timed his first season in the Polish top-flight with Panini's first domestic football sticker album in the country for a decade. Having served notice of his potential in the lower leagues with Znicz Pruszków, the striker joined Lech Poznań in 2008, taking his place in Panini's *Ekstraklasa 08–09* album.

After winning the Polish Cup in his first season, the emerging youngster's goals helped his team win the title in 2009–10. The Warsaw-born player also featured on the front of *Ekstraklasa 09–10*, his last season in his homeland before he moved to Germany. Nonetheless he popped up again in the following campaign's *Ekstraklasa* album to mark his top-scoring exploits.

Although Panini were not producing the Bundesliga album by the time of Lewandowski's move to Borussia Dortmund, they were releasing a dedicated album for the club. During his time there he won the Bundesliga twice and reached the Champions League final in 2013. That season marked the second of his four successive Panini Champions League album appearances, but Dortmund lost at Wembley to Bayern Munich, the club he joined a year later.

By this time Lewandowski had made his first national team sticker appearance, in the Panini *Euro 2012* collection, and was well on the way to breaking the previous record of 48 international goals for Poland. His nation returned for the next Euro album in 2016, going out on penalties in the quarter-final to eventual winners Portugal, before their star man scored a remarkable 16 goals in qualifying to send his team to Russia 2018. A third Panini Euro album sticker followed in the tournament delayed until 2021, ahead of a second World Cup in a finals tournament during which he scored twice.

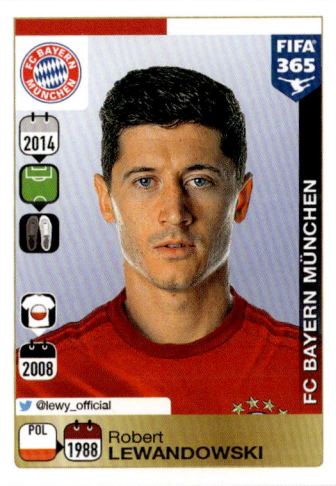

FIFA 365 2016

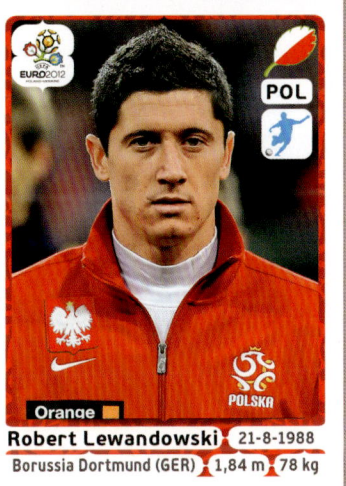

Euro 2012

Euro 2016

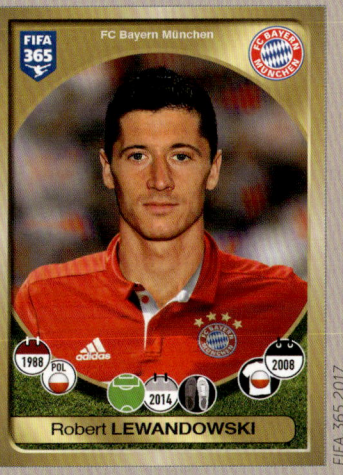

FIFA 365 2017

Playing Career

Delta Warsaw (2005); Legia Warsaw II (2005–2006); Znicz Pruszków (2006–2008); Lech Poznań (2008–2010); Borussia Dortmund (2010–2014); Bayern Munich (2014–2022); Barcelona (2022–) and Poland (2008–)

Panini Album Rookie Appearances

First club album appearance: Ekstraklasa 08–09 (Poland) (128)
First World Cup album appearance: Russia 2018 (609)

Selected Panini Appearances

Ekstraklasa 08–09 (Poland) (128); Ekstraklasa 09-10 (Poland) (10, 341); Ekstraklasa 2011 (Poland) (6, 8); Champions League 2011–2012 (412); Borussia Dortmund 2011–12 (147–152) Euro 2012 (74, 77, 38 – Dutch Special Edition); Champions League 2012–2013 (298); Futebol 2012–2013 (Portugal) (353); Borussia Dortmund 2012–13 (137 to 142); Champions League 2013–2014 (308, 447); Champions League 2014–2015 (355); FC Bayern Munich 2014–15 (136 to 141) Euro 2016 (312, 313, CC–C – Coca Cola); Dumni z Naszych (2018) (Poland) (82 to 85, C15); Russia 2018 (609); Liga 2022–23 (Colecciones ESTE) (Spain) (706); Qatar 2022 (POL16 and RL – Legend); Liga 2023–24 (Colecciones ESTE) (Spain) (150)

The Pole was a regular feature in Panini's *FIFA 365* albums during his eight seasons at Bayern Munich and twice a cover star in a period that saw him score a remarkable 238 goals in 253 Bundesliga appearances. Having been leading scorer in the German top flight in his last season at Dortmund, he topped the charts in six seasons out of eight in Munich, winning the league title every season and the Champions League in 2020.

Having scored more than 300 Bundesliga goals and with nothing left to achieve, 'Lewangoalski' moved to Barcelona in 2022, adding another chapter to his Panini career in the Colecciones ESTE Spanish Liga albums. The serial winner was top scorer in his first La Liga season, helping Barça to the league title and Supercopa de España.

FIFA 365 2018

KYLIAN MBAPPÉ

Foot 2016–17

Kylian Mbappé's rookie sticker appeared in French *Foot 2016–17* and is one of the last mass-produced stickers to be greatly sought after. The Paris-born striker had made his Ligue 1 debut for Monaco in December 2015 when still a few weeks short of his 17th birthday and his rapid progress over the second half of the 2015–16 campaign was enough to win selection for the following season's Panini album. Even though that turned out to be his only Panini sticker for the Principality, the prodigy was one of the leading lights in a Monaco side that won Ligue 1 and also enjoyed a run to the semi-finals of the Champions League.

Mbappé's senior international debut in March 2017 capped a remarkable first full season and he appeared on the cover of that year's *Fiers d'être Bleus* Panini album to celebrate the national team. A first international tournament Panini sticker came the following year in the *Russia 2018* album – by which time he was a Paris Saint-Germain player. Four goals, including one in the final victory over Croatia, was enough to win Mbappé the Best Young Player Award. A star was born.

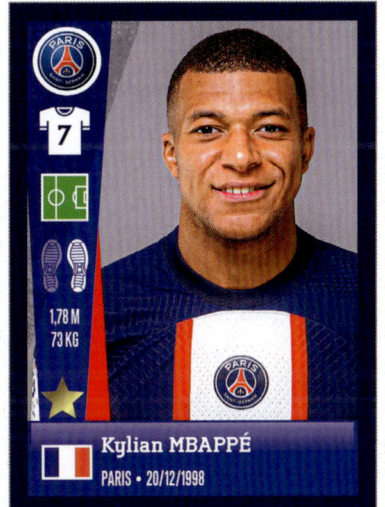

Foot 2023

Foot 2017-18

Russia 2018

Mbappé scored in the 2018 World Cup final and became the second teenager, after Pelé, to score in a World Cup final.

Kylian Mbappé's first international tournament Panini sticker came in the 2018 World Cup album, where he received the FIFA World Cup Best Young Player Award.

Mbappé first appeared on the Panini *FIFA 365* album cover in 2019 — an accolade bestowed only on the very finest players.

KYLIAN MBAPPÉ
20/12/1998 | Paris

Foot 2021

20-12-1998 Paris
Kylian **MBAPPÉ**

Foot 2018–2019

KYLIAN MBAPPÉ
20-12-1998

Qatar 2022

KYLIAN MBAPPÉ
FRA | Paris | 20/12/1998

Foot 2022

Kylian **MBAPPÉ**
20/12/1998 Paris

Foot 2019–2020

KYLIAN **MBAPPÉ**
20/12/1998
PARIS

Foot 2024

Euro 2020 Tournament Edition

A string of Panini *FIFA 365* album cover appearances – an accolade bestowed only on the very finest players – have since followed and he also joined Cristiano Ronaldo and Erling Haaland on the first *Top Class* release in 2022. That year saw Mbappé in his second Panini World Cup sticker collection, inevitably one of the Legends in the *Extra Stickers* produced for Qatar 2022. The French kingpin certainly lived up to his billing, securing the Golden Boot when he became only the second man to score a World Cup final hat-trick. While his country ultimately lost the final on penalties, it was only down to his sheer force of will that France even made it that far, as he had hauled his side back from the brink against Argentina at 0-2 and 2-3. Mbappé embarked on a new chapter in his career when he joined Real Madrid on a free transfer in June 2024.

RONALDINHO

Calciatori 2009-10

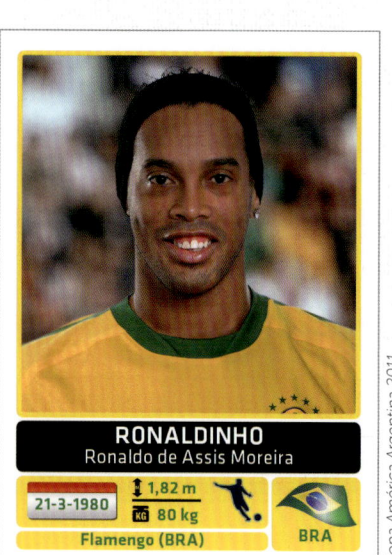

Copa América Argentina 2011

Ronaldinho burst onto the scene for Grêmio in 1998, earning himself a first Panini sticker in the *Campeonato Brasileiro 99* album, which now fetches thousands of pounds when in top condition. The playmaker added goals to his creativity in 1999, helping Grêmio to the Copa Sul and Campeonato Gaúcho, as well as earning his first Brazil cap. Then, after one further outing in Panini's Brazilian domestic football album, Ronaldinho made the move to Europe with Paris Saint-Germain, first appearing in *Foot 2002* for the French club.

That summer the attacker made his mark on the global stage, winning the World Cup in his first tournament. But he only appeared as an individual sticker in the Brazilian version of the Panini *Korea/Japan 2002* album – replacing Mauro Silva – although he did feature in the team group of the standard collection. Ronaldinho Gaúcho, as he was named on his Panini World Cup rookie, produced one of the most vivid memories of the co-hosted event when he floated a free kick over England goalkeeper David Seaman for the quarter-final winner.

It was in the following season's *Foot 2003* album that the longer hairstyle with which he would become synonymous during the golden phase of his career was unveiled. That elevation came following a move to Barcelona when those at Panini, clearly excited by the Brazilian's arrival, put him on the front of his first album. Among those joining him on the cover of *Superliga de Estrellas 2003–2004* were Ronaldo, Fernando Torres and Denilson.

There was no better player on the planet than Ronaldinho during his second and third seasons at Camp Nou in 2004–05 and 2005–06, winning two La Liga titles and the Champions League, as well as the Confederations Cup with his country. That Champions League triumph of 2006 – in which he scored seven goals along the way to the final victory over Arsenal – coincided with the first of five Panini Champions League album appearances.

Foot 2002

Champions of Europe 1955-2005

South Africa 2010

Germany 2006

Playing Career

Grêmio (1998–2001); Paris Saint-Germain (2001–2003); Barcelona (2003–2008); AC Milan (2008–2011); Flamengo (2011–2012); Atlético Mineiro (2012–2014); Querétaro (2014–2015); Fluminense (2015) and Brazil (1999–2013)

Panini Album Rookie Appearances

First club album appearance: *Campeonato Brasileiro 99* (124) First World Cup album appearance: *Korea/Japan 2002* (179 – Brazil version)

Selected Panini Appearances

Campeonato Brasileiro 99 (124); *Foot 2002* (France) (300); *Korea/Japan 2002* (179 – Brazil version); *Foot 2003* (France) (2006, 308); *Superliga de Estrellas 2003–2004* (Spain) (42, 120); *Liga 2003–2004* (Colecciones ESTE) (Spain) (523, 524); *Liga 2004–2005* (Colecciones ESTE) (Spain) (94); *Liga 2005–2006* (Colecciones ESTE) (Spain) (91); *Champions of Europe 1955–2005* (73) *Germany 2006* (393); *Liga 2006–2007 Colecciones ESTE* (Spain) (80); *Copa América Venezuela 2007* (117); *Liga 07–08* (Colecciones ESTE) (Spain) (109); *Calciatori 2008–09* (Italy) (283); *Calciatori 2009–10* (Italy) (307); *South Africa 2010* (500); *Calciatori 2010–11* (Italy) (332); *Campeonato Brasileiro 2011* (225); *Copa America Argentina 2011* (131, 343); *Campeonato Brasileiro 2012* (22, 31); *Campeonato Brasileiro 2012* (22, 31); *Campeonato Brasileiro 2013* (11); *BBVA Liga Bancomer Clausura 2015* (Mexico) (92)

Once the success dried up in Spain he moved to Italy, his third and final *Calciatori* album appearance coming in an AC Milan title-winning season, although the Brazilian left midway through. Ronaldinho went on to feature in *Campeonato Brasileiro* albums for Flamengo and Atlético Mineiro, winning trophies with both. A final playing sticker came for Mexican side Querétaro in Panini's *Liga BBVA Bancomer Clausura 2015*.

Ronaldinho's later appearances in Panini international albums proved to be premature: he was not picked for either the 2010 World Cup or the 2013 Confederations Cup. He didn't take part in the 2007 or 2011 Copa América either – the former after he asked to be left out due to fatigue – despite making Panini's *seleção* list.

LUÍS FIGO

Panini has produced football sticker albums for the Portuguese league since *Futebol 92–93* and in that album, in a collection divided by position rather than club, was a winger named Figo, a straggly-haired Sporting Lisbon youngster whose locks would become more styled as the years went on. A move to Barcelona beckoned and the midfield schemer went under the longer title of Luís Filipe Madeira Figo in his first Panini La Liga album for the 1995–96 season.

It was then back to the abbreviated Figo in his first Panini international tournament album – *European Football Championship England '96* – when he helped his country reach the quarter-finals. After Portugal missed out on France 98, Figo appeared in four consecutive Panini Euro and World Cup albums, up to his international retirement in 2006. The Iberian nation reached two semi-finals and one final during that time – the defeat to Greece in the Euro 2004 final the closest he got to a winner's medal.

Futebol 93–94

European Football Championship England '96

There were fewer disappointments on the club stage, however, as Figo won seven trophies in his five seasons at Barcelona. His final season at Camp Nou brought him a cover appearance on the Colecciones Este album, in action against Real Madrid – the side he would join in the summer – pursued by Fernando Morientes. Figo won the Ballon d'Or at the end of 2000, having carried his Barça form into Euro 2000 and his early months in Madrid, to begin a period of riches with seven trophies in his first three seasons. A move to Internazionale in Italy then followed in 2005, where he was deployed more centrally, orchestrating play, rather than in the wide role he had been in for most of his career. Four Panini *Calciatori* album appearances resulted in as many Serie A titles – the perfect ending for this stylish footballer.

FIGO

Calciatori 2005–06

FIGO

Calciatori 07–08

REAL MADRID CF

FIGO

Champions League 2000/2001

POR

FIGO

Germany 2006

FIGO
F.C. BARCELONA

Liga 95–96 (Colecciones ESTE)

Playing Career
Sporting Lisbon (1989–1995);
Barcelona (1995–2000);
Real Madrid (2000–2005);
Internazionale (2005–2009)
and Portugal (1991–2006)

Panini Album
Rookie Appearances
First club album appearance:
Futebol 92–93 (Portugal) (119)
First World Cup album
appearance: *Korea/Japan 2002*
(307)

Selected Panini
Appearances
Futebol 92–93 (Portugal) (119);
Futebol 93–94 (Portugal) (47);
Futebol 94–95 (Portugal) (187,
323); *Futebol 95–96* (Portugal)
(180); *Liga 95–96* (Colecciones
ESTE) (Spain) (39); *European
Football Championship England
'96* (307); *Futebol 96/97* (Portugal)
(360); *Liga 96–97* (Colecciones
ESTE)(Spain) (40); *Futebol
97–98* (Portugal) (177, 193); *Liga
97–98* (Colecciones ESTE)
(Spain) (48); *Futebol 98–99*
(Portugal) (179, 195); *Liga 98–99*
(Colecciones ESTE)(Spain) (70);
Euro Super Clubs 1999 (60);
Liga 1999–2000 (Colecciones
ESTE) (73); *Euro 2000* (66);
Futebol 2000–01 (Portugal) (335);
Liga 2000–2001 (Colecciones
ESTE) (Spain) (203); *Champions
League 2000/2001* (16); *Futebol
2001–2002* (Portugal) (435);
Liga 2001–2002 (Colecciones
ESTE) (Spain) (208); *Champions
League 2001/2002* (15);
Korea/Japan 2002 (307) *Liga
02–203* (Colecciones ESTE)
(Spain) (214); *Liga 2003–2004*
(Colecciones ESTE) (Spain)
(225); *Euro 2004* (20); *Liga
2004–2005* (Colecciones ESTE)
(Spain) (244); *Liga 2005–06*
(Colecciones ESTE) (Spain)
(257); *Calciatori 2005–2006*
(Italy) (134); *Germany 2006* (293);
Calciatori 2006–07 (Italy) (168);
Calciatori 07–08 (Italy) (163);
Calciatori 2008–09 (Italy) (187)

Playing Career

Bellmare Hiratsuka (1995–1998); Perugia (1998–2000); Roma (2000–2001); Parma (2001–2004); Bologna (loan) (2004); Fiorentina (2004–2006); Bolton Wanderers (loan) (2005–2006) and Japan (1997–2006)

Panini Album Rookie Appearances

First club album appearance: Calciatori 1998–99 (246)
First World Cup album appearance: France 98 (524)

Selected Panini Appearances

France 98 (524); Calciatori 1998–99 (Italy) (246); Calciatori 2000 (Italy) (258); Supercalcio 1999–2000 (Italy) (109); Roma 1999–2000 (29, 30) Super Football 99 (116); Calciatori 2000–2001 (Italy) (349); Roma 2000–01 (38, 39); Calciatori 2001–2002 (Italy) (260); Noi Campioni 2001–2002 (84); Road to FIFA World Cup 2002 (75); Korea/Japan 2002 (541); Calciatori 2002–2003 (Italy) (293); Supercalcio 2002–03 (Italy) (118); Calciatori 2003–2004 (Italy) (282, A22); Calcio Coppe 2003-2004 (Italy) (88); Liga Italiana e Nossas Estrelas (Italy) (2004) (33); Superalbum.: Storia e miti del calcio italiano (Italy) (2004) (215); Calciatori 2004-2005 (Italy) (136); Germany 2006 (Mini–sticker set) (107); Germany 2006 (447)

HIDETOSHI NAKATA

JAPAN

2002 FIFA WORLD CUP

Korea/Japan 2002

Nakata played in all four of Japan's matches at the 2002 World Cup, scoring in the 2–0 first round win against Tunisia.

HIDETOSHI NAKATA
JAPAN

France 98

PERUGIA

HIDETOSHI NAKATA

Calciatori 1998–99

ROMA

HIDETOSHI NAKATA

Calciatori 2000–2001

HIDETOSHI NAKATA

Calciatori 2002-2003

Calciatori 2004-2005

One of the first Asian-born players to become a global star, Hidetoshi Nakata blazed a trail for today's rich crop of talent from the continent. After finding his feet in his Japanese homeland with Bellmare Hiratsuka, the attacking midfielder became only the second player from his country to play in Serie A, when he joined Perugia in 1998.

Nakata had earned his first Panini sticker that summer as part of Japan's squad for France 98 – the first time the country had reached the finals. He then excelled in the co-hosted Korea/Japan 2002 World Cup, helping Japan top their group before exiting in the first knockout phase. He again played in all of Japan's games in Germany 2006.

The Yamanashi-born player proved a popular import during his time in Italy, featuring in seven consecutive *Calciatori* albums between 1998–99 and 2004–05. A move to Roma provided some of the fondest memories because he was part of the side that won the Serie A title and joined star names such as Cafu, Francesco Totti and Gabriel Batistuta among I Giallorossi in *Calciatori 2000–2001*. That year ended with him being nominated for the Ballon d'Or for the third time – the first Asian player to receive that accolade.

JÜRGEN KLINSMANN

JÜRGEN KLINSMANN

Italia '90

Jürgen
Klinsmann
VfB STUTTGART

Fussball 87

Famed for his acrobatic finishing and flamboyant goal celebrations, Jürgen Klinsmann began his career in his home city with the then-second-tier Stuttgarter Kickers, before starting his top-flight Bundesliga days with VFB Stuttgart. That 1984–85 campaign was also the start of his life as a Panini sticker – the familiar blond mop of hair that endured throughout his playing days already established. Klinsmann averaged a goal every other game at Stuttgart, but he went trophy-less over five seasons before moving to Internazionale for the 1989–90 season. The highlight of his three seasons in Milan came in the middle when he contributed important goals along the way to his side winning the UEFA Cup.

Two appearances in the French *Foot* album playing for Monaco followed in 1992–93 and 1993–94, and the German frontman played a season in England with Tottenham Hotspur before two seasons at Bayern Munich, winning the UEFA Cup in 1996 and the Bundesliga in 1997. In his last season at the top level, Klinsmann had time to fit in half a campaign at Sampdoria – and his final *Calciatori* sticker – as well as a return to Tottenham.

Klinsmann's first international Panini sticker had come in *Euro 88*. The Netherlands ended West Germany's dreams of glory at the semi-final stage, but nothing would impede the side's progress at Italia 90 with Klinsmann scoring three goals on the way to winning the tournament. He also scored in three European Championships, winning in Euro 96.

After his playing retirement, Klinsmann returned to his national team as manager, leading them to the semi-final of Germany 2006 and featuring in his own page of the special release Panini album *Deutsches Nationalteam 2006*.

JÜRGEN KLINSMANN

MONACO

Foot 93

INTER

JÜRGEN KLINSMANN

Calciatori 1989–90

JÜRGEN KLINSMANN
DEUTSCHLAND - BRD

Euro 88

INTER

JÜRGEN KLINSMANN

Calciatori 1990–91

VfB STUTTGART

JÜRGEN KLINSMANN

Fussball 89

SAMPDORIA

JÜRGEN KLINSMANN

Calciatori 1997–98

Playing Career

Stuttgarter Kickers (1981–1984); VfB Stuttgart (1984–1989); Internazionale (1989–1992); Monaco (1992–1994); Tottenham Hotspur (1994–1995); Bayern Munich (1995–1997); Sampdoria (1997–1998); Tottenham Hotspur (loan) (1997–1998); Orange County Blue Star (2003) and West Germany/Germany (1987–1998)

Panini Album Rookie Appearances

First club album appearance: Fussball 85 (Germany) (299)
First World Cup album appearance: *Italia '90* (265)

Selected Panini Appearances

Fussball 85 (Germany) (299); *Fussball 86* (Germany) (288); *Fussball 87* (Germany) (296); *Fussball 88* (Germany) (303); *Euro 88* (71); *Fussball 89* (Germany) (288); *Calciatori 1989–90* (Italy) (164); *Italia '90* (265); *Calciatori 1990–91* (Italy) (145); *Calciatori 1991–92* (Italy) (162); *Euro '92* (210); *Foot 93* (France) (137); *Foot 1994* (France) (190); *USA '94* (183); *Fussball 96* (Germany) (155, 161, 162); *German Football Bundesliga 1995–1996. Final phase* (1, 2, 145) (Germany); *European Football Championship England '96* (210); *Fussball 97* (Germany) (11, 44, 53, 475); *Fussball Bundesliga zur Endphase der Saison 1996/1997* (Germany) (173, 265, 266); *Calciatori 1997–1998* (Italy) (335); *France 98* (386); *Deutsches Nationalteam 2006* (4, 168, 171, 177, T24); *FIFA 365 2017* (16); *Premier League 2022* (England) (338)

NEYMAR JÚNIOR

Campeonato Brasileiro 2012

Campeonato Brasileiro 2010

Brazil's record goalscorer has been exciting audiences with his attacking play since bursting on to the scene in his homeland as a 17-year-old. In his debut season of 2009, such was his impact for Santos, he was given a rookie sticker in the following year's *Campeonato Brasileiro 2010* Panini album. Sporting a mohawk on his first sticker, Neymar won three successive Campeonato Paulista and the 2010 Copa do Brasil, but his crowning glory came when he scored in the second leg of the 2011 Copa Libertadores final – the first time Santos had won the trophy since the days of Pelé in 1963.

The tricky forward was by now a member of Brazil's national side, going on to win the player of the tournament in the 2013 Confederations Cup victory, a triumph that would be captured in Panini's *Brasil de Todas as Copas* album later that year. By the time of his first Panini World Cup album sticker, for the 2014 tournament in Brazil, the hopes of his nation were mostly pinned on the 22-year-old striker. He scored four goals up to the quarter-final, but a back injury sustained in that game ended his World Cup prematurely with Brazil exiting ignominiously in his absence.

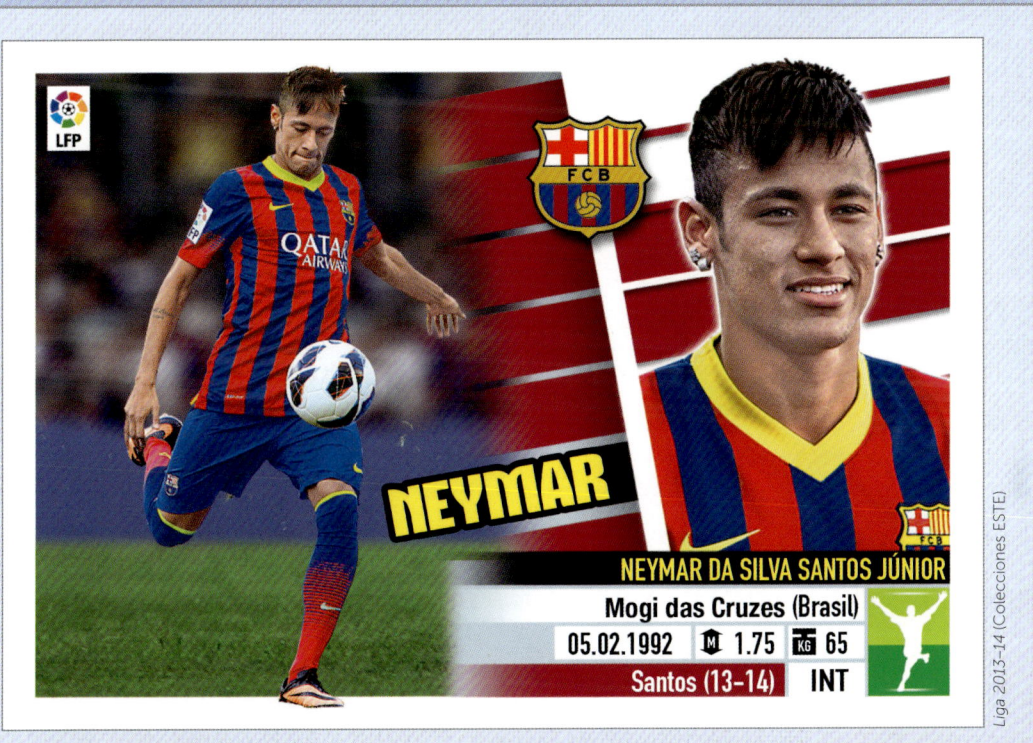

NEYMAR

NEYMAR DA SILVA SANTOS JÚNIOR

Mogi das Cruzes (Brasil)

05.02.1992 | M 1.75 | KG 65

Santos (13–14) | INT

Liga 2013–14 (Colecciones ESTE)

NEYMAR JR.

5-2-1992 | 1,75 m | 64 kg

Brasil 2014

NEYMAR JR

5-2-1992

2010

m 1,75

kg 68

Paris Saint-Germain (FRA)

Russia 2018

NEYMAR JR

5-2-1992

2010

1,75 | 68

Qatar 2022

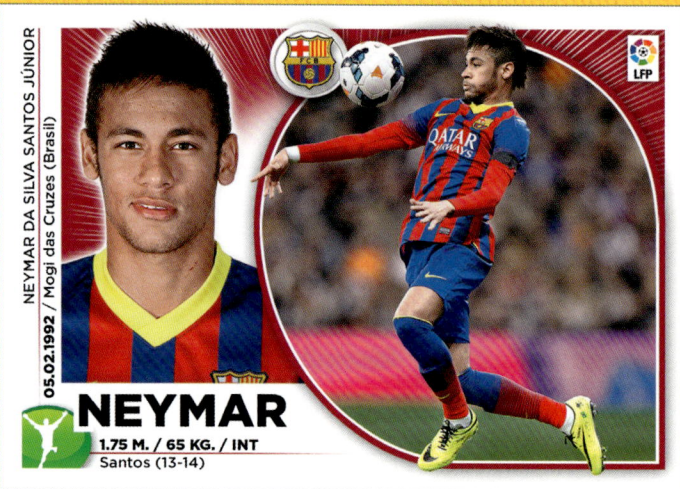

NEYMAR DA SILVA SANTOS JÚNIOR / Mogi das Cruzes (Brasil)

05.02.1992

NEYMAR

LFP

1.75 M. / 65 KG. / INT
Santos (13-14)

Colecciones ESTE Liga 2014-15

NEYMAR
Neymar da Silva Santos Júnior
Mogi das Cruzes (Brasil)
05.02.1992 / 1.75 M. / 65 KG.
Santos (13-14) / INT

Liga 2016-17 (Colecciones ESTE)

10
1,75 m
68 kg

NEYMAR JR.
05/02/1992 | Mogi das Cruzes (BRA)

Foot 2021

6
6

10
A

M 1,75
KG 68

NEYMAR JR.
05-02-1992 Mogi das Cruzes (BRA)

Foot 2017-18

10
A
M 1,75
KG 68

05-02-1992 Mogi das Cruzes (BRA)
NEYMAR JR

Foot 2018-2019

10
cm 1,75
kg 68

NEYMAR JR.
05/02/1992 Mogi das Cruzes (BRA)

Foot 2019-2020

Foot 2022

In the summer of 2013 Neymar had moved to Barcelona, making a first appearance in that season's Colecciones ESTE *Liga 2013-14* album. He missed out on major honours in that campaign, but better luck was to come in the next domestic season, 2014–15, as he was in irresistible form as part of a three-pronged attack with Lionel Messi and Luis Suárez. Neymar scored 22 goals in Barça's La Liga win and a further 10 to add the Champions League.

After securing the FIFA Club World Cup at the end of 2015, Barça secured another La Liga title in 2016, with Neymar once more in a lead role. There was time for one final trophy in his last season at Camp Nou – a third Copa del Rey – before he moved to Paris Saint-Germain for a world record fee of €222 million and a Panini appearance in the Ligue 1 album. In September 2023 he scored his 78th international goal to break Pelé's Brazilian national team record.

ROBERTO BAGGIO

Calciatori 1990–91

Calciatori 1992–93

As a creator and contributor of goals in equally high proportions, Roberto Baggio was, not surprisingly, a regular feature in his heyday on the cover of Panini's *Calciatori* albums. Yet the Panini career of *Il Divin Codino* (The Divine Ponytail) began in less conspicuous circumstances, in the back row of Serie C1 team Vicenza in *Calciatori 1984–85*.

Baggio was plucked from the lower leagues as an 18-year-old by Fiorentina and on his first individual Panini sticker, in *Calciatori 1985–86*, sported a bounteous mullet. Injuries ruined his first two seasons with La Viola before he established himself during the 1987–88 campaign. But it was in 1988–89 when a promising talent became a star – Baggio scored 15 goals to help his side win a UEFA Cup place.

His first international tournament sticker came for Italia 90, a World Cup which, agonisingly, saw the Italians go out on penalties to Argentina in the last four. However, Juventus rated him highly enough to splash out a then-record £8 million that summer, and he scored more than 100 goals for the club over the next five seasons. During that period Baggio was given the accolade of being Panini's cover star on *Calciatori 1991–92* and *Calciatori 1993–94*. Serie A, UEFA Cup and Coppa Italia winner's medals were achieved during his time in Turin, as well as the Ballon d'Or of 1993.

There would be further World Cup disappointment in 1994 when Italy lost the final to Brazil with Baggio missing his team's fifth penalty. Consecutive Serie A titles

ROBERTO BAGGIO

fiorentina

Calciatori 1985–86

FIORENTINA

ROBERTO BAGGIO

Calciatori 1988–89

INTER

ROBERTO BAGGIO

Calciatori 1998–99

USA '94

ROBERTO BAGGIO

ITALIA

USA '94

Playing Career
Vicenza (1982–1985); Fiorentina (1985–1990); Juventus (1990–1995); AC Milan (1995–1997); Bologna (1997–1998); Internazionale (1998–2000); Brescia (2000–2004) and Italy (1988–2004)

Panini Album Rookie Appearances
First club album appearance: Calciatori 1985–86 (Italy) (93)
First World Cup album appearance: *Italia '90* (53)

Selected Panini Appearances
Calciatori 1985–86 (Italy) (93); Calciatori 1986–87 (Italy) (129); Calciatori 1987–88 (Italy) (104); Calciatori 1988–89 (Italy) (112); Calciatori 1989–90 (Italy) (127); *Italia '90* (53); Calciatori 1990–91 (Italy) (165); Calciatori 1991–92 (Italy) (183, 347); Euro '92 (251); Calciatori 1992–93 (Italy) (2, 187); Calciatori 1993–94 (Italy)(127); USA '94 (259); Calciatori 1994–95 (Italy) (174); Calciatori 1995–96 (Italy) (168); European Football Championship England '96 (251); Calciatori 1996–97 (Italy) (185); Calciatori 1997–98 (Italy) (60); Calciatori 1998–99 (Italy) (135, 416); Calciatori 2000 (Italy) (115); Calciatori 2000–01 (Italy) (92); Calciatori 2001–02 (Italy) (69); *Azzurro Mondiale 1910–2002* (Italy) (74, 75, 90, 108, N5); Calciatori 2002–03 (Italy) (74); Calciatori 2003–04 (Italy) (71); Calciatori 2010–11 (Italy) 7 (Top Team Panini 50)

in his last season at Juventus and first with AC Milan were some consolation, but he missed out on Euro 96 after falling out with coach Arrigo Sacchi, though he did make Panini's *European Football Championship England '96* album. Baggio returned to international favour in time for a third Panini World Cup appearance in *France 98*, on the back of his best-ever haul of 22 Serie A goals during his only season with Bologna. Two unfulfilled seasons with Internazionale were followed by a renaissance at Brescia, whom he joined on a free transfer at the age of 33.

MILAN

Roberto BAGGIO

Calciatori 1996–97

DIDIER DESCHAMPS

Football 88

Foot 90

One of only three people to have won the World Cup as a player and manager, Didier Deschamps can lay claim to an active Panini sticker career of 35 years and counting. Making his Nantes first-team debut in 1985–86, the defensive midfielder got his Panini rookie only in *Football 88*, where he was joined in the squad by some high-profile imports in Maurice Johnston, Franky Vercauteren and Jorge Burruchaga, who scored the winning goal in the 1986 World Cup final.

Although by now an established member of the side, Deschamps missed the cut in *Foot 89*. He then returned in *Foot 90*, but midway through that season was signed by Marseille. After helping his new club win Ligue 1, he was loaned to Bordeaux the following season, appearing for Les Girondins in *Foot 91*. Deschamps could finally consider himself a fully fledged member of the Marseille squad in 1991–92, winning the league title, before captaining the club to the Champions League the year after. It was in 1992 that the tough tackler earned his first Panini international sticker in the *Euro '92* album, only for his country to miss out on the USA 94 World Cup after a last-gasp defeat in their final qualifier against Bulgaria.

Foot 91

Foot 93

Calciatori 1995-96

Calciatori 1996-97

Calciatori 1997-98

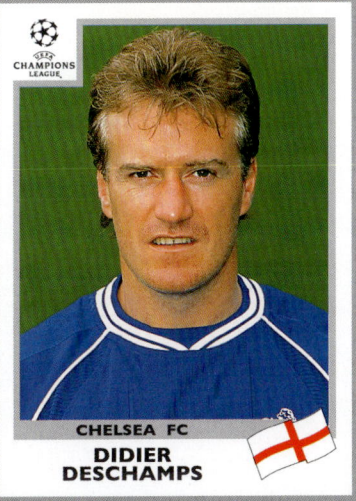

Champions League 1999-2000

Playing Career

Nantes (1985–1989); Marseille (1989–1994); Bordeaux (loan) (1990–1991); Juventus (1994–1999); Chelsea (1999–2000); Valencia (2000–2001) and France (1989–2000)

Panini Album Rookie Appearances

First club album appearance: *Football 88 (France)* (250)
First World Cup album appearance: *France 98* (165)

Selected Panini Appearances

Football 88 (France) (250); *Foot 90 (France)* (223); *Foot 91* (25); *Foot 92 (France)* (111); *Euro '92* (54); *Foot 93 (France)* (105, I); *Foot 1994 (France)* (140); *Supercalcio 94–95 (Italy)* (170); *Calciatori 1995–96 (Italy)* (126); *European Football Championship England '96* (186); *Calciatori 1996-97 (Italy)* (143); *Supercalcio 96–97* (103); *Türkiye 1. Futbol Ligi 1996–1997* (250); *Calciatori 1997–98 (Italy)* (161); *France 98* (165); *Champions 98 (France)* (27, 28, 29); *Superfoot 1998/99 (France)* (165, 186); *Calciatori 1998–99 (Italy)* (151); *Scottish Premier League 99* (214); *Super Football 99* (94); *Champions League 1999/2000* (281); *Olympique de Marseille 1999–2000* (125); *Euro 2000* (346); *Champions League 2000/2001* (167); *Valencia CF 2000–01* (89–92); *Superfoot 2003–04 (France)* (7 – as manager); *Foot 2005 (France)* (224 – as manager); *Superfoot 2005–06 (France)* (31 – as manager, 150); *Foot 2010 (France)* (238 – as manager); *Foot 2011–12 (France)* (26, 254 – as manager); *Team France 2018: Fiers d'être Bleus* (8, 9, 10 – as manager); *Team France 2023: Fiers d'être Bleus* (215, 216, 217 – as manager)

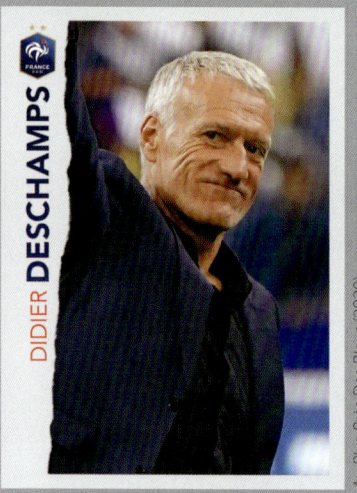

Au Plus Près Des Bleus (2020)

Didier Deschamps is one of only three people to have won the FIFA World Cup as a player (1998) and a coach (2018).

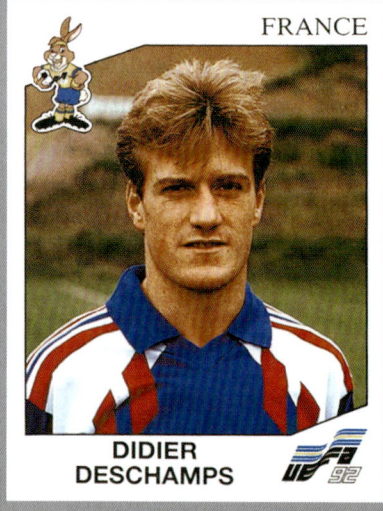

FRANCE

DIDIER DESCHAMPS

Euro '92

FRANCE

DIDIER DESCHAMPS

European Football Championship England 96

DIDIER DESCHAMPS

FRA

Euro 2000

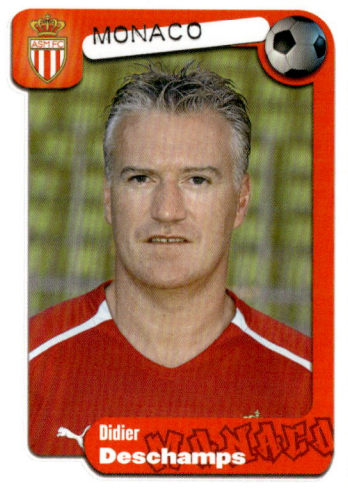

MONACO

Didier Deschamps

Foot 2005

France 98

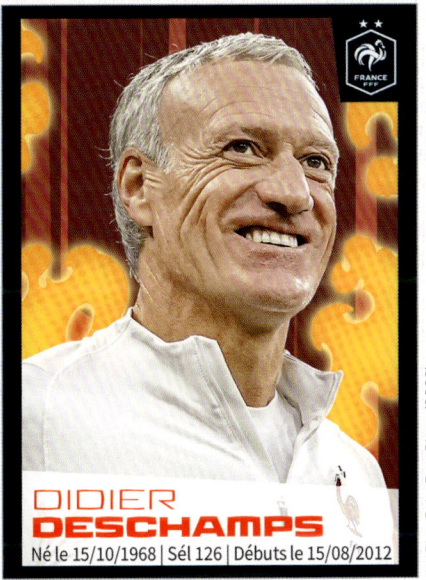

DIDIER
DESCHAMPS
Né le 15/10/1968 | Sél 126 | Débuts le 15/08/2012

Au Plus Près Des Bleus (2022)

Deschamps moved to Italy during the 1994–95 campaign, winning the first of three Serie A titles in his first season at Juventus. As the glue that held together a star-studded line-up around him, the Frenchman appeared in three consecutive Champions League finals, winning the first in 1996. His crowning glory as a player came late on, captaining France to the 1998 World Cup and Euro 2000, retiring a year after the second of those triumphs. Late club moves as a veteran performer saw him appear in successive Panini Champions League albums as a Chelsea and Valencia player.

After management spells with Monaco and Marseille, sandwiched by one season at Juventus when he got them promoted from Serie B, the man from Bayonne achieved his destiny in the summer of 2012 when he was appointed manager of the France national side. As well as winning the World Cup in 2018 and the Nations League in 2021, Les Bleus under Deschamps have so far also been runners-up at Euro 2016 and at the 2022 World Cup in Qatar.

ROGER MILLA

ROGER MILLA
VALENCIENNES

Football 79

While Cameroon's 38-year-old Roger Milla became a global phenomenon for his goalscoring heroics during Italia 90, his late call-up meant one of the tournament's stars was not part of the Panini sticker album. The Indomitable Lions caused one of the biggest World Cup shocks of all time in the opening match by defeating holders Argentina and, fired on by Milla's four goals, went on to reach the quarter-finals, where they were narrowly defeated by England.

Milla's two Panini World Cup sticker appearances came either side of his Italia 90 glory and 12 years apart – *España 82* and *USA '94*. At the latter tournament he cemented his record as the oldest World Cup finals goalscorer ever by hitting the back of the net against Russia at the age of 42.

Having been a prolific scorer in Cameroonian domestic football with Léopard Douala and Tonnerre during his formative years, Milla transferred to France in 1977, appearing in 11 successive Panini French domestic football albums, from *Football 79* to *Foot 89*. The striker's longevity as a force to be reckoned with is evidenced by the 14-year gap between his two African Footballer of the Year awards, which he received in 1976 and 1990.

MONACO

ROGER MILLA

ASM

Football 80

ESPAÑA 82

ROGER MILLA

CAM

MARTIN MAYA

España 82

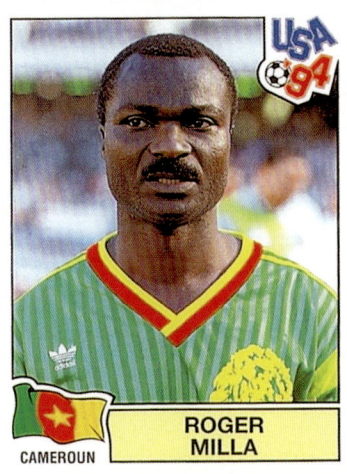

ROGER MILLA
CAMEROUN

USA 94

ROGER MILLA
BASTIA

Football 84

MONTPELLIER

ROGER MILLA

Foot 89

BASTIA

ROGER MILLA

Football 81

BASTIA

ROGER MILLA

Football 82

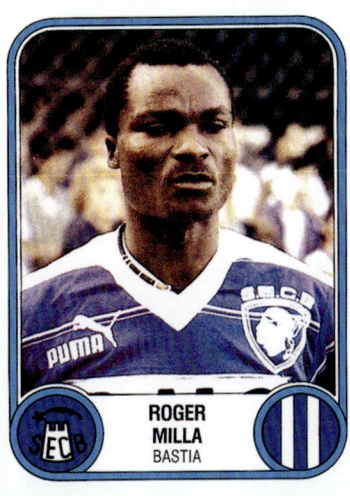

ROGER MILLA
BASTIA

Football 83

Playing Career

Eclair de Douala (1967–1970); Léopard Douala (1970–1974); Tonnerre (1974–1977); Valenciennes (1977–1979); Monaco (1979–1980); Bastia (1980–1984); Saint-Étienne (1984–1985); Montpellier (1986–1989); Saint-Pierroise (1989–1990); Tonnerre (1990–1994); Pelita Jaya (1994–1995); Putra Samarinda (1995–1996) and Cameroon (1973–1994)

Panini Album Rookie Appearances

First club album appearance: Football 79 (France) (315) First World Cup album appearance: España 82 (98)

Selected Panini Appearances

Football 79 (France) (315); Football 80 (France) (188); Football 81 (France) (46); Football 82 (France) (30); España 82 (98); Football 83 (France) (31); Panini Futbol 83 (Spain) (406); Football 84 (France) (33); Football 85 (France) (459); Football 86 (France) (386); Football 87 (France) (437); Football 88 (France) (228); Foot 89 (France) (212); Football 1991 (UK) (529, 553); USA '94 (144); Africa '96 (9)

PAOLO ROSSI

Having started the Spain 82 World Cup in underwhelming fashion, Paolo Rossi scored six goals in Italy's last three matches to win his nation the trophy and himself the Golden Shoe. At the end of that year he was awarded the Ballon d'Or but the Prato-born attacker had endured a lot of heartache on the way to glory.

He started life at Juventus as a frustrated winger, but his Panini rookie sticker came in *Calciatori 1975–76*, while on loan at Como, and it wasn't until a move to Serie B team Vicenza that he began to make waves in the game. Injuries to others meant he was shifted from the wing to a central striking role and he scored 21 league goals in his first season to help win Vicenza the Serie B title. Rossi's first Panini sticker with Vicenza was shared with teammates Renato Faloppa and Giancarlo Salvi, but he was restored to individual sticker status in *Calciatori 1977–78*.

Despite the step up in class, Rossi scored even more league goals than in the previous campaign – 24 – taking the promoted side to second place, their highest-ever Serie A finish. However, the following season the club were relegated and he was loaned to Perugia to maintain his Serie A presence now that he was an established Azzurri player. Rossi earned his first Panini World Cup sticker in *Argentina 78*, a tournament in which he scored three goals. His only individual European Championships sticker came two years later in *Europa 80* – a tournament he missed while serving a two-year ban for alleged match-fixing – but that was followed by another World Cup appearance in *España 82*.

In 1981 he moved to Juventus, where he spent four trophy-laden years, winning the European Cup in his final season. Single seasons with Milan and Verona were intersected by a third Panini World Cup sticker in *Mexico 86*, although he didn't play in the tournament despite making the squad. One of Italy's most intelligent and skilful forwards was also immortalised on the cover of Panini's *Azzurro Mondiale 1910–2002*, where he was depicted arms aloft in exultation, during that never-to-be-forgotten summer in Spain.

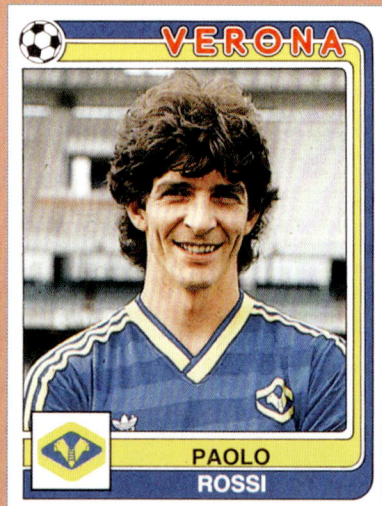

Calciatori 1986-87

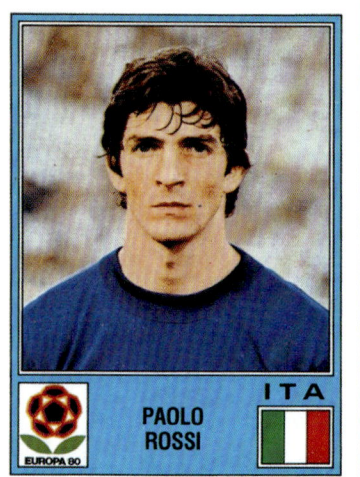

Europa 80

PAOLO
ROSSI
L.R. VICENZA

Calciatori 1978–79

ROSSI P.
COMO

Calciatori 1975–76

JUVENTUS

PAOLO
ROSSI

Calciatori 1982–83

PAOLO
ROSSI

milan

Calciatori 1985–86

ESPAÑA 82

PAOLO
ROSSI
ITALIA

España 82

ITALIA

PAOLO ROSSI

Mexico 86

Playing Career
Juventus (1973–1976); Como (loan) (1975–1976); Vincenza (1976–1980); Perugia (loan) (1979–1980); Juventus (1981–1985); Milan (1985–1986); Verona (1986–1987) and Italy (1977–1986)

Panini Album Rookie Appearances
First club album appearance: Calciatori 1975–76 (Italy) (98)
First World Cup album appearance: Argentina 78 (112)

Selected Panini Appearances
Calciatori 1975–76 (Italy) (98); *Calciatori 1976–77* (Italy) (376); *Calciatori 1977–78* (Italy) (153); *Argentina 78* (112); *Calciatori 1978–79* (Italy) (156); *Calciatori 1979–80* (Italy) (221); *Europa 80* (149); *Calciatori 1981–82* (Italy) (209); *España 82* (50); *Calciatori 1982–83* (Italy) (165, 314); *Panini Futbol 83* (Spain) (383); *Voetbal 83* (Netherlands) (1); *Football 83* (Switzerland) (437); *Calciatori 1983–84* (Italy) (121); *Calciatori 1984–85* (Italy) (145); *Football 85* (UK) (252); *Calciatori 1985–86* (Italy) (157); *Supercalcio 1985–86* (Italy) (144); *Mexico 86* (50); *Calciatori 1986–87* (Italy) (313); *Fussball 87* (Germany) (396); *Azzurro Mondiale 1910–2002* (Italy) (41, 49, N1); *Superalbum: Storia e miti del calcio italiano* (2004) (86, 112, 116); *Superalbum In Azzurro* (Italy) (2006) (167, 175); *Calciatori 2010–11* (Italy) (P15); *Azzurri 2023* (Italy) (221)

BOBBY CHARLTON

Calciatori 1966-67

BOBBY CHARLTON

Calciatori 1968-69

BOBBY CHARLTON

At the age of 20, the Manchester United goal-scoring midfielder was one of the lynchpins of the side that was rebuilt by manager Matt Busby after the tragic Munich air disaster of 1958, in which eight players were among the 23 who died. It took until 1963 for the team to experience success – an FA Cup final victory against Leicester – but that was followed by Division One titles in 1965 and 1967.

The pinnacle of Busby's side's achievements was a first European Cup for the Red Devils in 1968. Bobby Charlton was naturally among the goals in that final against Benfica at Wembley, opening the scoring before adding the last in a 4-1 extra-time win. The first of those goals – a glancing header – featured in the *Victory in Europe* section of Panini's *Football 86*.

That night came two years after England's 1966 World Cup win and, while there was no Panini collection for that tournament, subsequent albums commemorated the role of the Ashington-born player in that triumph. The England great may have missed out on significant Panini recognition during his playing days, but a number of albums have since made up for lost time by acknowledging his contribution to club and country.

Mexico 70

Football 85

Playing Career
Manchester United (1956–1973); Preston North End (1974–75); Waterford (1976); Newcastle KB United (1978); Perth Azzurri (1980); Blacktown City (1980) and England (1958–1970)

Panini Album Rookie Appearances
First club album appearance: *Calciatori 1966–67* (Italy) (459) First World Cup album appearance: *Mexico 70* (197)

Selected Panini Appearances
Calciatori 1966–67 (Italy) (459); *Campioni dello Sport 1966–67* (Italy) (160); *Calciatori 1968–69* (Italy) (547); *Fotboll 71* (Sweden) (Williams Förlags/Panini) (326); *Fotboll 72* (Sweden) (Williams Förlags/Panini) (160, 175); *Football 72* (UK) (Top Sellers/Panini) (214); *Football 73* (UK) (Top Sellers/ Panini) (202, 214); *Football 1972–73* (Belgium) (327); *Football 74* (UK) (Top Sellers/Panini) (201); *München 74* (45); *Argentina 78* (24); *Football 85* (UK) (376); *Football 86* (UK) (263); *The All-Time Greats 1920–1990* (UK) (43); *Champions of Europe 1955–2005* (7); *Manchester United 2006–07* (D); *Manchester United 2009–10* (121); *Manchester United 2014–15* (175, 176); *England 2016* (261)

Argentina 78

GLENN HODDLE

Europa 80

GLENN HODDLE

ENG

Football 80

GLENN HODDLE
TOTTENHAM HOTSPUR

Few players could get supporters out of their seats like the technically gifted midfielder Glenn Hoddle. He made his debut for Tottenham at the age of 17 in August 1975 and established himself in the side the following season, with his first appearance on a Panini sticker coming in a team photo as Second Division clubs were only afforded a group shot and foil badge in *Football 78*.

There then followed the curious case of Glenn Hoddle's moustachioed period, which was short-lived, but captured for eternity in Panini's *Football 80* and *Europa 80* albums, just after he had made his international debut at the tail end of 1979 in a qualifier for Europa 80 (as it was called at the time).

The ball-master then played a major role in Spurs winning consecutive FA Cups in 1981 and 1982, scoring the winning goal in the latter final replay against Queens Park Rangers.

For England, Hoddle made the *España 82* collection and was a mainstay of *Mexico 86*. His final England appearance came in the last group match of Euro 88 against the Soviet Union, which was a dead rubber after his side had already been doomed to elimination from the tournament.

The Hayes-born footballer had by then moved to Monaco and, managed by Arsène Wenger, he won Ligue 1 in his first season, although injury curtailed his time in the Principality. He returned to England to play for Swindon, and the final Panini sticker of his playing career placed him in the 'Twelve of the best from the Second Division' in *English Football 1992*.

ESPAÑA 82

**GLENN
HODDLE**
ENGLAND

España 82

Hoddle appeared in Panini's *España 82* and *Mexico 86* World Cup collections as well as English and French domestic albums.

Playing Career
Tottenham Hotspur (1975–1987); Monaco (1987–1991); Swindon Town (1991–1993); Chelsea (1993–1995) and England (1979–1988)

Panini Album Rookie Appearances
First club album appearance: Football 79 (UK) (341)
First World Cup album appearance: *España 82* (249)

Selected Panini Appearances
Football 79 (UK) (341); *Football 80* (UK) (335); *Europa 80* (133); *Football 81* (UK) (320); *Football 82* (UK) (283); *España 82* (249); *Football 83* (UK) (302); *Football 84* (UK) (305); *Football 85* (UK) (323); *Football 86* (UK) (334, 398); *Mexico 86* (441); *Football 87* (UK) (335); *Fussball 87* (Germany) (409); *Supersport* (UK) (1987) (UK) (80, 234); *Football 88* (France) (209); *Football 88* (UK) (389, 448); *Euro 88* (172); *Supersport* (Spain) (1988) (100); *Foot 89* (France) (192); *Foot 90* (France) (175); *The All-Time Greats 1920–1990* (UK) (65); *English Football 1992* (267)

**GLENN
HODDLE**
TOTTENHAM HOTSPUR

Football 84

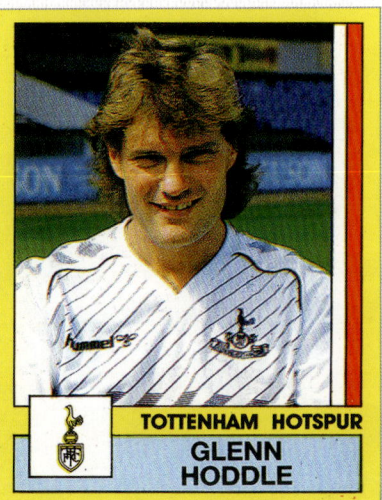
TOTTENHAM HOTSPUR
**GLENN
HODDLE**

Football 87

MONACO
**GLENN
HODDLE**
ASM

Football 88

CAROLINE GRAHAM HANSEN

France 2019

Caroline Graham Hansen was destined for stardom from an early age, making her Norwegian top-flight debut at 15 in 2010. Three years later, still only 18, Graham Hansen took her place on the right-wing for the Euro 2013 final against Germany. The teenager more than held her own, winning a second-half penalty, only for the Scandinavians to miss from the spot for the second time in the game as Germany ran out 1-0 victors.

Graham Hansen's Panini sticker debut came in the 2015 World Cup album, but a knee injury kept her out of the tournament. Consequently, she put all her frustrations into ensuring Norway made it to the 2019 World Cup, scoring six goals in qualifying.

Once in France, Graham Hansen was on top of her game, earning two Player of the Match awards on the way to reaching the quarter-finals. Her exciting wing play led to an appearance in 'The Best' section at the start of Panini's *FIFA 365 2020*, sharing a sticker with Megan Rapinoe and Virgil van Dijk. A second successive Panini Euro album appearance came in 2022, before she made it a hat-trick of Panini World Cup stickers the following year.

Graham Hansen's domestic career has been laden with silverware at Stabæk, VFL Wolfsburg and, most recently, Barcelona. After winning two Champions Leagues in her first four seasons in Spain, she was given three stickers in Panini's *Liga F 2023–24* collection. A third Champions League was secured at the end of that campaign, having already been a star performer in Barcelona's domestic treble.

CAROLINE GRAHAM HANSEN
⚽ VfL Wolfsburg (GER)
1,74 m 18-2-1995   DEBUT 2011

NOR

Euro 2017

Playing Career
Stabæk (2010–2013); Tyresö
FF (2013); Stabæk (2014);
VfL Wolfsburg (2014–2019);
Barcelona (2019–) and
Norway (2011–)

Panini Album
Rookie Appearances
First club album appearance:
Liga F 2023–24 (Spain) (61, 329,
Premium Sticker)
First World Cup album
appearance: Canada 2015 (145)

Selected Panini
Appearances
Canada 2015 (145); Euro 2017
(49); France 2019 (73); FIFA 365
2020 (8); Euro 2022 (92); Australia
and New Zealand 2023 (34);
Liga F 2023–24 (Spain) (61, 329,
Premium Sticker)

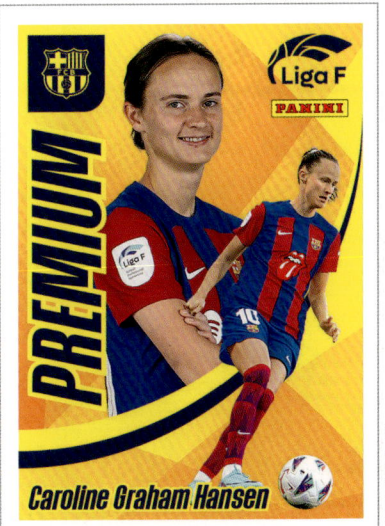

Liga F 2023-24

Liga F 2023-24

Canada 2015

PELÉ

Santos 100 Años

Calciatori 1968–69

Mexico 70

109 - CALCIO
PELE'

Campioni dello Sport 1973–74

Calciatori 1965–66

Edson Arantes do Nascimento, better known as Pelé, was football's first global superstar. An attacker who excelled in feints and tricks, as well as scoring spectacular goals, the Brazilian has made more than 30 appearances in various Panini albums. He made his debut for the Brazilian club Santos as a 15-year-old, in 1956, and inspired a golden era: the club won two Copa Libertadores and two Intercontinental Cups. He remains Santos' all-time top goalscorer with 643 goals. Pelé appeared as a Panini rookie in the *Calciatori 1964–65* album (when there were cards to collect, rather than stickers), while his card in Panini's first World Cup album – *Mexico 70* – is treasured by collectors.

Synonymous with the number 10 shirt of the Brazil national team, Pelé is the youngest player to win a World Cup – he was 17 years and eight months old in 1958, when he scored twice in the final against Sweden, including flicking the ball over a defender before volleying home. After missing Brazil's 1962 triumph through injury, he crowned his international career with the opening goal in the 1970 World Cup final demolition of Italy. Even his near misses in that tournament, such as a shot from the halfway line against Czechoslovakia and a header that produced a flying save from Gordon Banks, have become iconic football memories.

In 2017, a complete *Mexico 70* Panini album sold at auction for a record sum. The album had been signed twice by Pelé at the tournament in 1970.

Grandi club - SANTOS - Brasile
EDSON ARANTES (PELE')
nato a Baurù il 23-10-1940

Calciatori 1967-68

Rimet 1970

München 74

PELÉ 1970

Argentina 78

PELÉ
LEGENDS

Russia 2018

Pelé's international career was coming to a close as Panini sticker albums became a global phenomenon, his number of album appearances over the years befitting the mark he left on the game. He featured in Panini's *München 74* World Cup album, seen being held aloft by his teammates following Brazil's 1970 triumph, and appeared in *Argentina 78* as a black-and-white portrait. He was also honoured with a Legends foil in the Russia 2018 World Cup album. In addition, having played for Brazilian team Santos for most of his career, he featured heavily in the club's special *100 Años* (100 years) anniversary album.

Calciatori 1964–65

PELE' (Coppe)

Playing Career
Santos (1956–1974); New York Cosmos (1975–1977) and Brazil (1957–1971)

Panini Album Rookie Appearances
First club album appearance: Calciatori 1964–65 (Italy) (415); First World Cup album appearance: Mexico 70 (180)

Selected Panini Appearances
Calciatori 1964–65 (Italy) (415); Calciatori 1965–66 (Italy) (450); Campioni dello Sport 1966–67 (Italy) (168); Calciatori 1967–68 (Italy) (642); Calciatori 1968–69 (Italy) (537); Mexico 70 (180); Campioni dello Sport 1970–71 (Italy) (93); Panini Gran Varietà (Italy) (1972) (53); Fotboll 72 (Williams Förlags/Panini) (Sweden) (162); Football 1972–73 (Belgium) (331); Football 73 (Top Sellers/Panini) (UK) (204); OK VIP (Italy) (1973) (156); Campioni dello Sport 1973–74 (109); München 74 (50); Argentina 78 (27); Uomini Illustri (Italy) (1980) (323); Football 90 (UK) (309); Calcio (Italy) (1990) (27); The Official PFA Collection '97 (England) (145); Panini Supergol 2000 (Israel) (391); Santos 100 Años (90, 95, 96, 103–109, 124–126, 221); Campeonato Brasileiro 2013 (a20); Brasil de Todas as Copas 2013 (34, 35, 60, 61, 64, 65, 68, 69, 82, 147, A14); Russia 2018 (680, CA1 - Coca Cola Austria); Seleção Brasileira – Rússia 2018 (23, 91); Conmebol Copa Libertadores 2023 (CL10 to CL13); CONMEBOL Copa América USA 2024 (LEG3)

Santos 100 Años

Pelé's rookie Panini card appeared in the *Calciatori 1964—65* album while his card in Panini's first World Cup album — *Mexico 70* — is treasured by most collectors.

TIM CAHILL

Tim Cahill's career really kick-started in 2004. Not only did he score Millwall's winning goal in the FA Cup semi-final against Sunderland (they lost the final to Manchester United), but he also made his debut for Australia, at the age of 24, and represented his country in the Olympics.

He then ended that summer by moving to Premier League Everton, having secured his legendary status at Millwall with more than 200 league appearances and in excess of 50 goals. The Sydney-born player went on to achieve equal acclaim at Goodison Park, with very similar statistics, before moving around the world during the latter phase of his career.

However, he remained a constant for his national side, scoring 50 goals in 108 games – a terrific record for someone who was primarily deployed as an attacking midfielder. He may have worn a furrowed brow on his first Panini World Cup sticker (*Germany 2006*), but it was Australia's first opponents, Japan, that would have most cause for concern. Coming on as a second-half substitute, Cahill became the first player to score for Australia in the World Cup finals, adding another in a 3-1 win.

After scoring crucial goals in qualifying, Cahill got off to the worst possible start in the 2010 World Cup when he was controversially sent off against Germany, although he returned to score in the final group match win against Serbia. He was 34 at the 2014 World Cup, but rolled back the years by scoring two goals – the second, a left-foot volley against the Netherlands, one of the best ever scored at a World Cup finals. Despite approaching his 40s, there was still time for appearances in the Panini *FIFA Confederations Cup 2017* and *Russia 2018* World Cup albums, although Australia's record goalscorer was largely restricted to coming on from the bench.

TIM CAHILL

Germany 2006

Playing Career
Millwall (1998–2004); Everton 2004–2012; New York Red Bulls (2012–2015); Hangzhou Greentown (2015–2016); Melbourne City (2016–17); Millwall (2018); Jamshedpur (2018–2019) and Australia (2004–2018)

Panini Album Rookie Appearances
First club album appearance: N/A
First World Cup album appearance:
Germany 2006 (428)

Selected Panini Appearances
Germany 2006 (428); Germany 2006 (Pocket Album) (241); South Africa 2010 (290); South Africa 2010 (Mini-sticker set) (95); Brasil 2014 (178); FIFA Confederations Cup 2017 (223); Road to Russia 2018 (448); Russia 2018 (228)

TIM CAHILL

South Africa 2010

New York Red Bulls (USA)
6-12-1979 | 1,78 m | 67 kg

TIM CAHILL

Brasil 2014

OLIVER KAHN

OLIVER KAHN
KARLSRUHER SC

Fussball 89

Karlsruher SC
Oliver Kahn

Fussball '94

German goalkeeper Oliver Kahn made his senior debut for Karlsruher at 18 in the 1987–88 season and his Panini debut in the following campaign's *Fussball 89* collection, sporting his trademark blond thatch. The larger-than-life character secured the number 1 spot in 1991–92, spending two more seasons representing his hometown club until a high-profile move to Bayern Munich in the summer of 1994.

A Germany debut and Panini Euro and World Cup sticker album appearances came in *European Football Championship England '96* and *France 98*, but he was understudy on both occasions. However, he was the main keeper in Euro 2000 and led Germany to the World Cup final in Korea and Japan.

Kahn's experiences in his two Champions League finals were mixed, losing in dramatic fashion to Manchester United in 1999, then atoning with victory over Valencia in 2001. That win over Spanish opposition came in the season of Panini's second Champions League release.

Kahn did not appear on the Bayern pages of *Fussball 03–04* or *Fussball 04/05*, but the stalwart kept his place as number 1 in both seasons and a further three thereafter, returning to Panini duty between *Fussball 2005–2006* and *Bundesliga Fussball 2007/2008*. It was a successful climax to his career as he won an eighth Bundesliga title and sixth German Cup in that final year before retirement.

Playing Career
Karlsruher SC (1987–1994); Bayern Munich (1994–2008) and Germany (1995–2006)

Panini Album
Rookie Appearances
First club album appearance: Fussball 89 (Germany) (150)
First World Cup album appearance: France 98 (388)

Selected Panini Appearances
Fussball 89 (Germany) (150); Fussball 90 (Germany) (148); Fussball 92 (Germany) (165); Fussball '94 (Germany) (85); Fussball '95 (Germany) (5); Fussball 96 (Germany) (139); European Football Championship England '96 (214); Fussball 97 (Germany) (31); Fussball 98 (9, 12); France 98 (388); Fussball 99 (Germany) (38); Super Football 99 (3); Champions League 1999/2000 (223); Fussball 2000 (Germany) (13); Euro 2000 (6); Fussball 2001 (334, 354); Bayern Munich 2000–01 (1, 4–9); Champions League 2000/2001 (211); Fussball 2002 (332, 334, A); Champions League 2001/2002 (230); Korea-Japan 2002 (315); Fussball 2002–2003 (Germany) (334, 353, 498); Fussball 2005–2006 (Germany) (392); Germany 2006 (19); Deutsches Nationalteam 2006 (31, 52–55, 185, T22); Fussball 2006/2007 (Germany) (365); Fussball 2007/2008 (Germany) (340)

Fussball '95

Champions League 1999/2000

Fussball 99

Champions League 2001/2002

France 98

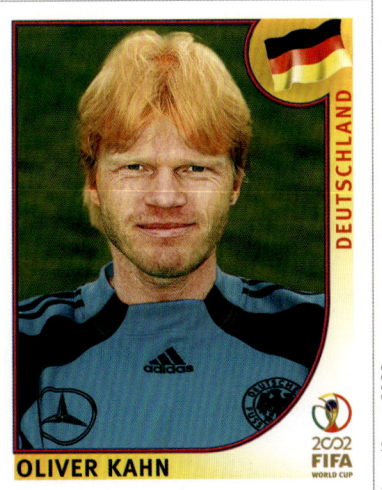
Korea/Japan 2002

Germany 2006

BOBBY MOORE

Mexico 70

München 74

A mid-sixties heyday saw the composed England defender lead West Ham to victory in the 1964 FA Cup – their first – followed by the Cup Winners' Cup a year later, with both finals at Wembley. Those triumphs were particularly enjoyed in east London, but Bobby Moore's encore has gone down in English football folklore.

As one of three West Ham players in the side, Moore led his country out for the 1966 World Cup final against West Germany. In a 4-2 win, all three Hammers made a huge impression, Geoff Hurst scoring three, Martin Peters the other and Moore's pinpoint accuracy providing two assists. There was no Panini album for that tournament, but the Italian collectables producers were keen to honour Moore's achievement, placing him in both the *Calciatori* and *Campioni dello Sport* collections in 1966–67.

Those were his first Panini appearances and his first Panini World Cup album came for *Mexico 70*, a tournament in which Moore excelled, only for West Germany to knock the holders out in the quarter-final. A second Panini World Cup appearance came in the *München 74* collection, but only as part of the section for excluded nations, as on this occasion England had failed to qualify.

Moore's 1966 triumph led to his first Panini appearances in *Calciatori* and *Campioni dello Sport* collections in 1966–67.

EUROCALCIO   INGHILTERRA

Calciatori 1966-67

BOBBY MOORE

A composed central defender, best known for reading the game, Moore made 108 appearances for England.

Playing Career
West Ham United (1958–1974); Fulham (1974–1977); San Antonio Thunder (loan) (1976); Seattle Sounders (1978); Herning Fremad (1978); Carolina Lightnin' (1983) and England (1962–1973)

Panini Album Rookie Appearances
First club album appearance: Calciatori 1966–67 (Italy) (456) First World Cup album appearance: Mexico 70 (194)

Selected Panini Appearances
Calciatori 1966–67 (Italy) (456); *Campioni dello Sport 1966–67* (Italy) (161); *Mexico 70* (194); *Fotboll 1972* (Sweden) (Williams Förlags/Panini) (157, 210); *Football 72* (UK) (Top Sellers/Panini) (331); *Football 1972–73* (Belgium) (326); *Football 73* (UK) (Top Sellers/Panini) (199, 344); *Football 74* (UK) (Top Sellers/Panini) (333); *Campioni dello Sport 1973–74* (113); *München 74* (366); *Football 85* (UK) (377); *The All-Time Greats 1920–1990* (UK) (45); *England 2016* (67)

München 74

Rimet 1966

STARS OF THE PAST

BOBBY MOORE

Football 85

ALLY McCOIST

Football 82

Football 1991

If a player's first Panini appearance is on a team sticker, many collectors are likely to pass over it, but for Ally McCoist the 1980–81 season was a breakthrough campaign and came at a time when Panini made a rare foray into Scottish League Division One. In the *Football 81* album the young forward can be spotted front row, second from the left, in a St Johnstone team that only missed out on promotion to the Scottish Premier Division on goal difference.

After continuing his goalscoring form with St Johnstone in the early part of the 1981–82 season, McCoist became Sunderland's record signing, joining the North East club early enough to make it into *Football 82*. Then, after one further Panini appearance in Sunderland colours, it was back to Scotland with Rangers.

The undoubted stand-out moment of his first season at Ibrox was a hat-trick in the League Cup final win over Celtic, but it wasn't until his third season, in 1985–86, that McCoist became a real fan favourite. April 1986 was a turning point for both the player and the club, as it was the month the prolific McCoist made his full international debut for Scotland and Graeme Souness became manager of the Glasgow club, transforming their fortunes.

McCoist won his first Scottish Premier Division title the following season and then, after Celtic won it in 1987–88, he was a mainstay of the team that won a further nine in a row. Naturally, McCoist was also a regular in the Rangers section of Panini's UK releases, although he was a surprise omission from the Scottish Football 1992 album, having struggled to cement his place the previous season. That year saw a massive return

RANGERS

ALLY McCOIST

Football 89

Playing Career
St Johnstone (1978–1981);
Sunderland (1981–1983); Rangers
(1983–1998); Kilmarnock (1998–
2001) and Scotland (1986–1998)

**Panini Album
Rookie Appearances**
First club album appearance:
Football 82 (UK) (255)
First World Cup album appearance:
Italia '90 (226)

**Selected Panini
Appearances**
Football 82 (UK) (255); *Football 83*
(UK) (274); *Football 84* (UK) (507);
Football 85 (UK) (516); *Football 86*
(UK) (533); *Football 87* (UK) (554);
Football 88 (UK) (565); *Football 89*
(UK) (454); *Football 90* (UK) (454);
Italia '90 (226); *Football 1991* (UK)
(484); *Euro '92* (162); *Futebol 92–93*
(Portugal) (199); *Panini Futbol 92–
93* (Spain) (203); *Scottish Premier
Division 95* (291, 296); *Scottish
Premier Division 96* (301, 305);
*European Football Championship
England '96* (110); *Scottish Premier
Division 97* (156, 291); *Scottish
Premier Division '98* (202, 322,
336, 337); *France 98* (45); *Scottish
Premier League 99* (285, 297);
Scottish Premier League 2000 (284,
302); *Rangers FC 1999–2000* (167,
168); *Rangers FC 2000–01* (171)

to form, however, and he won the European Golden Shoe with 34 league goals, repeating the trick the following year.

At international level McCoist made it into two Panini World Cup and two Euro albums, but it was in the latter of those European tournaments, Euro 96, that he scored his final Scottish goal. He signed off with two Panini Scottish Premier Division appearances for Kilmarnock before returning to Rangers on the coaching side and then moving on to a successful media career.

SCOTLAND
ALLY McCOIST

Italia '90

SCOTLAND
ALLY McCOIST

European Football Championship England '96

ALLY McCOIST
SCOTLAND

France 98

OLIVIER GIROUD

Foot 2011

Olivier GIROUD

Foot 2011-12

Olivier GIROUD

Olivier Giroud didn't make his French top-flight debut until one month short of his 24th birthday, but he made up for lost time after that. Having plied his trade in the lower leagues with Grenoble, Istres and Tours (making his Panini debut for the latter in *Foot 2010*), Giroud adapted quickly to Ligue 1 when he moved to Montpellier, going on to finish as the league's top scorer in 2011–12 as the club won their first-ever league title.

Giroud made the squad for Euro 2012, the first of three consecutive Panini album appearances for the European Championships. The forward joined Arsenal soon after France's quarter-final exit to Spain, appearing in red and white in Panini's 2012–13 and 2013–14 Champions League albums.

By then a regular starter for his national side, Giroud scored three goals and provided two assists along the way to France's Euro 2016 final loss to Portugal. His country went one better in 2018, though, by winning the World Cup in Russia.

A move to Chelsea brought further silverware, including the Europa League and Champions League. After making Panini's first two Premier League collections, Giroud moved to AC Milan – and the *Calciatori* album – from 2021-22. The Serie A title followed in his first season, before his second consecutive World Cup final, in December 2022. During that tournament, he broke Thierry Henry's record to become the France national team's all-time leading goalscorer.

Champions League 2013–2014

FIFA 365 2020

Calciatori 2022–2023

Playing Career

Grenoble (2005–2008); Istres (loan) (2007–2008); Tours (2008–2010); Montpellier (2010–2012); Arsenal (2012–2018); Chelsea (2018–2021); AC Milan (2021–2024); Los Angeles FC (2024–) and France (2011–2024)

Panini Album Rookie Appearances

First club album appearance: *Foot 2010* (France) (653)
First World Cup album appearance: *Brasil 2014* (391)

Selected Panini Appearances

Foot 2010 (France) (653); *Foot 2011* (France) (309, 312); *Foot 2012* (France) (297, V3, V9); *Euro 2012* (477, 108 in Dutch edition); *Champions League 2012–2013* (100); *Champions League 2013–2014* (410); *Road to 2014 World Cup* (107); *Brasil 2014* (391); *Euro France 2016* (33, 42 plus FR-9 – Coca-Cola); *Foot 2017* (France) (P18); *Road to 2018 World Cup* (95); *Russia 2018* (194); *Football 2020* (England) (188); *FIFA 365 2020* (19); *Euro 2020 Preview Edition* (FRA22); *Premier League 2021* (England) (161); *Euro 2020 Tournament Edition* (564, 572); *Calciatori 2021–22* (Italy) (286, C11); *Qatar 2022* (Fra15x – International Update Set); *Calciatori 2022–23* (Italy) (295); *Calciatori 2023–24* (324)

Euro 2012

Russia 2018

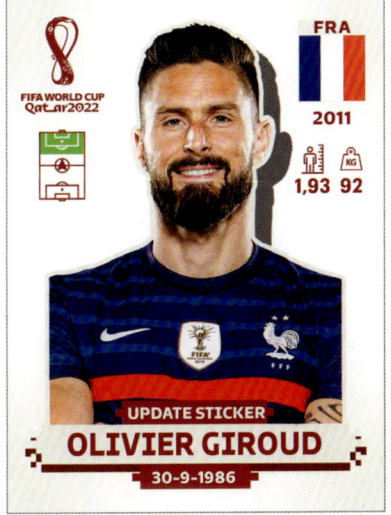

Qatar 2022

ERLING HAALAND

FIFA 365 2021

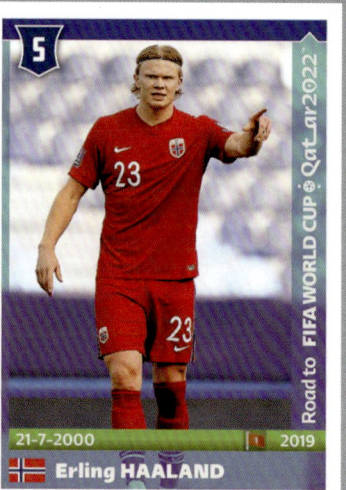

Road to Qatar 2022

As well as being a goalscoring phenomenon in recent years, Erling Haaland found himself at the forefront of a seismic change in Panini sticker collecting. In 2020, and seemingly out of nowhere (at least for most European collectors), that year's global pandemic heralded a sudden chase for rookie stickers.

When the Austrian league's *Fussball 19–20* collection was released, there was little clamour from outside its homeland, but making his first Panini appearance in the album was a young Norwegian striker who had joined Red Bull Salzburg from Molde the previous season. A blistering start in the Austrian Bundesliga was augmented by an astonishing six goals in his first three Champions League games – at the age of 19. The early part of the campaign also saw a full international debut.

Haaland's rapid elevation took on greater proportions when he moved to Borussia Dortmund at the end of 2019, coming off the bench to score a hat-trick in 23 minutes on his debut against Augsburg the following January. By the time Dortmund's season was halted in March – due to covid – the Leeds-born attacker was a household name. It seemed that fame had filtered through to sports collectables fans around the globe, as Haaland's first Panini sticker was beginning to generate unexpected levels of demand.

The powerful forward's strike rate hasn't diminished his popularity either and by the time he left Dortmund for

Fussball 19–20

Playing Career
Bryne 2 (2015–2016); Bryne (2016–2017); Molde 2 (2017); Molde (2017–2019); Red Bull Salzburg (2019–2020); Borussia Dortmund (2020–2022); Manchester City (2022–) and Norway (2019–)

Panini Album Rookie Appearances
First club album appearance: Fussball 19–20 (Austria) (32) First World Cup album appearance: N/A

Selected Panini Appearances
Fussball 19–20 (Austria) (32); FIFA 365 2021 (8, 181, 208); Road to Qatar 2022 (358); FIFA 365 2022 (206, 210); Top Class 2022 (279); Premier League 2023 (England) (325, 424, 428); FIFA 365 2023 (SAL–HAA, 97, 99) Premier League 2024 (England) (425, 427, 429); FIFA 365 2024 (HAA, 97, 99)

Manchester City in the summer of 2022 he had scored nearly a goal a game. It was in 2022 that Haaland made his first Panini sticker album cover appearance, too, and he has since made it a habit (the debut *Top Class* collection, *FIFA 365 2023* and *FIFA 365 2024*, along with *Premier League 2024* being his early impressions). The first of those covers saw the Scandinavian in the yellow of Dortmund, but he was in the sky blue of City from the second release onwards. Haaland's first season at the Etihad was a triumph, scoring 52 goals in 53 games as City won the Champions League, Premier League and FA Cup. Another Golden Boot followed in 2023-24 as Man City won their fourth successive Premier League title. While more silverware beckons on the domestic front, a Panini World Cup album appearance would be another landmark to achieve in the years ahead.

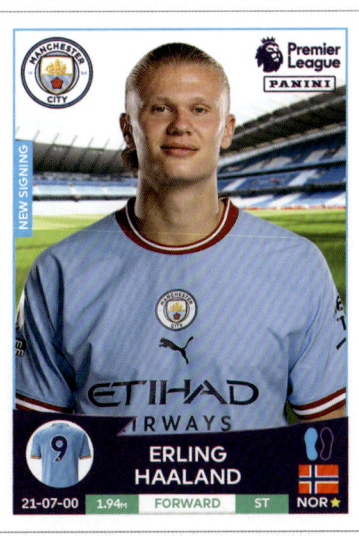

Premier League 2023

FRANCO BARESI

FRANCO BARESI
ITALIA

Euro 88

FRANCO BARESI
ITALIA

USA '94

A one-club man, Franco Baresi was the long-term captain of one of the most redoubtable backlines in history. Having made his Serie A debut for AC Milan at 17 in April 1978, Baresi enjoyed 19 consecutive *Calciatori* appearances, from his 1978–79 rookie to 1996–97. The photo on that first sticker – in the famous red and black stripes – was taken at a distance that captured the number 6 on his shorts, a digit that would ultimately be retired by the club when Baresi finished playing.

That debut season ended in triumph, with the first of his six Scudetto, but the nine-year wait for his second coincided with some difficult times for Milan. Two demotions early in the 1980s led to some high-profile departures from the club, but elevated the defender to captain at the age of 22. From the time of their return to the top flight in 1983–84, however, there was a steady improvement, built on the solid foundation of Baresi at centre-back or sweeper. After title success in 1987–88, Dutch trio Marco van Basten, Frank Rijkaard and Ruud Gullit then made their presence felt further up the pitch over the next two seasons, resulting in back-to-back European and Intercontinental Cups.

Four more domestic titles were gained between 1991–92 and 1995–96 and, while the team lacked some of their previous flamboyance, a Serie A and Champions League double was achieved in 1993–94 when the defence conceded only 15 goals in 36 league games.

Baresi featured in the second of his two Panini World Cup albums that year, captaining the side and playing alongside club mate Paolo Maldini in the final penalty shoot-out defeat

Calciatori 1979–80

Calciatori 1981–82

FRANCO
BARESI
MILAN

Calciatori 1978–79

against Brazil. Acknowledgement of his poise throughout
the 90 minutes and extra time of the final was encapsulated
on the cover of *Calciatori 1994–95*. Winning a sixth league
title in his penultimate season enabled the consummate
defender to go out on a high, a few years later being named
AC Milan's Player of the Century.

Calciatori 1987–88

Calciatori 1992–93

Calciatori 1995–96

KEVIN DE BRUYNE

Euro 2016

Football 2020

In a constellation of stars in the all-conquering Manchester City side of recent years, Kevin De Bruyne is perhaps the pick of the bunch. The playmaker's beginnings were humble, back in his Belgian homeland, and he started off with a couple of appearances for Genk towards the end of the 2008–09 season, establishing himself in the line-up in 2009–10.

Panini Belgium took note of the exciting young talent in their midst, placing him on the cover of *Football 2011*. Their faith paid off because the attacking midfielder was the creative hub of Genk's league title success that year. De Bruyne was also given his senior Belgium international debut at the start of the season, in August 2010, and has since gone on to win more than a hundred caps for the Red Devils. The Belgian *Football 2011* album also marked the youngster's first Panini stickers and he earned a second position in the Genk section as Top Joueur (Top Player).

He moved to Chelsea in 2012, but fairly swiftly went on loan to Werder Bremen before moving to Wolfsburg in January 2014 for a successful spell. That summer brought the midfielder his debut Panini World Cup sticker, having scored four goals to help Belgium qualify for Brazil 2014 – their first major tournament finals in 12 years.

De Bruyne joined Manchester City at the end of the 2015 summer transfer window, winning the League Cup in his first season. He has won countless honours since, including the Champions League, Premier League and FA Cup treble in 2022–23, and a fourth successive Premier League title in 2023-24.

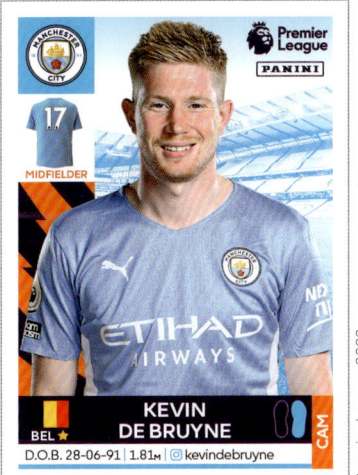

Premier League 2022

Premier League 2024

Champions League 2011–2012

Qatar 2022

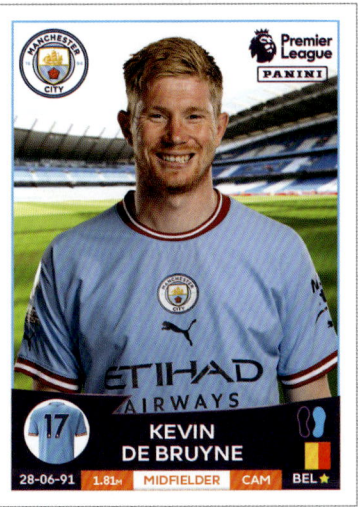

Premier League 2023

Playing Career

Genk (2008–2012); Chelsea (2012–2014); Werder Bremen (loan) (2012–13); VfL Wolfsburg (2014–2015); Manchester City (2015–) and Belgium (2010–)

Panini Album Rookie Appearances

First club album appearance: *Football 2011* (Belgium) (153, 163) First World Cup album appearance: *Brasil 2014* (575)

Selected Panini Appearances

Football 2011 (Belgium) (153, 163); *Foot 2012* (Belgium) (95); *Champions League 2011–2012* (338); *Champions League 2013–2014* (342); *Road to World Cup 2014* (262); *Belgian Red Devils 2014* (11, 21, 30, 94–98); *Brasil 2014* (575); *Road to Euro 2016* (8); *Belgian Red Devils 2016* (200–205); *Euro 2016* (476, 490, H9 – Coca Cola); *Road to 2018 World Cup* (11); *Russia 2018* (522); *FIFA 365 2019* (58); *Pro League 2019–2020* (Belgium) (380); *Football 2020* (England) (323, 360); *Euro 2020 Preview Edition* (BEL21); *Premier League 2021* (England) (324, 397); *FIFA 365 2021* (54, 80) *Euro 2020 Tournament Edition* (132, 146); *Premier League 2022* (England) (391, 403); *FIFA 365 2022* (69, 75, 354); *Qatar 2022* (BEL10 or BEL11, KDB, C3 – Coca Cola); *Premier League 2023* (England) (421, 433); *Top Class 2022* (83); *FIFA 365 2023* (91, 94, FOD–KDB); *Premier League 2024* (England) (421, 433); *FIFA 365 2024* (KDB, 94)

Playing Career

Leicester City (1966–1974); Stoke City (1974–1977); Nottingham Forest (1977–1982); Southampton (1982–1987); Derby County (1987–1992); Plymouth Argyle (1992–1995); Wimbledon (1995); Bolton Wanderers (1995); Coventry (1995–1996); West Ham United (1996); Leyton Orient (1996–1997) and England (1970–1990)

Panini Album Rookie Appearances

First club album appearance: Football 72 (UK) (Top Sellers/Panini) (162)
First World Cup album appearance: España 82 (240)

Selected Panini Appearances

Football 72 (UK) (Top Sellers/Panini) (162); Football 73 (UK) (Top Sellers/Panini) (151); Football 74 (UK) (Top Sellers/Panini) (151); Football 75 (UK) (Top Sellers/Panini) (141); Football 76 (UK) (Top Sellers/Panini) (295); Football 77 (UK) (Top Sellers/Panini) (253); Football 78 (UK) (297); Football 79 (UK) (282); Football 80 (UK) (276); Europa 80 (128); Football 81 (UK) (247); Football 82 (UK) (184); España 82 (240); Football 83 (UK) (232); Football 84 (UK) (232); Football 85 (UK) (267); Football 86 (UK) (311); Mexico 86 (402); Football 87 (UK) (313); Football 88 (UK) (77, 446); Euro 88 (160); Football 89 (UK) (66); Football 90 (UK) (97); Italia '90 (383); The All-Time Greats 1920–1990 (62); Football 1991 (UK) (97, 529, 531); English Football 1992 (265)

Football 78

Football 79

Football 85

Football 89

Europa 80

España 82

PETER SHILTON

ENGLAND

PETER SHILTON

Mexico 86

ENGLAND

PETER SHILTON

Italia '90

As befits for a man whose career spanned 125 England caps and more than 1,000 football league appearances, Peter Shilton can also lay claim to having one of the most stellar Panini sticker careers. The goalkeeper appeared in every Panini UK domestic football album from *Football 78* to *English Football 1992* (the last of which was in a 'Twelve of the best from the Second Division' section). Panini produced the stickers for all the Top Sellers releases between *Football 72* and *Football 77*, so if you add those in that's an unbroken run of two decades.

Shilton's appearances in those early albums came when he was playing for Leicester City and then Stoke City. In fact, he was still wearing the latter's jersey in the Nottingham Forest section of *Football 78*, having arrived too late to facilitate an image for his new club. It was at Forest that he enjoyed his greatest successes, collecting two European Cups, the European Super Cup, a First Division title and the League Cup in the space of three seasons between 1977–78 and 1979–80. What's more, Shilton was part of Southampton's side when they achieved their best-ever league placing in 1983–84 (second) and was also between the posts for a Derby County side that enjoyed a revival in the late 1980s.

He made it into three consecutive Panini World Cup albums, remaining as England's number one from *España 82* through to *Italia '90*, after which he retired from international football at the age of 40.

ROY KEANE

Nottingham Forest snapped up Roy Keane from Cobh Ramblers over the summer of 1990, but, as an unknown quantity, he missed out on Panini's *Football 1991* album despite quickly becoming a regular in Brian Clough's side. His first Panini stickers duly came in the 1991–92 season: first in the *Soccer's Super Sevens* album and then the grander *English Football 1992*. In 1993, a move to Manchester United showed the shape of things to come, with Keane winning a Premier League and FA Cup double in his first season at the club.

Panini's first Champions League album came the season after United's 1999 victory. Although Keane was suspended for the final against Bayern Munich, his contribution in the semi-final second leg, to haul the team back from 0-2 against Juventus, goes down as one of the greatest midfield performances in the tournament's history.

The Cork-born player had made his Panini World Cup album debut in *USA '94*, a tournament in which he impressed, despite the Republic of Ireland's last-16 exit to the Netherlands. Keane also made the Panini Korea/Japan 2002 World Cup collection despite leaving the training camp before the tournament had started.

In between there was plenty of silverware at domestic level, with Keane's eventual tally of seven Premier League titles and four FA Cups.

Roy Keane's first Panini stickers came in the *Soccer's Super Sevens* collection and then *English Football 1992*.

USA '94

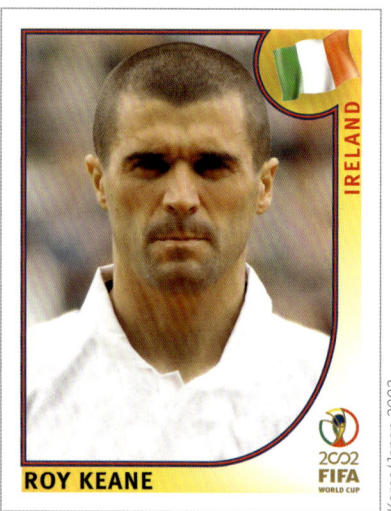

Korea/Japan 2002

ROY KEANE
NOTTINGHAM FOREST

Football '93

Playing Career
Cobh Ramblers (1989–1990); Nottingham Forest (1990–1993); Manchester United (1993–2005); Celtic (2005–2006) and Republic of Ireland (1991–2005)

Panini Album Rookie Appearances
First club album appearance: Soccer's Super Sevens (1991–92) (UK) (88)/English Football 1992 (150)
First World Cup album appearance: USA '94 (330)

Selected Panini Appearances
Soccer's Super Sevens (1991–92) (UK) (88); English Football 1992 (England) (150); Football '93 (England) (174); USA '94 (330); Superplayers '96 (England) (170); The Official PFA Collection '97 (England) (137); Superplayers 98 (England) (170, P9); Champions League 1999/2000 (128); Champions League 2000/2001 (257); Champions League Finale 2000/2001 (122); Champions League 2001/2002 (184); Korea/Japan 2002 (361); Champions of Europe 1955–2005 (221); Manchester United 2006–07 (T); Manchester United 2008–09 (122)

NOTTINGHAM FOREST

ROY KEANE

English Football 1992

MANCHESTER UNITED FC

ROY KEANE

Champions League 2000/2001

ROY KEANE
MANCHESTER UNITED FC

Champions League 2001/2002

ROY KEANE | **137**

ALEXIA PUTELLAS

Few players have influenced the rise of women's football more than Alexia Putellas. She was earmarked for the top from an early age, starring in Spain's successive UEFA U-17 Women's Championship wins in 2010 and 2011. She then captained her side to the final of the UEFA U-19 Women's Championship in 2012, losing to Sweden in extra time.

The left-footer's senior career began with Espanyol, before she joined Levante for the 2011–12 season. Her 15 league goals caught the eye of that year's champions, Barcelona, who snapped her up for the following campaign. The Catalan club were embarking on a period of dominance that would see them rule the roost in the Primera División (now Liga F) and win the Champions League in 2020–21 and 2022–23. It was no surprise when Putellas won consecutive Ballon d'Or and FIFA Best Women's Player awards in 2021 and 2022, and she was pictured in Panini's *FIFA 365 2024* album with her second FIFA trophy.

After making her senior international debut just before Euro 2013, Putellas received her first Panini sticker in the 2015 World Cup album. A first Panini Euro sticker followed in 2017 and while injury prevented her from appearing in the 2023 World Cup album, she returned to make Spain's triumphant squad and be given an update sticker.

ESP

WOMEN'S WORLD CUP
FRANCE 2019

ALEXIA PUTELLAS

1,72 m
4-2-1994
FC Barcelona (ESP)

France 2019

Alexia Putellas has won all the major club and individual awards.
She is one of the best female footballers of her generation.

Playing Career
Espanyol (2010–2011); Levante
(2011–2012); Barcelona (2012–)
and Spain (2012–)

**Panini Album
Rookie Appearances**
First club album appearance:
Liga F 2022–23 (Spain) (129,
324, 357)
First World Cup album
appearance:
Canada 2015 (377)

**Selected Panini
Appearances**
Canada 2015 (377); *Euro 2017*
(313); *France 2019* (155); *Euro
2022* (171); *Liga F 2022–23*
(Spain) (129, 324, 357); *Australia
and New Zealand 2023* (J7 –
Spain update); *Liga F 2023–24*
(Spain) (56, 324, Premium
Sticker); *FIFA 365 2024* (407, 426)

However, there was no chance of Putellas being excluded
when Panini made history by producing their first-ever
domestic women's football sticker album for *Liga F 2022–
23*. As well as three stickers inside, the Barcelona star was
given the honour of featuring on the cover. Another trio
of stickers then followed in Liga F 2023–24, as Barcelona
once more dominated, winning a domestic treble and the
Champions League (Putellas coming off the bench to score
in the final victory against Lyon).

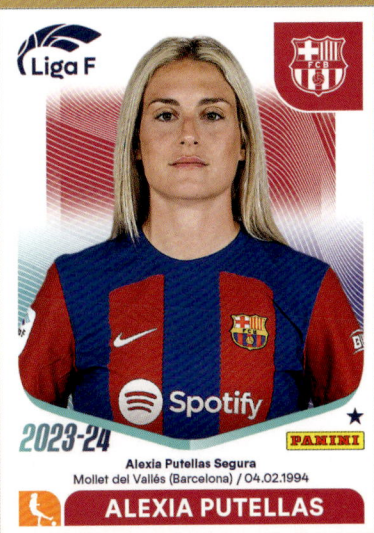

Liga F

2023-24

Alexia Putellas Segura
Mollet del Vallès (Barcelona) / 04.02.1994

ALEXIA PUTELLAS

Liga F 2023–24

BRYAN ROBSON

Football 78

España 82

He endured many serious injuries, but if proof of Bryan Robson's durability in the professional game was needed, then his claim to being the only player to have an individual sticker in every Panini UK album from *Football 78* to *Football '93* is as good as any. The combative midfielder's Panini career didn't even start – or end – there, because he had already featured under the Top Sellers banner for West Bromwich Albion in *Football 77* and was present as player-manager for Middlesbrough as late as *Superplayers '96*.

However, it is at Manchester United where he is best remembered and for whom he captained the side to three FA Cup triumphs, in 1983, 1985 and 1990, and the European Cup Winners' Cup in 1991. He finally left the club in 1994 after 13 years, almost 500 games, 100 goals and Premier League title medals in his last two seasons, going to Middlesbrough as player-manager. Despite turning 38 midway through the footballing year, he nonetheless played a significant role on the pitch in leading Middlesbrough back to the top flight in that first season in charge. He also featured in Panini's first album for the restructured football league in 1994–95.

Robson won 90 England caps between 1980 and 1991, earning appearances in three consecutive Panini World Cup albums as well as *Euro 88*. His *España 82* sticker preceded his goal in England's opening game against France, when he scored after just 27 seconds.

Bryan Robson won 90 caps for England and appeared in the 1982, 1986 and 1990 Panini World Cup collections.

Euro 88

Playing Career
West Bromwich Albion (1975–1981); Manchester United (1981–1994); Middlesbrough (1994–1997) and England (1980–1991)

Panini Album Rookie Appearances
First club album appearance: *Football 77* (UK) (Top Sellers/Panini) (342)
First World Cup album appearance: *España 82* (246)

Selected Panini Appearances
Football 77 (UK) (Top Sellers/Panini) (342); *Football 78* (UK) (335); *Football 79* (UK) (356); *Football 80* (UK) (351); *Football 81* (UK) (335); *Football 82* (UK) (299); *España 82* (246); *Football 83* (UK) (174); *Football 84* (UK) (160); *Football 85* (UK) (158); *Football 86* (192); *Mexico 86* (412); *Football 87* (UK) (174); *Football 88* (UK) (143, 445); *Euro 88* (174); *Football 89* (UK) (132); *Foot 89* (France) (397); *Football 90* (UK) (178, 319); *Italia '90* (395); *The All-Time Greats 1920–1990* (UK) (63); *Football 1991* (UK) (203); *Soccer's Super Sevens* (1991–92) (UK) (74); *English Football 1992* (121); *Football '93* (England) (138); *Football League 95* (England) (136); *Superplayers '96* (England) (189, 192); *One England* (2023) (116)

Football 87

Football 86

Football '93

Playing Career
Team Viborg (2007–2010);
IK Skovbakken (2010–2012);
Linköping FC (2012–2016);
VfL Wolfsburg (2017–2020);
Chelsea (2020–2023); Bayern
Munich (2023–) and Denmark
(2009–)

**Panini Album
Rookie Appearances**
First club album appearance:
Frauen Bundesliga 2023–24
(Germany) (77, 271)
First World Cup album
appearance: *Australia and New
Zealand 2023* (255, 291)

**Selected Panini
Appearances**
Euro 2017 (72); *Euro 2022* (149);
Australia and New Zealand 2023
(255, 291); *Frauen Bundesliga
2023–2024* (Germany) (77, 271)

Harder has made in excess of 150 appearances for Denmark.
She is considered one of the best footballers in the world.

Euro 2017

Australia and New Zealand 2023

Pernille Harder has won nine successive league titles up to the end of the 2023-24 season, playing for Linköping, Wolfsburg, Chelsea and Bayern Munich.

PERNILLE HARDER

Euro 2022

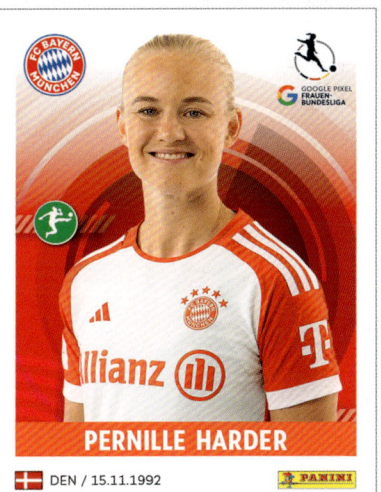

Frauen Bundesliga 2023–2024

Landmarks in women's football are being set all the time and Denmark star Pernille Harder was at the forefront of another during the 2023–24 season. She transferred to Bayern Munich that summer, and her status in the game made her an obvious choice to take pride of place at the front of Panini's first-ever *Frauen Bundesliga* sticker album cover. While that was her first Panini domestic football sticker, the free-scoring attacker has been building up an international portfolio since the first Euro album in 2017.

Her first major tournament exposure came in Euro 2013, when she led the line as Denmark reached the semi-finals, losing on penalties to Norway. Four years later, with Harder by now captain, the Danes went one stage further to the Euro 2017 final, pushing hosts the Netherlands all the way. Harder's stunning left-footed strike pegged the Dutch back to 2-2, but it was not to be and it ended 4-2 to Oranje. Harder's first Panini World Cup stickers featured in the *Australia and New Zealand 2023* collection – her country's first appearance in the finals since 2007.

Since beginning her domestic career in Denmark, Harder has gone on to play for Swedish club Linköping, Wolfsburg and Bayern Munich in Germany and English team Chelsea, winning nine successive league titles up to the end of the 2023-24 season.

GEORGE BEST

Football 85

Football 88

Panini's output beyond Italy began only in the 1970s, meaning Northern Ireland and Manchester United's George Best, one of the greatest talents to have graced the game, is comparatively underrepresented in sticker form. However, the winger did feature as part of a Manchester United team group in three consecutive *Calciatori* albums, from 1966–67 to 1968–69, as well as on his first individual Panini card in the 1967–68 release.

That season climaxed with Best scoring in United's 4-1 European Cup final win over Benfica, and he also bagged a career high of 28 league goals in that same campaign. He had also been to the fore the previous season when helping his side to a second First Division title in three seasons. His first Panini UK album presence, though, came in the Top Sellers collaboration *Football 72* and he appeared once more in *Football 73*.

His Red Devils career finally came to an end in January 1974 and Best spent the next decade globe-trotting, making appearances in the North American Soccer League (NASL) and a string of other clubs, including Fulham. His international career, meanwhile, spanned the years 1964 to 1977, playing on 37 occasions. Fittingly, Northern Ireland's finest ever outfield player also appeared on the cover of Panini's *All-Time Greats 1920–1990*.

Grandi club · MANCHESTER · Inghilterra
GEORGE BEST
nato a Belfast (Irl. del N.) il 22-5-1946

Calciatori 1967–68

Regarded as Northern Ireland's greatest player, George Best played for his national side 37 times and scored 9 goals.

Playing Career
Manchester United (1963–1974); Jewish Guild (1974); Stockport County (1975); Cork Celtic (1975–76); Los Angeles Aztecs (1976); Fulham (1976–1977); Los Angeles Aztecs (1977–1978); Fort Lauderdale Strikers (1978–1979); Hibernian (1979–1980); San Jose Earthquakes (1980–81); AFC Bournemouth (1982–83); Brisbane Lions (1983) and Northern Ireland (1964–1977)

Panini Album Rookie Appearances
First club album appearance: Calciatori 1967–68 (Italy) (630) First World Cup album appearance: N/A

Selected Panini Appearances
Calciatori 1967–68 (Italy) (630); Fotboll 71 (Sweden) (Williams Förlags/Panini) (325); Fotboll 72 (Sweden) (Williams Förlags/Panini) (177); Football 72 (UK) (Top Sellers/Panini) (216, 57A–57P puzzle); Football 73 (UK) (Top Sellers/Panini) (216); Football 1972–73 (Belgium) (338); Football 85 (UK) (379); Football 88 (UK) (286); The All–Time Greats 1920–1990 (UK) (48); Manchester United 2006–07 (G); Manchester United 2008–09 (120); Manchester United 2014–15 (175, 176)

The All-Time Greats 1920–1990

George Best's first Panini UK album apperance came in the Top Sellers collaboration *Football 72*.

KARL-HEINZ RUMMENIGGE

BAYERN MÜNCHEN

Fussball Bundesliga 79

Time and again, when a goal was most needed, Karl-Heinz Rummenigge would deliver. His Panini rookie appearance came in the *Euro Football 78* album, swiftly followed by a first World Cup sticker in *Argentina 78*. He also appeared in the *Europa 80* album where his all-round attributes were crucial to his nation lifting the trophy.

   The Lippstadt-born player rediscovered his scoring touch at the 1982 World Cup in Spain, finishing second only to Paolo Rossi for the Golden Boot, and by this point he was the football darling of the nation, appearing on the cover of *Fussball 82* and *Fussball 84*. The latter was his last year in the Bundesliga with Bayern Munich, scoring 26 goals in 29 league games, as well as being part of a German Cup-winning side, to cap a spectacular decade at the club.

   A move to Internazionale brought a cover appearance on *Calciatori 1984–85*, although his three seasons with Inter didn't quite reach the heights anticipated. He captained West Germany in the Mexico 86 World Cup final, but, despite scoring, ended up on the losing side. There was time, though, for a final hurrah with Servette in Switzerland and he appeared on a Panini sticker for his final club in the Swiss *Football 88* album.

KARL-HEINZ RUMMENIGGE

FC BAYERN MÜNCHEN

Fussball 82

FC BAYERN MÜNCHEN

KARL-HEINZ
RUMMENIGGE

Fussball 84

SERVETTE
KARL-HEINZ
RUMMENIGGE

Football 88

INTER

MiSURA

KARL-HEINZ
RUMMENIGGE

Calciatori 1984–85

INTER

KARL-HEINZ
RUMMENIGGE

Calciatori 1986–87

Playing Career
Bayern Munich (1974–1984);
Internazionale (1984–1987);
Servette (1987–1989) and West
Germany (1976–1986)

Panini Album
Rookie Appearances
First club album appearance:
Euro Football 78 (32)
First World Cup album appearance:
Argentina 78 (149)

Selected Panini
Appearances
Euro Football 78 (32); *Argentina
78* (149); *Fussball Bundesliga '79*
(Germany) (261); *Calciatori 1979–80*
(Italy) (315); *Fussball 80* (Germany)
(244, 374, 375); *Europa 80* (45);
Fussball 81 (Germany) (345); *Fussball
82* (Germany) (303); *Sport Superstars
Euro Football 82* (1982) (147); *España
82* (127); *Fussball 83* (Germany) (334);
Fussball 84 (Germany) (220–251,
294, 453); *Euro 84* (155); *Calciatori
1984–85* (Italy) (128); *Football 85*
(UK) (250); *Calciatori 1985–86* (Italy)
(106); *Fussball 86* (Germany) (322);
Mexico 86 (307); *Supercalcio 1985–
86* (Italy) (173); *Calciatori 1986–87*
(Italy) (154); *Fussball 87* (Germany)
(379, 387); *Football 88* (Switzerland)
(170); *Fussball 88* (Germany) (329,
330); *Euro 88* (15); *Fussball 89*
(Germany) (342); *European
Football Championship England '96*
(11); *Russia 2018* (Austria) (CA4 –
Coca Cola)

ARGENTINA 78

KARLHEINZ
RUMMENIGGE

BRD

Argentina 78

ESPAÑA 82

KARL-HEINZ
RUMMENIGGE
DEUTSCHLAND-BRD

España 82

DEUTSCHLAND-BRD

KARL-HEINZ RUMMENIGGE

Mexico 86

ALESSANDRO DEL PIERO

Calciatori 1995–96

ALESSANDRO
DEL PIERO
JUVENTUS

European Football Championship England '96

ITALIA

ALESSANDRO
DEL PIERO

Alessandro Del Piero began professional life in Serie B with Padova, making his first appearance on a Panini sticker alongside teammate Gaetano Fontana in *Calciatori 1992–93*. Still only 18, Del Piero was transferred to Juventus in the summer of 1993 and became a regular in the following campaign. In a memorable breakthrough year, he helped Juve win the 1995 Serie A title, as well as making his Italy debut in March. The following season once again ended in triumph when Ajax were beaten on penalties in the Champions League final.

That led to a first Panini international tournament sticker for Euro 96, although he featured in only the first half of his country's opening match against Russia. After winning a second Scudetto in 1996–97, Del Piero hit new heights in 1997–98 when he struck a career best of 21 goals as Juventus once again won Serie A (he equalled that figure 10 years later).

On the international front, Italy would suffer penalty shoot-out and golden goal heartbreak against France in the 1998 World Cup and Euro 2000, but revenge would be exacted for the Azzurri and Del Piero further down the line. The deep-lying striker would mark appearances on the front of both *Calciatori 2001–2002* and *Calciatori 2002–2003* (having undergone a drastic haircut in between) by winning his fourth and fifth Serie A titles respectively.

Success on the international stage was finally added to his vast array of domestic honours in his third and last Panini World Cup album appearance. Although by now not a regular starter for his country, Del Piero came on as a substitute in the 2006 final against arch-nemesis France, going on to score in the penalty shoot-out victory.

A fourth Panini Euro sticker came two years later, with a quarter-final penalty shoot-out loss to Spain ushering in his international retirement soon after. Del Piero's career in his homeland ended after 18 consecutive appearances in the *Calciatori* album, right up to his departure in 2012, winning another Serie A title in his final season.

Calciatori 1994-95

Calciatori 1992-93

Calciatori 2001-2002

Playing Career
Padova (1991–1993); Juventus (1993–2012); Sydney FC (2012–2014); Delhi Dynamos (2014) and Italy (1995–2008)

Panini Album Rookie Appearances
First club album appearance: *Calciatori 1992–93* (Italy) (442) First World Cup album appearance: *France 98* (97)

Selected Panini Appearances
Calciatori 1992–93 (Italy) (442); *Calciatori 1994–95* (Italy) (180); *Calciatori 1995–96* (Italy) (131); *European Football Championship England '96* (249) *Calciatori 1996–97* (Italy) (145); *Calciatori 1997–98* (Italy) (165, 393); *France 98* (97) *Calciatori 1998–99* (Italy) (157); *Calciatori 2000* (Italy) (140, 451); *Euro 2000* (184); *Calciatori 2000–2001* (Italy) (164); *Calciatori 2001–2002* (Italy) (166); *Korea/Japan 2002* (471); *Calciatori 2002–2003* (Italy) (199); *Calciatori 2003–2004* (Italy) (166); *Euro 2004* (236); *Calciatori 2004–2005* (Italy) (189); *Calciatori 2005–06* (Italy) (166, 776); *Germany 2006* (335); *Calciatori 2006–07* (Italy) (599); *Calciatori 07–08* (Italy) (189); *Euro 2008* (303); *Calciatori 2008–09* (Italy) (214, X9, V9); *Calciatori 2009–10* (Italy) (236, X10); *Calciatori 2010-2011* (261, X18); *Calciatori 2011-2012* (237, V14)

ELLEN WHITE

Ellen White started her football life as part of Arsenal's youth set-up. In 2005, with competition for places strong in the senior team, she departed for Chelsea aged 16. The striker immediately became part of the west London club's first team, with a best-place Women's Premier League (WPL) finish of fifth in her third season.

She moved to Leeds Carnegie in 2008, enjoying a particularly successful campaign in 2009–10 when she finished as the WPL's joint-second top scorer. It was around this time that White made her senior England debut, coming on as a substitute to score against Austria.

She then returned to Arsenal and during three seasons with the Gunners she greatly increased her medal haul, picking up two Women's Super League (WSL) titles, two FA Cups and three WSL Cups. Her best season in front of goal for Arsenal came in her first year, 2011, during which she appeared in Panini's first Women's World Cup sticker album.

Injury hampered the Aylesbury-born forward's England career for a while, but she was a regular starter again by the time of Euro 2017, taking her place in Panini's debut album for the tournament. Having moved to Notts County in 2014, White moved club again in 2017 as she joined Birmingham. She helped the Blues to the 2017 FA Cup final and was then WSL top scorer in 2017–18 with 15 goals in 14 games.

Ellen White was a member of the England team that triumphed at Euro 2022.

Ellen White

England

Germany 2011

ENG

ELLEN WHITE
9-5-1989 / 1,70 m
Manchester City WFC (ENG)

DEBUT 2010

Euro 2022

France 2019

1,70 m
9-5-1989
Birmingham City WFC (ENG)

Ellen White appeared in two Panini Women's World Cup albums. She scored 52 goals in 113 games for England.

Playing Career
Chelsea (2005–2008); Leeds Carnegie (2008–2010); Arsenal (2010–2013); Notts County (2014–2016); Birmingham City (2017–2019); Manchester City (2019–2022) and England (2010–2022)

Panini Album Rookie Appearances
First club album appearance: N/A
First World Cup album appearance:
Germany 2011 (176)

Selected Panini Appearances
Germany 2011 (176); *Euro 2017* (274); *France 2019* (269); *Euro 2022* (51); *One England* (2023) (9, 159)

ELLEN WHITE
Birmingham City LFC (ENG)
1,70 m 9-5-1989 DEBUT 2010

Euro 2017

By now at the peak of her powers, White finished as joint leading scorer at the 2019 World Cup in France. A final club stint at Manchester City, where she won the FA Cup and WSL Cup, was crowned during the final summer of her playing career at Euro 2022. Going into the tournament with more than 100 caps and a half-century of goals, White led the line diligently and added two more goals to her England women's record tally. She was also a member of the starting XI on the day when England ran out 2-1 extra-time winners over Germany in the final at Wembley.

LIAM BRADY

Arsenal was undergoing a period of struggle when left-footed, attacking midfielder Liam Brady came into the side, but his presence helped to restore the Gunners' place among the trophy contenders. Brady was the lynchpin of the side that reached three FA Cup finals in successive seasons between 1978–1980.

The Republic of Ireland international had made his Panini sticker debut under the Top Sellers banner in 1975, but was still in red and white when Panini released its first UK domestic album in 1978. The following year he was named the PFA Players' Player of the Year, inspiring Arsenal to that season's FA Cup. The Irishman then moved to Serie A in 1980, where he won successive Italian league titles in his two seasons with Juventus.

Brady also went on to feature in subsequent Panini *Calciatori* albums for Sampdoria, Internazionale and Ascoli – almost all under his full name of William – before returning to the UK for two further appearances in *Football 88* and *Football 89* with West Ham United. He also graced the *Europa 80* album, despite Republic of Ireland missing out on qualification, and the *Euro 88* album, even though on that occasion he was ruled out of a much-deserved appearance at a major international tournament by suspension.

Calciatori 1981–82

Calciatori 1985–86

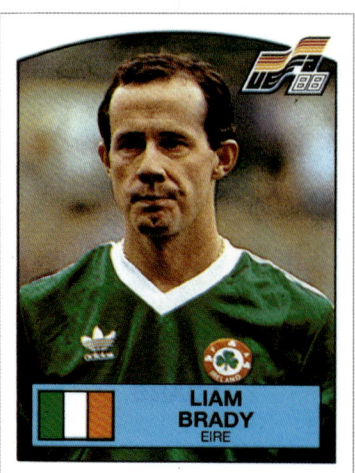

Euro 88

Calciatori 1986–87

Playing Career

Arsenal (1973–1980); Juventus (1980–1982); Sampdoria (1982–1984); Internazionale (1984–1986); Ascoli (1986–1987); West Ham United (1987–1990) and Republic of Ireland (1974–1990)

Panini Album Rookie Appearances

First club album appearance: *Football 75 (UK)* (Top Sellers/Panini) (14); First World Cup album appearance: N/A

Selected Panini Appearances

Football 75 (UK) (Top Sellers/ Panini) (14); *Football 77 (UK)* (Top Sellers/Panini) (6); *Football 78 (UK)* (16); *Football 79 (UK)* (18); *Euro Football 79* (371); *Football 80 (UK)* (13); *Europa 80* (200) *Calciatori 1980–81 (Italy)* (200); *Calciatori 1981–82 (Italy)* (199); *Sport Superstars Euro Football 82* (150); *Calciatori 1982–83 (Italy)* (237); *Calciatori 1983–84 (Italy)* (231); *Calciatori 1984–85 (Italy)* (127); *Football 85 (UK)* (254); *Calciatori 1985–86* (102); *Calciatori 1986–87* (9); *Football 88 (UK)* (349, 453); *Euro 88* (199); *Football 89 (UK)* (281); *The All–Time Greats 1920–1990 (UK)* (60); *Superalbum: Storia e miti del calcio italiano (2004)* (103)

Europa 80

LIAM BRADY

EIR

Brady played for Arsenal, Juventus, Sampdoria, Internazionale, Ascoli and West Ham United in a career that spanned 17 years.

JUVENTUS

WILLIAM BRADY
Serie A · 1980-81

Calciatori 1980–81

SAMPDORIA

LIAM BRADY

Calciatori 1982–83

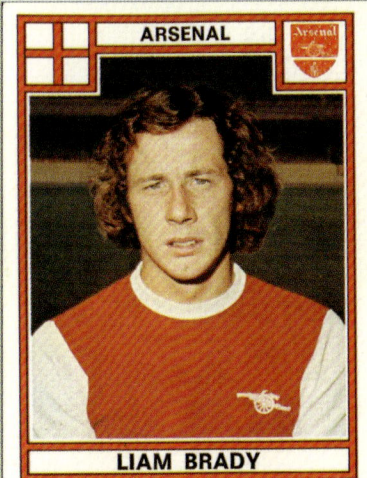

ARSENAL

LIAM BRADY

Football 78

Playing Career
Gladsaxe–Hero (1981–1984); Hvidovre (1984–1987); Brøndby (1987–1991); Manchester United (1991–1999); Sporting Lisbon (1999–2001); Aston Villa (2001–2002); Manchester City (2002–2003) and Denmark (1987–2001)

Panini Album Rookie Appearances
First club/domestic album appearance:
Soccer's Super Sevens (1991–92) (UK) (71)/ *English Football 1992* (122)
First World Cup album appearance:
France 98 (212)

Selected Panini Appearances
Soccer's Super Sevens (1991–92) (UK) (71); *English Football 1992* (122); *Euro '92* (216); *Football '93* (England) (133); *Futebol 92–93* (Portugal) (209); *Superplayers '96* (UK) (163); *European Football Championship England '96* (277); *The Official PFA Collection '97* (England) (221); *Futebol 96/97* (Portugal) (354); *Superplayers 98* (UK) (284, P16); *France 98* (212); *Futebol 1999–2000* (Portugal) (53, 167); *Euro 2000* (320); *Futebol 2000–2001* (Portugal) (1); *Champions League 2000/2001* (59); *Manchester United 2006–07* (N); *Manchester United 2008–09* (115)

Euro '92

Peter Schmeichel was Denmark's starting goalkeeper at the Euro 92 tournament, which they went on to win.

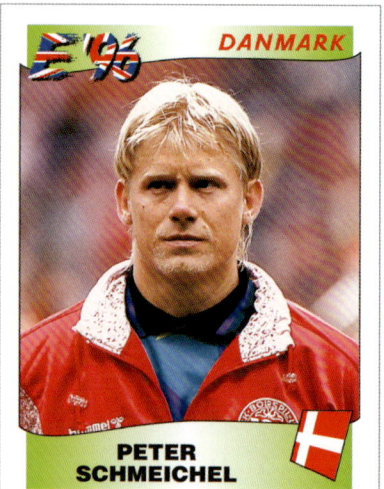

European Football Championship England '96

France 98

Euro 2000

PETER SCHMEICHEL

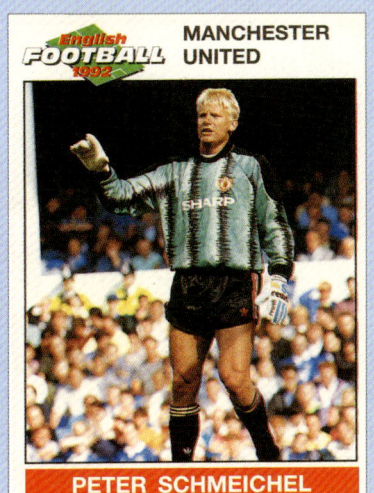

English Football 1992

Football '93

Peter Schmeichel's early playing days took him to Gladsaxe-Hero, Hvidovre and Brøndby, but as Panini produced no Danish league sticker albums it wasn't until Schmeichel was nearly 28 that he first appeared in Panini form. He might have made it into the *Euro 88* collection, but Panini selected Lars Høgh as the back-up goalkeeper to the Denmark team's first choice, Troels Rasmussen. As it transpired, Schmeichel did make the trip to West Germany and by the second game had displaced Rasmussen, never relinquishing his position as Denmark's number 1 until he retired in 2001 after winning 129 caps.

Schmeichel's opening Panini domestic stickers arrived during his first season at Manchester United, first in the experimental *Soccer's Super Sevens* album and then the more familiar *English Football 1992* collection. Denmark was a late replacement for Yugoslavia at Euro 92 and Schmeichel's saves were pivotal in the Danes' fairytale success.

Schmeichel's years with Manchester United delivered an almost unsurpassed decade of riches, his time at the club ending in 1998–99 on the highest of high notes with a last-gasp Champions League final victory over Bayern Munich. Along with his fifth Premier League and third FA Cup, that completed a historic treble in his final season with the Reds.

Schmeichel made his only World Cup finals Panini sticker appearance in *France 98*. The commanding stopper played a key role as Denmark reached the last eight, pushing Brazil all the way in the quarter-final. Schmeichel pulled the curtain down on a glittering career with seasons at Sporting Lisbon, Aston Villa and Manchester City.

DINO ZOFF

Calciatori 1963–64

Calciatori 1973–74

As well as picking up a wealth of team and individual accolades over a two-decade top-class career, legendary Italian goalkeeper Dino Zoff is also part of Panini folklore. He is the only player to feature as a current player in Panini's first four World Cup albums – *Mexico 70*, *München 74*, *Argentina 78* and *España 82* – all four stickers depicting him in a grey jersey with blue collars, the hairstyle also differing little over the 12-year period. The last of those appearances saw Zoff captain his country to the trophy at the age of 40. That triumph resulted in his presence on the following season's *Calciatori* album cover, along with his Azzurri teammates.

Zoff retired at the end of that 1982–83 campaign, ending an astonishing run of 20 consecutive *Calciatori* albums since 1963–64, his Serie A debut having come for Udinese in 1961–62. He established himself the following season, although by then they had dropped down a division and he moved on to Mantova and then, in 1967, Napoli, earning the first of his 112 Italy caps the following year. He later transferred to Juventus, where he enjoyed great success, winning six Serie A titles, two Coppa Italia and the UEFA Cup.

He appeared on the cover of *Calciatori 1975–76*, seen plucking the ball out of the air during a European Championship qualifier versus Poland in April 1975, although a smaller image of a black-shirted Zoff had already featured in a montage cover shot on *Calciatori 1974–75*. The evergreen stopper was also part of the first-ever Panini album for the European Championships – *Europa 80* – where he kept three clean sheets, only for a lack of goals to eliminate the hosts.

Zoff also made several Panini appearances as manager in a career that took in spells at Juventus, Lazio and Fiorentina, as well as the Italian national team. Unsurprisingly, one of the best goalkeepers in history still regularly shows up whenever the all-time greats are honoured in sticker form.

Calciatori 1972–73

Mexico 70

Münchner 74

Argentina 78

España 82

Playing Career
Udinese (1961–1963); Mantova
(1963–1967); Napoli (1967–1972);
Juventus (1972–1983) and Italy
(1968–1983)

**Panini Album
Rookie Appearances**
First club album appearance:
Calciatori 1963–64 (Italy) (164);
First World Cup album
appearance: Mexico 70 (112)

**Selected Panini
Appearances**
Calciatori 1963–64 (Italy) (164);
Calciatori 1964–65 (Italy) (180);
Calciatori 1965–66 (Italy) (345);
Calciatori 1966–67 (Italy) (191);
Calciatori 1967–68 (Italy) (161);
Campioni dello Sport 1967–68
(Italy) (178); Calciatori 1968–69
(Italy) (147); Campioni dello
Sport 1968–69 (Italy) (133);
Calciatori 1969–70 (Italy) (163);
Campioni dello Sport 1969–70
(Italy) (142); Mexico 70 (112);
Calciatori 1970–71 (Italy) (205);
Calciatori 1971–72 (Italy) (211);
Calciatori 1972–73 (Italy) (135);
Calciatori 1973–74 (Italy) (161,
300); München 74 (288);
Calciatori 1974–75 (Italy) (181);
Calciatori 1975–76 (Italy) (141);
Calciatori 1976–77 (Italy) (151);
Calciatori 1977–78 (Italy) (125);
Argentina 78 (99); Calciatori
1978–79 (Italy) (129); Calciatori
1979–80 (Italy) (136); Europa 80
(140); Calciatori 1980–81 (Italy)
(193); Calciatori 1981–82 (Italy)
(192); España 82 (38); Calciatori
1982–83 (Italy) (154, 304);
Calciatori 2010–11 (Italy) (Top
Team Panini 50) (X12); Calciatori
2021 (Italy) (Top Team Panini
60) (X2)

'JAY-JAY' OKOCHA

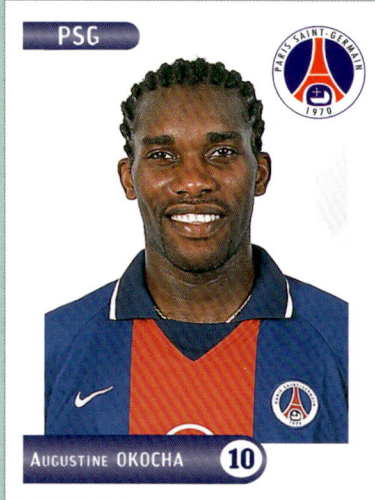

Foot 2001

Fussball '94

Augustine 'Jay-Jay' Okocha thrilled supporters wherever he went during a career that saw him shine around Europe and on the international stage. A holiday to West Germany in 1990 led to the Nigerian earning a contract with a third division club, before his meteoric rise landed a deal with Bundesliga-side Eintracht Frankfurt by the end of the following year.

The attacking midfielder's first Panini sticker came during his second full season at Frankfurt, in *Fussball '94*. Already going by his nickname of 'Jay-Jay', Okocha stayed at the club until the summer of 1996. He then lit up the Turkish league with Fenerbahçe, scoring 30 league goals in two seasons. The first of those campaigns, in 1996–97, coincided with an early Panini release in the country: *Türkiye 1. Futbol Ligi*.

Okocha made his Nigeria debut against Ivory Coast in a World Cup qualifier for USA '94, and scored a free-kick in his next outing against Algeria to help his nation secure their first-ever World Cup appearance. The second of three Panini World Cup stickers then came in *France 98*, when Nigeria matched their 1994 run by reaching the last 16.

Okocha moved to the French capital that summer to represent Paris Saint-Germain, appearing in four consecutive *Foot* albums. The showman subsequently took his expansive talent to the Premier League, proving a huge crowd favourite during four seasons at Bolton Wanderers.

PARIS SAINT GERMAIN

Jayjay OKOCHA

Foot 99

PARIS SAINT-GERMAIN

Augustine OKOCHA

Foot 2000

P.S.G.

AUGUSTINE OKOCHA

Foot 2002

Playing Career

Borussia Neunkirchen (1990–1992); Eintracht Frankfurt (1992–1996); Fenerbahçe (1996–1998); Paris Saint-Germain (1998–2002); Bolton Wanderers (2002–2006); Qatar SC (2006–2007); Hull City (2007–2008) and Nigeria (1993–2006)

Panini Album Rookie Appearances

First club album appearance: *Fussball '94* (Germany) (64) First World Cup album appearance: *USA '94* (241)

Selected Panini Appearances

Fussball '94 (Germany) (64); *USA '94* (241) *Fussball '95* (Germany) (88); *Fussball Bundesliga 1994–1995 – Final phase* (Germany) (117); *Fussball 96* (Germany) (230, 242, 243); *Fussball Bundesliga 1995–1996 – Final phase* (Germany) (44, 229, 230); *Africa '96* (197); *Türkiye 1. Futbol Ligi 1996–1997* (105); *African All-Star 97* (122); *France 98* (253); *SuperFoot 1998/99* (France) (84); *Euro Super Clubs 1999* (266); *Foot 99* (France) (287); *Foot 2000* (France) (268); *Champions League 2000/2001* (240); *Foot 2001* (France) (225); *Foot 2002* (France) (295); *Road to FIFA World Cup 2002* (79); *Korea/ Japan 2002* (414)

USA '94 NIGERIA

AUGUSTINE OKOCHA

EMMANUEL AMUNEKE

USA '94

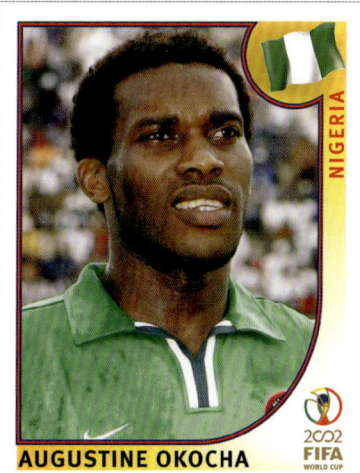

NIGERIA

AUGUSTINE OKOCHA

2002 FIFA WORLD CUP

Korea/Japan 2002

SERGIO RAMOS

As a breakthrough star with his hometown club in the 2004–2005 season, Sergio Ramos was part of a Sevilla squad that also contained Dani Alves, Jesús Navas and Júlio Baptista. However, the versatile defender had moved to Real Madrid in the summer of 2005, so featured for two teams in his debut *Colecciones ESTE* album in 2005–06, first with Sevilla and then, later in the album, in white as part of the Últimos Fichajes (Latest Signings) section.

Switching between the middle and right side of defence, the committed performer won the first two of his five La Liga titles in 2006–07 and 2007–08, and he had his first World Cup experience at Germany 2006, when he played three of Spain's four games at right-back, exiting in the round of 16 versus France.

Euro success came with the first two of his four tournament album appearances in 2008 and 2012. In between came a World Cup winner's medal in South Africa as a Spanish

Liga 2005–2006 (Colecciones ESTE)

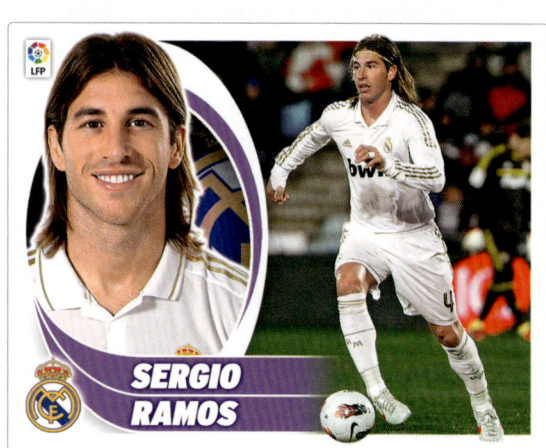

Liga 2012–13 (Colecciones ESTE)

side largely made up of Real Madrid and Barcelona players dominated the era. His international career ended in 2021, having given his all over 16 years and 180 appearances.

Domestic honours continued to pour in over this latter period. The first of his four Champions League victories with Madrid occurred during the 2013–14 season, the seventh of eight Panini album appearances for the competition. A move to Paris Saint-Germain in 2021 brought another two league titles, before he returned to where it all began at Sevilla.

Euro 2012

Brasil 2014

Foot 2022

Germany 2006

Playing Career
Sevilla (2004–2005); Real Madrid (2005–2021); Paris Saint-Germain (2021–2023); Sevilla (2023–) and Spain (2005–2021)

Panini Album Rookie Appearances
First club album appearance: Liga 2005–2006 (Colecciones ESTE) (Spain) (359, 525)
First World Cup album appearance: Germany 2006 (538)

Selected Panini Appearances
Liga 2005–2006 (Colecciones ESTE) (Spain) (359, 525); Germany 2006 (538); Liga 2006–2007 (Colecciones ESTE) (Spain) (310); Liga 07–08 (Colecciones ESTE) (Spain) (278); Euro 2008 (420); Liga 08–09 (Colecciones ESTE) (Spain) (205); Liga 09–10 (Colecciones ESTE) (Spain) (215); South Africa 2010 (567); Liga 2010–2011 (Colecciones ESTE) (Spain) (275); Liga 2011–12 (Colecciones ESTE) (Spain) (245); Euro 2012 (291); Liga 2012–13 (Colecciones ESTE) (Spain) (307, 613); Liga 2013–14 (Colecciones ESTE) (Spain) (365); Brasil 2014 (111); Liga 2014–15 (Colecciones ESTE) (Spain) (396); Liga 2015–16 (Colecciones ESTE) (Spain) (367); France 2016 (355, 375); Liga 2016–17 (Colecciones ESTE) (Spain) (406, 655); Liga 2017–18 (Colecciones ESTE) (Spain) (467, 664); Russia 2018 (139); Liga 2018–19 (Colecciones ESTE) (Spain) (434); Liga 2019–20 (Colecciones ESTE) (Spain) (407, 653); Euro 2020 Preview Edition (ESP4, C8 – Coca Cola); Liga 2020–21 (Colecciones ESTE) (Spain) (378); Euro 2020 Tournament Edition (521, 535); Foot 2022 (France) (347); Liga 2021–22 (Colecciones ESTE) (Spain) (637); Foot 2023 (France) (332); Liga 2023–24 (Colecciones ESTE) (Spain) (718)

MOHAMED SALAH

Thanks to his phenomenal goalscoring record over the last decade, Mohamed Salah has become one of the players opposition teams and fans alike most fear. Salah made his Egyptian Premier League debut for Al Mokawloon Al Arab a month short of his 18th birthday in May 2010. After establishing himself the following season, the Nagrig-born player made great strides during the 2011–12 campaign, making his senior Egypt debut in September 2011 and then moving to Swiss club Basel.

The winger's first campaign in Europe was a success and he helped his club win the league and reach the semi-finals of the Europa League. That led to his Panini sticker debut the following season in the 2013–14 *Champions League* album. Salah scored in group stage Champions League wins over Chelsea that season, clearly making a strong impression on manager José Mourinho: he joined the Blues in January 2014.

The pacy attacker made just a handful of starts during his year at Stamford Bridge, eventually being shipped out on loan to Fiorentina in February 2015. Given a transfer update sticker in *Calciatori 2014–2015*, Salah was an instant hit in Italy. The following season he went on loan to Roma, who signed him permanently the season after that, a campaign in which the capital city club finished second in Serie A. However, they were unable to keep Salah from moving on again.

A return to England with Liverpool in 2017 could not have started in better fashion, as he scored 32 Premier League goals to win the Golden Boot. He then earned a first Panini World Cup sticker in 2018, but Egypt missed out in 2022. Salah appeared in Panini's debut *Premier League* album in 2019–20, which coincided with Liverpool's first league title for 30 years.

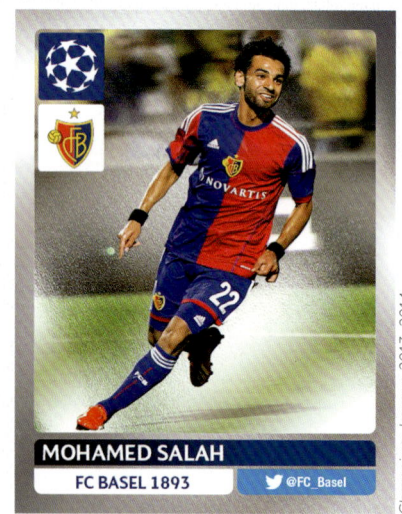

MOHAMED SALAH
FC BASEL 1893 — @FC_Basel

Champions League 2013–2014

Playing Career

Al Mokawloon Al Arab (2010–2012); Basel (2012–2014); Chelsea (2014–2016); Fiorentina (loan) (2015); Roma (loan) (2015–2016); Roma (2016–2017); Liverpool (2017–) and Egypt (2011–)

Panini Album Rookie Appearances

First club album appearance: Champions League 2013–2014 (302, 372)
First World Cup album appearance: *Russia 2018* (90)

Selected Panini Appearances

Champions League 2013–2014 (302, 372); *Calciatori 2014–2015* (Italy) (A11); *Calciatori 2015–2016* (Italy) (464); *FIFA 365 2016* (R86); *Calciatori 2016–2017* (Italy) (443); *FIFA 365 2017* (283); *Russia 2018* (90); *Panini Tabloid* (2019) (England) (103); *Football 2020* (England) (304, 322); *Premier League 2021* (England) (323, 373); *FIFA 365 2021* (75, 446); *Premier League 2022* (England) (368); *FIFA 365 2022* (60); *Top Class* (2022) (45, 48, 61); *Premier League 2023* (England) (394, 404); *FIFA 365 2023* (SAL–HAA, 81 83); *Premier League 2024* (England) (366, 375); *FIFA 365 2024* (83)

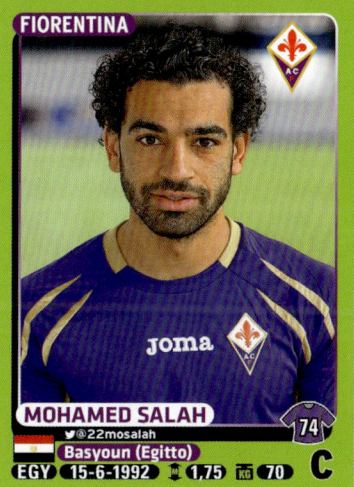

Calciatori 2014–2015

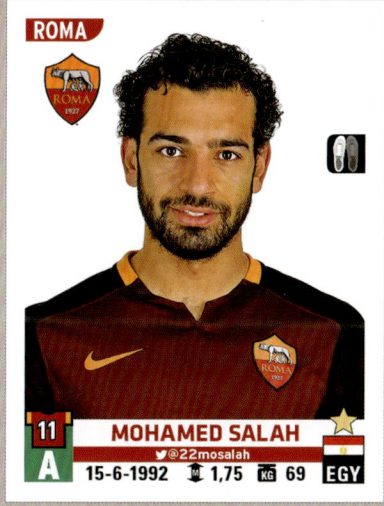

Calciatori 2015–2016

Russia 2018

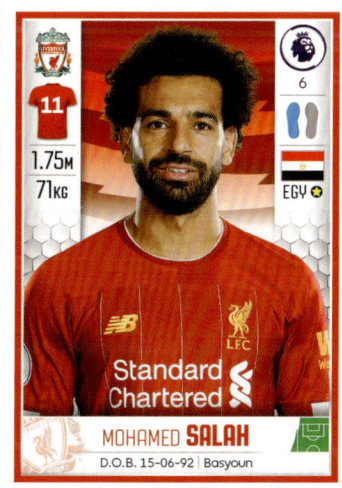

Football 2020

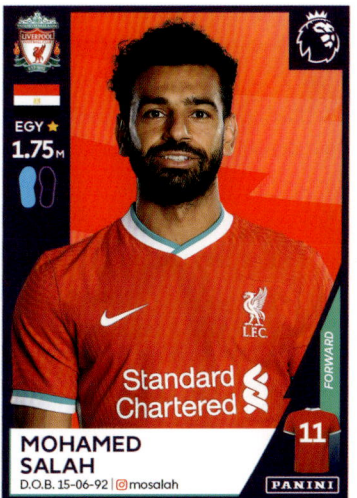

Premier League 2021

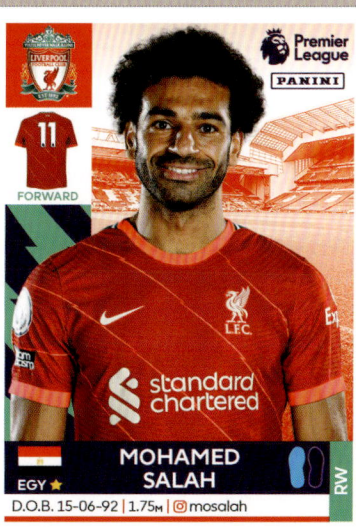

Premier League 2022

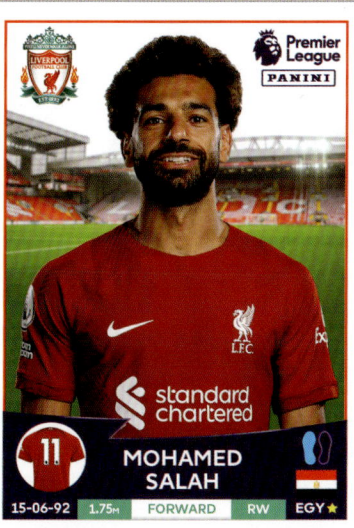

Premier League 2023

TREVOR FRANCIS

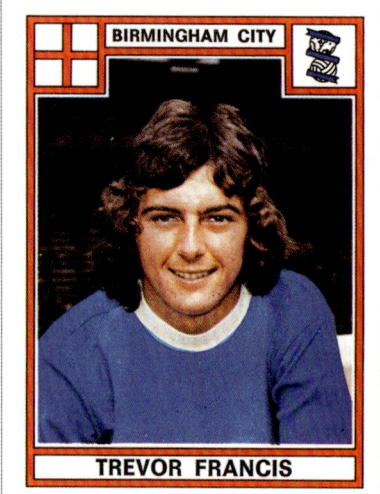

Football 78

Europa 80

Trevor Francis burst onto the scene at Birmingham City as a 16-year-old, scoring four goals against Bolton Wanderers in his first season of senior football. The Plymouth-born attacker helped the Blues win promotion to Division One in 1972, leading to his first appearance in a Panini collaboration the following season, when he was pictured in *Football 73* (published by Top Sellers).

Francis had his most prolific season in 1977–78 (scoring 25 league goals), coinciding with Panini's full debut in the UK with *Football 78*. The Devonian was still in Blue for Panini's *Football 79* follow-up, but by the end of the season he was scoring the winning goal for Nottingham Forest against Malmö in the European Cup final, following a record-breaking £1 million move. Francis's stooping header to win the game is neatly captured in the 'Victory in Europe' section of Panini's *Football 86*.

The forward made his first appearance in the Forest section of a Panini album in *Football 80*, but a serious injury, one that forced him to miss that season's European Cup final win over Hamburg, meant he was overlooked for the following collection.

Trevor Francis represented England in the *Europa 80* and *España 82* albums, and he appeared in domestic albums for a range of clubs over the next eight years, including Manchester City, Sampdoria, Atalanta and Queens Park Rangers.

Playing Career
Birmingham City (1970–1979); Detroit Express (loan) (1978); Nottingham Forest (1979–1981); Detroit Express (1979); Manchester City (1981–1982); Sampdoria (1982–1986); Atalanta (1986–1987); Rangers (1987–1988); Queens Park Rangers (1988–1990); Woolongong City (loan) (1988); Sheffield Wednesday (1990–1994) and England (1977–1986)

Panini Album Rookie Appearances
First club album appearance: Football 73 (UK) (Top Sellers/Panini) (25)
First World Cup album appearance: *España 82* (253)

Selected Panini Appearances
Football 73 (UK) (Top Sellers/Panini) (25); Football 74 (UK) (Top Sellers/Panini) (21); Football 75 (UK) (Top Sellers/Panini) (20); Football 76 (UK) (Top Sellers/Panini) (35); Football 77 (UK) (Top Sellers/Panini) (41); Football 78 (UK) (54); Football 79 (UK) (55); Football 80 (UK) (286); Calciatori 1979–80 (Italy) (307); Europa 80 (135); Football 82 (UK) (151); España 82 (253); Calciatori 1982–83 (Italy) (241); Calciatori 1983–84 (Italy) (235); Calciatori 1984–85 (Italy) (240); Calciatori 1985–86 (Italy) (235); Supercalcio 1985–86 (Italy) (140); Football 86 (UK) (266); Calciatori 1986–87 (Italy) (39); Football 87 (UK) (456); Football 89 (UK) (227); Football 90 (UK) (231 – as player-manager)

Football 80

España 82

Calciatori 1982–83

Calciatori 1984–85

Football 89

Football 90

GIANLUIGI BUFFON

Euro 2000

Calciatori 1995–96

Gianluigi Buffon's final Panini appearance in a goalkeeper jersey, for Serie B team Parma, came in *Calciatori 2022–2023*. His first, also for Parma, but this time in Serie A, was as far back as 1995–96, the season he turned 18 and understudied Luca Bucci. The Italian missed out on only one *Calciatori* album during that 28-year period, making a quick detour to Panini's *Foot 2018–2019* collection with Paris Saint-Germain.

Buffon impressed sufficiently during the nine Serie A appearances he had during that 1995–96 campaign to become first choice the following year and, making six appearances in the Parma section of *Calciatori* up to 2000–01, the precocious stopper was a key member of a competitive side, winning the UEFA Cup and Coppa Italia in that time.

His early international experience also came during this period, with his debut in a crucial World Cup qualification play-off match against Russia in October 1997. Italy made it to France 98, as did Buffon, but he made neither the Panini sticker album nor an appearance in the tournament. However, the 1.88 m/6 ft 2 in-tall keeper, known for his preference for short-sleeved shirts, did make Panini's *Euro 2000* collection and was due to be Italy's first choice in the Netherlands and Belgium until he broke his hand in a warm-up game.

Buffon moved to Juventus the following summer, winning the first of 10 Serie A titles in his first season. The first of three Champions League final appearances – all ending in defeat – arrived the following year. That 2002–03

ITA

GIANLUIGI BUFFON

Germany 2006

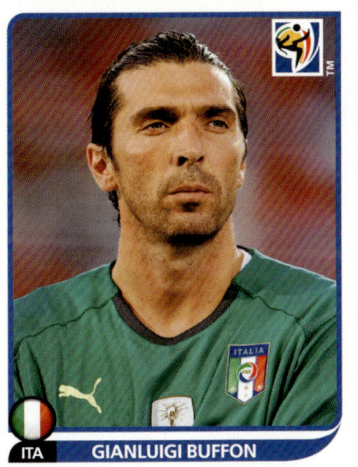

ITA GIANLUIGI BUFFON

South Africa 2010

GIANLUIGI BUFFON

JUVENTUS

Calciatori 2003–2004

PARMA

Gianluigi BUFFON

PARMA A.C.

Calciatori 1996–97

campaign also saw him win UEFA Club Footballer and Goalkeeper of the Year.

Buffon's first Panini World Cup sticker was for Korea/ Japan 2002, but it was for his second of four such album appearances that he most assured his legacy. Italy's 2006 World Cup triumph was underpinned by their solidity at the back, with Buffon as a redoubtable last line. He kept five clean sheets in seven games and a remarkable extra-time save in the final from a Zinedine Zidane effort enabled the subsequent win on penalties.

Playing Career
Parma (1995–2001); Juventus (2001–2018); Paris Saint-Germain (2018–2019); Juventus (2019–2021); Parma (2021–2023) and Italy (1997–2018)

Panini Album Rookie Appearances
First club album appearance: *Calciatori 1995–96* (Italy) (228) First World Cup album appearance: *Korea/Japan 2002* (459)

Selected Panini Appearances
Calciatori 1995–96 (Italy) (228); *Calciatori 1996–97* (Italy) (225); *Calciatori 1997–98* (Italy) (256); *Calciatori 1998–99* (Italy) (211); *Calciatori 2000* (Italy) (221, 447); *Euro 2000* (167); *Calciatori 2000–2001* (Italy) (269); *Calciatori 2001–2002* (Italy) (149); *Korea/ Japan 2002* (459); *Calciatori 2002–2003* (Italy) (181); *Calciatori 2003–2004* (Italy) (149); *Euro 2004* (222); *Calciatori 2004–2005* (Italy) (173); *Calciatori 2005–06* (Italy) (149); *Germany 2006* (323); *Calciatori 2006–07* (Italy) (587); *Calciatori 07–08* (Italy) (173, T1); *Euro 2008* (286, 462); *Calciatori 2008–09* (Italy) (194, X1, V4); *Calciatori 2009–10* (Italy) (X1, 221, 481); *South Africa 2010* (412); *Calciatori 2010–11* (Italy) (246, X1); *Calciatori 2011–2012* (Italy) (218, V6, X19, X20); *Euro 2012* (316); *Calciatori 2012–2013* (Italy) (201, V4); *Calciatori 2013–2014* (Italy) (280); *Brasil 2014* (319); *Calciatori 2014–2015* (Italy) (238, V4); *Calciatori 2015–2016* (Italy) (300, V15); *Euro 2016* (491, 497); *Calciatori 2016–2017* (Italy) (260, 566, 570); *Calciatori 2017–2018* (Italy) (C12, 290); *Foot 2018– 2019* (France) (353); *Calciatori 2019–2020* (Italy) (C1, 242, 263); *Calciatori 2021* (Italy) (271, X1); *Calciatori 2021–2022* (Italy) (654); *Calciatori 2022–2023* (Italy) (611); *Calciatori 2023–2024* (Italy) (1)

JOHN BARNES

WATFORD

JOHN BARNES

Football 83

WATFORD

JOHN BARNES

Football 87

John Barnes made his debut for Watford early in the 1981–82 season and the fleet-of-foot left-winger quickly became a regular in the side, scoring 13 goals to help the Hornets gain promotion to the top flight for the first time in their history.

There was no denying Barnes's right to a sticker in *Football 83* and he was honoured with one of the experimental full-length shots. It was back to the traditional head and shoulder images, though, in *Football 84*, and the youngster was an inspiration as Watford reached their first FA Cup final, losing to Everton. Three further Panini stickers followed in yellow before a big money move to Liverpool ahead of the 1987–88 season.

Barnes enjoyed a debut season to remember for Liverpool, helping them win the First Division at a canter, reaching the FA Cup final and winning both the PFA and FWA Player of the Year awards. The former of those individual accolades earned Barnes the first sticker in *Football 89*, followed by a place on the cover of *Football 90*, jostling with Everton's Pat Nevin during the 1989 FA Cup final, which Liverpool won 3-2.

Although he first played for England in 1983, Barnes had to wait a while for his first Panini international tournament sticker, as England failed to qualify for Euro 84 and then the wide man missed out on the *Mexico 86* album, despite making the squad. There then followed three England stickers between 1988 and 1992, but a groin injury ended his Italia 90 participation in the last 16 and an Achilles problem forced him to miss Euro 92 entirely.

LIVERPOOL

JOHN BARNES

Football 90

Considered one of England's most talented players, John Barnes represented the national side at the 1986 and 1990 World Cups.

Playing Career
Watford (1981–1987); Liverpool (1987–1997); Newcastle United (1997–1999); Charlton Athletic (1999) and England (1983–1995)

Panini Album Rookie Appearances
First club album appearance: Football 83 (UK) (321)
First World Cup album appearance: *Italia '90* (400)

Selected Panini Appearances
Football 83 (UK) (321); Football 84 (UK) (326); Football 85 (UK) (340); Football 86 (UK) (354); Football 87 (UK) (358); Supersport (UK) (1987) (226); Football 88 (UK) (115, 262); Euro 88 (179); Supersport (Spain) (1988) (89); Football 89 (UK) (1, 106); Football Egypt 1988–89 (363); Football 90 (UK) (137); *Italia '90* (400); *The All-Time Greats 1920–1990* (UK) (68); Football 1991 (UK) (160); *Soccer's Super Sevens* (1991–92) (UK) (54); *English Football 1992* (96); Euro '92 (109); Football '93 (UK) (118); Superplayers '96 (England) (130); European Football Championship England '96 (140–144); The Official PFA Collection '97 (England) (15); Superplayers 98 (17); Scottish Premier League 2000 (49 – as manager); Celtic 1999–2000 (6); Liverpool 2008–09 (183, 186, 195); Liverpool 2009–10 (212)

ENGLAND

JOHN BARNES

Euro '92

JOHN BARNES
LIVERPOOL

Football 88

ITALIA90

ENGLAND
JOHN BARNES

Italia '90

MIROSLAV KLOSE

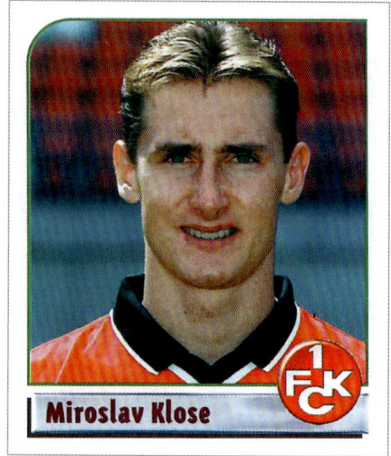

Miroslav Klose

Fussball 2002

MIROSLAV KLOSE

Fussball 2005–2006

Few have surpassed the consistency of Miroslav Klose. The German striker bowed out of his fourth tournament with a men's World Cup finals record high of 16 goals and he left the big stage in the grand manner, as a member of the starting XI that beat Argentina in the 2014 final.

The Polish-born attacker was a relatively late starter in top-level football, but once he got a foothold there was no stopping him. His first Panini album appearance – *Fussball 2002* – not only placed him on the Kaiserslautern pages, but also on a special poster for the predicted German national squad to go to Korea/Japan.

He scored five goals – all headers – at the tournament and another five on home soil in the 2006 World Cup. A further four goals in South Africa 2010 again placed him among the leading tournament scorers. Klose became the first man to play in four successive World Cup semi-finals when he scored in Germany's 7-1 win over Brazil in 2014. That proved to be his 16th and last World Cup goal. International retirement followed soon after, with a record of 71 goals in 137 matches.

Domestic trophies – and Panini stickers – were collected with Werder Bremen, Bayern Munich and Lazio, before Klose retired in 2016. A first managerial sticker came in Panini's *Österreichische Fussball Bundesliga 22–2023*, during his one season in charge of Rheindorf Altach.

Fussball 08/09

Calciatori 2015–2016

MIROSLAV KLOSE

Brasil 2014

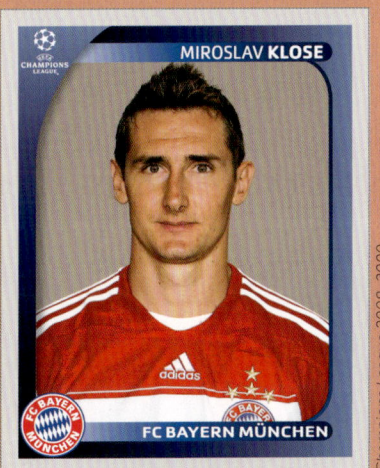

Champions League 2008-2009

MIROSLAV KLOSE

Germany 2006

MIROSLAV KLOSE

Euro 2008

Playing Career

FC 08 Homburg (1998–1999);
1. FC Kaiserslautern (1999–2004);
Werder Bremen (2004–2007);
Bayern Munich (2007–2011);
Lazio (2011–2016) and Germany
(2001–2014)

Panini Album
Rookie Appearances

First club album appearance:
Fussball 2002 (Germany) (241, X)
First World Cup album
appearance: *Germany 2006* (33)

Selected Panini
Appearances

Fussball 2002 (Germany) (241, X);
Fussball 2002–2003 (Germany)
(267); *Fussball 03–04 (Germany)*
(269, 272); *Euro 2004* (314);
Fussball 2005–2006 (Germany)
(83); *Germany 2006* (33); *Fussball
2006/2007 (Germany)* (3, 138);
Fussball 2007/2008 (Germany)
(354); *Euro 2008* (225, 519);
Fussball 08/09 (Germany) (406);
Champions League 2008–2009
(160); *South Africa 2010* (275,
DE1–DE4 Coca Cola); *Calciatori
2011–2012 (Italy)* (V4, 264); *Euro
2012* (247, D3, D16 in German
Edition); *Calciatori 2012–2013
(Italy)* (246, X15, X16); *Calciatori
2013-2014 (Italy)* (328); *Brasil
2014* (506); *Calciatori 2014–2015
(Italy)* (284, 288); *Calciatori
2015–2016 (Italy)* (350); *Russia
2018 World Cup* (681 – Legends,
CA-12 – Coca Cola Austria);
*Österreichische Fußball
Bundesliga 22–23 (Austria)* (214
– as manager)

SAMUEL ETO'O

Joining Real Madrid's youth academy at 16, Samuel Eto'o spent most of his time there on loan at other clubs. With little prospect of breaking into the star-studded line-up, the Cameroonian made his final transient spell permanent by joining Mallorca in 2000. Eto'o's first stickers came during his first season as a fully contracted Mallorca player and he appeared in both the Panini and ESTE 2000–2001 collections.

Calciatori 2009–10

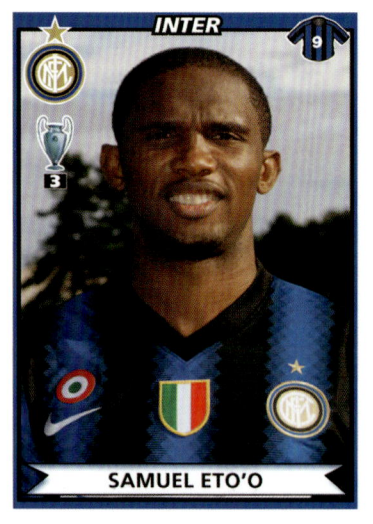

Calciatori 2010–11

Calciatori 2014–2015

Goals came at an increasing rate in Eto'o's final two seasons at Mallorca, including two in the 2003 Copa del Rey final win over Recreativo de Huelva. A big-money transfer to Barcelona was his reward in 2004, after which his scoring rate went to greater heights. The first two of his three La Liga title successes came in his opening two seasons at Camp Nou. Two Champions League victories followed in 2006 and 2009. He also won La Liga and the Copa del Rey in the latter year, contributing 36 goals to the cause, but surprisingly it turned out to be the end of his time at the club.

Another glorious chapter of success followed at Internazionale, however, where he won six trophies in two seasons, including a third Champions League in 2010. He then had spells with Anzhi Makhachkala, Chelsea and Sampdoria, and appeared on Panini stickers for those clubs. Eto'o also made World Cup album appearances in 2002, 2010 and 2014, as well as in the AFCON collections of 2008 and 2010.

Playing Career
Real Madrid (1997–2000); Leganés (1997–1998) (loan); Espanyol (1999) (loan); Mallorca 2000 (loan); Mallorca (2000–2004); Barcelona (2004–2009); Internazionale (2009–2011); Anzhi Makhachkala (2011–2013); Chelsea (2013–2014); Everton (2014–2015); Sampdoria (2015); Antalyaspor (2015–2018); Konyaspor (2018); Qatar SC (2018–2019) and Cameroon (1997–2014)

Panini Album Rookie Appearances
First club album appearance: Panini Liga 2000–2001 (Spain) (168a)/Liga 2000–2001 (Colecciones ESTE) (Spain) (248)
First World Cup album appearance: Korea/Japan 2002 (383)

Selected Panini Appearances
Panini Liga 2000–2001 (Spain) (168a); Liga 2000–2001 (Colecciones ESTE) (Spain) (248); Liga 2001–2002 (Colecciones ESTE) (Spain) (255); Korea/Japan 2002 (383); Liga 02–03 (Colecciones ESTE) (Spain) (262); Liga 2003–2004 (Colecciones ESTE) (Spain) (280); Liga 2004–2005 (Colecciones ESTE) (Spain) (293, 520, 541); Liga 2005–2006 (Colecciones ESTE) (Spain) (92); Champions of Europe 1955–2005 (75); Liga 2006–2007 (Colecciones ESTE) (Spain) (81); Champions League 2006–2007 (20); Liga 07–08 (Colecciones ESTE) (Spain) (110); Champions League 2007–2008 (56); Africa Cup 2008 (192); Liga 08–09 (Colecciones ESTE) (Spain) (96); Champions League 2008–2009 (110); Calciatori 2009–10 (Italy) (214, 487); Champions League 2009–2010 (376 and 559); Africa Cup 2010 (40); South Africa 2010 (408); Calciatori 2010–11 (Italy) (239); Champions League 2010–2011 (20); Russian Football Premier League 2012–2013 (100, 103); Champions League 2013–2014 (339); Brasil 2014 (107, P19); Calciatori 2014–2015 (Italy) (A40)

SAMUEL ETO'O

Korea/Japan 2002

SAMUEL ETO'O

South Africa 2010

ETO'O

F.C. BARCELONA

Liga 2006–2007 (Colecciones ESTE)

SON HEUNG-MIN

After spending his formative years in the Bundesliga, in recent times South Korean Son Heung-min has been one of the Premier League's shining lights. Having moved to Germany at 16, his first-team debut came as an 18-year-old for Hamburger SV during 2010–11.

Three seasons of increasing promise led to a move to Bayer Leverkusen in 2013–14 and a first Panini sticker in that season's *Champions League* album. A first Panini World Cup sticker followed in 2014, with Son scoring once in Brazil, and he also appeared in the 2018 and 2022 World Cup Panini albums.

Then came the big-money move to Tottenham, where Son established himself as a fan favourite during his second season, with 21 goals in all competitions, as Spurs finished second in 2016–17. As a scorer of great goals, as well as lots of them, Son also featured in Panini's first Premier League release of 2019–20. A Premier League Golden Boot came in 2021–22, shared with Liverpool's Mohamed Salah, to help earn Spurs a Champions League spot on the final day of the season.

Known for his speed, finishing, and link play, Son is regarded as one of the greatest Asian footballers of all time.

Premier League 2024

Russia 2018

Bayer 04 Leverkusen (GER) | 8-7-1992 | 1,83 m | 76 kg

SON HEUNG-MIN

Brasil 2014

Son Heung-min captains both his Premier League club Tottenham Hotspur and the South Korea national team.

Playing Career
Hamburger SV (2010–2013); Bayer Levekusen (2013–2015); Tottenham Hotspur (2015–) and South Korea (2010–)

Panini Album rookie appearances
First club album appearance: *Champions League 2013–2014* (61) First World Cup album appearance: *Brasil 2014* (635)

Selected Panini appearances
Champions League 2013–2014 (61); *Brasil 2014* (635); *Champions League 2014–2015* (226); *Russia 2018* (496); *Panini Tabloid* (2019) (England) (49); *Football 2020* (England) (19, 329, 542); *Premier League 2021* (England) (19, 546, 551, 553); *Road to Qatar 2022* (300); *Premier League 2022* (England) (542, 546); *Qatar 2022* (KOR19, HS – Extra Stiicker, C8 – Coca Cola Believers); *Premier League 2023* (England) (569, 577); *FIFA 365 2023* (129, 131, RON–SON); *Premier League 2024* (England) (568, 572)

Football 2020

Premier League 2023

Qatar 2022

MARCO VAN BASTEN

Calciatori 1988–89

MILAN

MARCO VAN BASTEN

Voetbal 83

AJAX

MARK VAN BASTEN

Having torn up the Eredivisie with Ajax for much of the 1980s, Marco van Basten moved to AC Milan in 1987 in an era when he was the greatest centre-forward on the planet.

The Dutchman made his Ajax debut towards the end of the 1981–82 season as a 17-year-old, scoring after coming on as a substitute for Johan Cruyff. Far more opportunities came the following campaign, during which he also earned his first Panini sticker in *Voetbal 83* – initially under the moniker of 'Mark'. At 1.88 m (6ft 2in), the attacker helped the Amsterdam club win the domestic league and cup double that season, before the goals really started to flow over the following years. Van Basten was Eredivisie top scorer four seasons in a row between 1983–84 and 1986–87, winning another league title, two KNVB cups and the Cup Winners' Cup in the process.

His move to AC Milan during the summer of 1987 saw him adorn the cover of that season's Panini *Calciatori* album. Although the striker was limited to only 11 Serie A appearances in his first year at the club, it was still enough to earn him a title medal. That success gave AC Milan a place in the following season's European Cup, with the Dutch master scoring 10 goals on the way to his side's victory. His ninth goal – the first of two in the final win over Steaua București – is pictured in Panini's *Champions of Europe 1955–2005* album. Another European Cup followed in 1990 before back-to-back Serie A titles in 1991–92 and 1992–93.

His crowning glory of an international career that spanned from 1983 to 1992 came during Euro 88, when he finished as top scorer and player of the tournament. A hat-trick in the group stage destroyed England before van Basten deftly carried his side to a semi-final win against West Germany. His coup de grâce was a stunning volley from an oblique angle to give the Dutch breathing space in the final against the Soviet Union.

That fortnight's momentum in West Germany led him to winning the Ballon d'Or three times between 1988 and 1992, but injuries were beginning to take their toll by the time of the last of those awards. There was barely a chink in the Utrecht-born striker's armoury, and it was only the savagery meted out to him by opponents that prevented him from dominating on the world stage for much longer.

His final professional match came in the 1993 Champions League final when another hefty tackle forced him to leave the field early, putting a premature end to the 28-year-old's career.

Playing Career
Ajax (1981–1987); AC Milan (1987–1995) and Netherlands (1983–1992)

Panini Album Rookie appearances
First club album appearance: Voetbal 83 (Netherlands) (21) First World Cup album appearance: *Italia '90* (417)

Selected Panini Appearances
Voetbal 83 (Netherlands) (21); *Voetbal 84* (Netherlands) (21); *Voetbal 85* (Netherlands) (18); *Voetbal 86* (Netherlands) (15); *Voetbal 87* (Netherlands) (14); *Voetbal 88* (Netherlands) (4); *Calciatori 1987–88* (Italy) (163); *Euro 88* (Italy) (230); *Calciatori 1988–89* (Italy) (211); *Panini Futbol 88* (Spain) (213); *Calciatori 1989–90* (Italy) (240); *Voetbal 90* (Netherlands) (330); *Italia '90* (417); *Calciatori 1990–91* (Italy) (221); *Voetbal '91* (Netherlands) (341 *Calciatori 1991–92* (Italy) (220, 377); *Voetbal '92* (Netherlands) (247); *Euro '92* (134); *Calciatori 1992–93* (Italy) (35, 220); *Futebol 92–93* (Portugal) (212); European Football Championship England '96 (16); *Tutto Milan* (1997) (177, 178); *Champions of Europe 1955–2005* (17); *Euro 2012* (Dutch edition) (17, 96)

Calciatori 1987–88

MARCO VAN BASTEN

MARCO VAN BASTEN

MILAN

Calciatori 1992–93

MARCO VAN BASTEN
NEDERLAND

Euro 88

NEDERLAND

MARCO VAN BASTEN

Italia '90

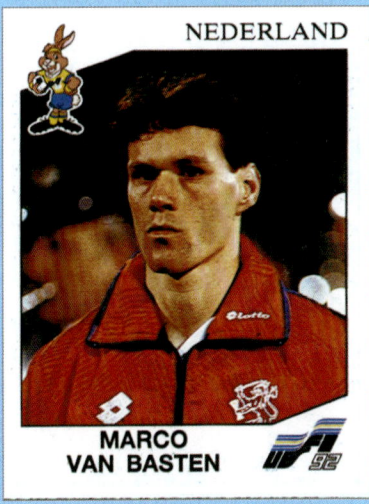

NEDERLAND

MARCO VAN BASTEN

Euro '92

LUKA MODRIĆ

Luka Modrić   9-9-1985
Tottenham Hotspur FC (ENG)   1,73 m   70 kg

Euro 2012

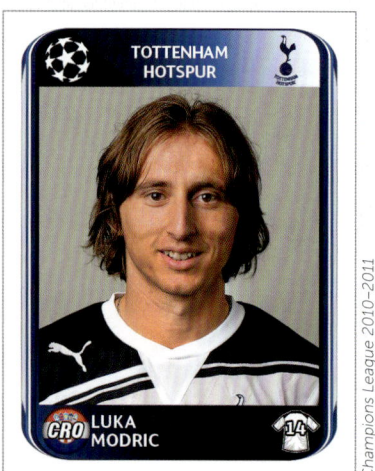

TOTTENHAM HOTSPUR

LUKA MODRIC

Champions League 2010–2011

Few players have displayed more composure and awareness on a football pitch over the last couple of decades than Croatian maestro Luka Modrić. The player from Zadar became a regular member of the Dinamo Zagreb line-up during the 2005–06 season, culminating in the first of a hat-trick of league titles. Two Croatian Cups and a Super Cup were also won before he departed for Tottenham Hotspur in 2008.

Modrić was handed his first Croatia cap in March 2006, too late to make that year's Panini World Cup album, but enough time to earn his place in the squad for the tournament in Germany. His first sticker under the Panini name, though, appeared in the *Euro 2008* collection.

After his fourth season with Spurs, Modrić joined Real Madrid and has since spent over a decade with the Spanish giants. By the end of the 2023–24 season, the playmaker had made 12 Colecciones ESTE Spanish Liga appearances in a row. Over that period he has been a mainstay in winning six Champions Leagues, five FIFA Club World Cups, four La Liga titles, two Copa del Rey and plenty more besides.

As captain of Croatia, he led his national side to their first-ever World Cup final at Russia 2018. Croatia lost to France, but the 2018 Ballon d'Or capped off a year of rare brilliance, during which he was also masterful in the middle of the park at club level as Real Madrid won the Champions League and FIFA Club World Cup.

Russia 2018

Euro 2008

Euro 2016

Qatar 2022

Liga 2014–15 (Colecciones ESTE)

Playing Career
Dinamo Zagreb (2003–2008); Zrinjski Mostar (loan) (2003–2004); Inter Zaprešić (loan) (2004–2005); Tottenham Hotspur (2008–2012); Real Madrid (2012–) and Croatia (2006–)

Panini Album Rookie Appearances
First club album appearance: Champions League 2010–2011 (49)
First World Cup album appearance: *Brasil 2014* (62)

Selected Panini Appearances
Euro 2008 (194); *Champions League 2010–2011* (49); *Euro 2012* (387, 395); *Liga 2012–13* (Colecciones ESTE) (Spain) (695); *Liga 2013–14* (Colecciones ESTE) (Spain) (374); *Brasil 2014* (62); *Liga 2014–15* (Colecciones ESTE) (Spain) (402); *Liga 2015–16* (Colecciones ESTE) (Spain) (374); *France 2016* (434, 448); *Liga 2016–17* (Colecciones ESTE) (Spain) (412); *Liga 2017–18* (Colecciones ESTE) (Spain) (470, 656); *Russia 2018* (322); *Liga 2018–19* (Colecciones ESTE) (442, 818); *Liga 2019–20* (Colecciones ESTE) (Spain) (411, 646, Q13); *Euro 2020 Preview Edition* (CRO6); *Liga 2020–21* (Colecciones ESTE) (Spain) (384); *Euro 2020 Tournament Edition* (360, 371); *Liga 2021–22* (Colecciones ESTE) (Spain) (386); *Liga 2022–23* (Colecciones ESTE) (Spain) (352); *Qatar 2022* (CRO13, LMO – Extra Sticker, C4 – Coca Cola); *Liga 2023–24* (Colecciones ESTE) (385, 735)

PEP GUARDIOLA

Few people can lay claim to having had a greater impact at the pinnacle of the men's game over the last four decades than Josep 'Pep' Guardiola. A graduate of Barcelona's youth academy at La Masia, the midfielder debuted in the first team in 1990–91 and has rarely misstepped since. Possessing an understanding of the game that belied his years, Guardiola became a regular during the 1991–92 season. Dictating the tempo from a deep-lying midfield position, he was part of the side that won La Liga and the club's first-ever European Cup.

The player from Santpedor also gained his first sticker that year, in the Colecciones ESTE *Liga 91–92* album. Guardiola went on to feature in a further nine Colecciones ESTE releases as a Barcelona player, along with the same number in Panini's rival album, including a cover appearance in the last of those in 2000–01. More league titles came in 1992–93 and 1993–94, as well as a European Super Cup. Copa del Rey and Cup Winners' Cup successes were achieved in 1996–97.

Injury kept him out of France 98, though he did feature in the Panini sticker album for the tournament. That was the middle of three Panini World Cup album appearances, but the midfielder played in only the first of the corresponding events, USA 94, as he retired from international football ahead of Korea/Japan 2002. Guardiola's only Panini Euro sticker came in 2000.

Liga 92–93 (Colecciones ESTE)

GUARDIOLA
FUTBOL C. BARCELONA

Liga 91–92 (Colecciones ESTE)

FUTBOL CLUB BARCELONA

GUARDIOLA

Liga 97–98 (Colecciones ESTE)

Guardiola
F. C. BARCELONA

Liga 2000–2001 (Colecciones ESTE)

Playing Career

Barcelona (1990–2001); Brescia (2001–2002); Roma (2002–2003); Brescia (2003); Al-Ahli (2003–2005); Dorados (2005–2006) and Spain (1992–2001)

Panini Album Rookie Appearances

First club album appearance: *Liga 91–92 (Colecciones ESTE) (Spain)* (34); First World Cup album appearance: *USA '94* (195)

Selected Panini Appearances

Liga 91–92 (Colecciones ESTE) (Spain) (34); *Panini Fútbol 92–93 (Spain)* (108); *Liga 92–93 (Colecciones ESTE) (Spain)* (27); *Liga 93–94 (Colecciones ESTE) (Spain)* (30); *Panini Fútbol 93–94 (Spain)* (79); *USA '94* (195); *Liga 94–95 (Colecciones ESTE) (Spain)* (36); *Panini Liga '94–'95 (Spain)* (61); *Panini Liga 95–96 (Spain)* (41); *Liga 95–96 (Colecciones ESTE) (Spain)* (37); *Liga 96–97 (Colecciones ESTE) (Spain)* (42); *Panini Liga 96/97 (Spain)* (40); *Liga 97–98 (Colecciones ESTE) (Spain)* (39); *Panini Liga 97/98 (Spain)* (24); *France 98* (238); *Panini Liga 98–99 (Spain)* (17); *Liga 98–99 (Colecciones ESTE) (Spain)* (60); *Panini Liga 1999–2000 (Spain)* (8); *Liga 1999–2000 (Colecciones ESTE) (Spain)* (66); *Champions League 1999/2000* (44); *Euro 2000* (200); *Liga 2000/2001 (Colecciones ESTE) (Spain)* (63); *Champions League 2000–2001* (295); *Calciatori 2001–2002 (Italy)* (67); *Korea/Japan 2002* (106); *Calciatori 2002–2003 (Italy)* (392, T13); *Liga 08–09 (Colecciones ESTE) (Spain)* (76 – as manager); *Liga 09–10 (Colecciones ESTE) (Spain – as manager)* (92); *Liga 2010–2011 (Colecciones ESTE) (Spain)* (92 – as manager); *FC Bayern München 2013–2014* (16–18 – as manager); *Panini Tabloid (England) (2019)* (79 – as manager)

JOSEP GUARDIOLA

ESPAÑA

JOSEP GUARDIOLA

ESPAÑA

JOSEP GUARDIOLA

ESP

JOSEP GUARDIOLA

ESPAÑA

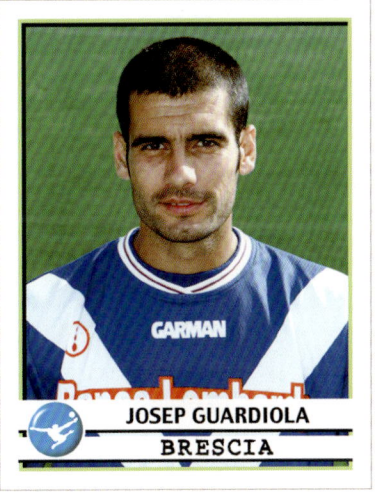

Calciatori 2001–2002

JOSEP GUARDIOLA
BRESCIA

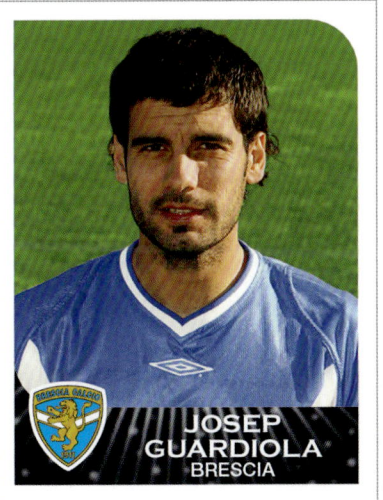

Calciatori 2002–2003

JOSEP GUARDIOLA
BRESCIA

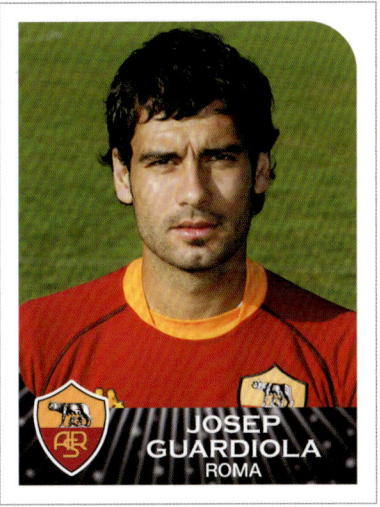

Calciatori 2002–2003

JOSEP GUARDIOLA
ROMA

One final league title at Barcelona in 1998–99 was followed by two Panini *Calciatori* appearances in the early 2000s, first with Brescia and then in both Brescia and Roma shirts in the next album. Guardiola returned to manage the Barcelona B team, and after just one season he was put in charge of the first team and became the most successful manager in the club's history, winning 14 trophies in just four seasons.

He later managed Bayern Munich, winning seven trophies in three seasons, before taking over at Manchester City in the summer of 2016, where his trophy haul included six Premier League titles, a Champions League and two FA Cups by the end of the 2023–24 season.

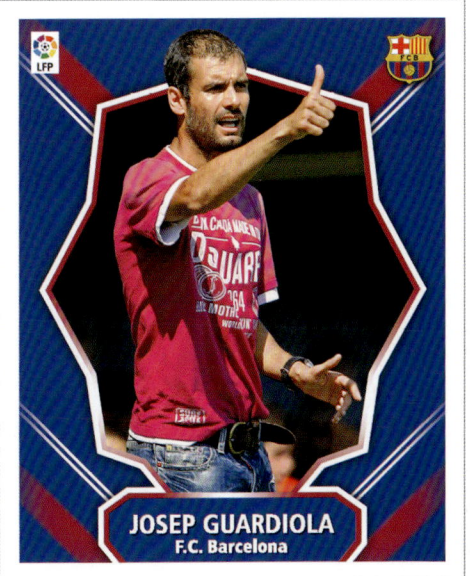

Liga 08–09 (Colecciones ESTE)

JOSEP GUARDIOLA
F.C. Barcelona

HARRY KANE

All-time record England goal-scorer and World Cup Golden Boot winner, Harry Kane is one of the world's leading strikers, but he needed all his powers of perseverance and patience to recover from being released as a youngster by Arsenal and then being loaned out four times by Tottenham, before finally getting his chance at White Hart Lane.

However, in his full Premier League debut for Tottenham in April 2014, he did grab a first Premier League goal in the win over Sunderland. He finished the next campaign with 21 Premier League goals, 31 in total, and was named the PFA Young Player of the Year. Over a decade or so he would score 213 goals in 317 league games for the north London club.

A senior England debut arrived in March 2015, when he came off the bench to score after 79 seconds against Lithuania. Kane's header was depicted in Panini's *England 2016* release, the first album dedicated to the Three Lions after the licence was regained in 2015.

The rising England star was given his first four Panini stickers in that *England 2016* collection and he went on to make a Panini international tournament album debut in *Euro 2016*. He was England captain by the time of his first Panini World Cup sticker, for Russia 2018, and his six goals helped England to the semi-finals and won him the Golden Boot. Another two goals came in the 2022 World Cup, although he suffered a mixed night in England's quarter-final loss to France, scoring and missing from the penalty spot.

A move to Bayern Munich in the summer of 2023 earned Kane a spot on the cover of Panini's *FIFA 365 2024* during his first season in Germany.

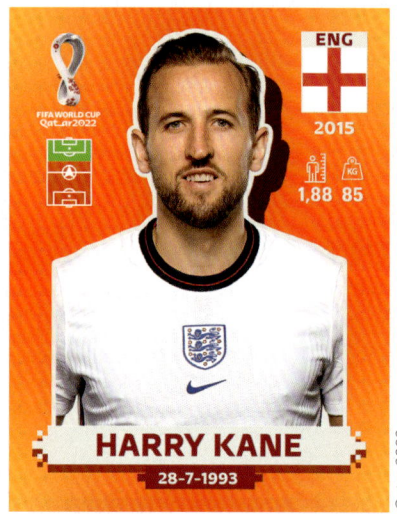

Qatar 2022

Premier League 2022

HARRY KANE

Tottenham Hotspur FC (ENG)

28-7-1993

m 1,88

kg 85

ENG

2015

Russia 2018

Harry Kane is England's all-time top goal-scorer and received the FIFA World Cup Golden Boot at Russia 2018 with six goals.

Playing Career
Tottenham Hotspur (2009–2023); Leyton Orient (loan) (2011); Millwall (loan) (2012); Norwich City (loan) (2012–2013); Leicester City (loan) (2013); Bayern Munich (2023–) and England (2015–)

Panini Album Rookie Appearances
First club album appearance: *Football 2020* (England) (543)
First World Cup album appearance: *Russia 2018* (589)

Selected Panini Appearances
Euro 2016 (148, 154, CC–F); Football 2017 (UK) (48); Road to Russia 2018 (63); Kellogg's Football Superstars (2018) (54); Russia 2018 (589); FIFA 365 2019 (417 and 437); *Panini Tabloid* (2019) (England) (35, 62, 83); Football 2020 (England) (543); Road to Euro 2020 (82); Euro 2020 Preview Edition (ENG4); Premier League 2021 (England) (329, 548); Euro 2020 Tournament Edition (418, 426); Premier League 2022 (England) (543, 548); Los Ídolos de la Roja 2022 (Spain) (55); FIFA 365 2022 (366); Qatar 2022 (ENG18); Premier League 2023 (England) (330, 571); FIFA 365 2023 (129, 130); One England (2023) (151, 153, 155, 213–217); FIFA 365 2024 (KAN, 239); World Class (2024) (287, 289, 291, 307)

10

1.88M

86KG

11

ENG

HARRY KANE

D.O.B. 28-07-93 | Walthamstow

Football 2020

ENG

SINCE 2015

1993

1,88 m

85 Kg

HARRY KANE

Euro 2020 Tournament Edition

PAOLO MALDINI

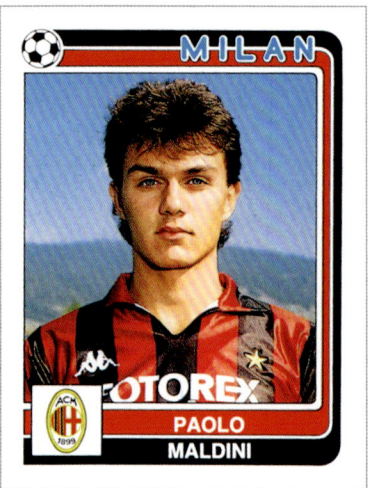

Calciatori 1986–87

Calciatori 1989–90

While Paolo Maldini achieved untold accolades during his career, a record-breaking run of 24 consecutive appearances in Panini's *Calciatori* albums is as impressive a record as any. The consummate defender made his AC Milan debut at 16 during the 1984–85 campaign, becoming a regular from the following season onwards, initially at right-back, and it was in *Calciatori 1985–86* that Maldini began his unprecedented run in sticker form.

Arrigo Sacchi's arrival as coach in 1987, along with key player acquisitions in the form of Dutch pair Ruud Gullit and Marco van Basten, transformed AC Milan from contenders to the greatest club side in Europe. After winning the Serie A title that year, AC Milan achieved successive European Cup victories in 1989 and 1990.

Maldini's contribution led to a senior international call-up in March 1988 and, starting in *Euro 88*, the first of four Euro sticker appearances. Also making the first of four Panini World Cup album appearances, Maldini was part of the best defence at Italia 90 and was picked for the Team of the Tournament. A semi-final penalty shoot-out loss to Argentina was scant reward for his efforts. More heartbreak came in USA 94 when Italy were losing finalists, and Maldini took over as captain of Italy later that year, retaining the position up to his international retirement after the 2002 World Cup.

Hanging up his boots in 2009, Maldini could look back on a club trophy haul that included seven Serie A titles and f ive Champions Leagues. In a fitting tribute to more than two decades of defensive brilliance, Maldini was given a 24-sticker album to commemorate his career – one for every *Calciatori* appearance.

Paolo Maldini

milan

Calciatori 1985–86

PAOLO MALDINI

MILAN

Calciatori 1992–93

MILAN

Paolo MALDINI

Calciatori 1996–97

milan

PAOLO MALDINI

Calciatori 2006–07

Playing Career

AC Milan (1984–2009) and Italy (1988–2002)

Panini Album Rookie Appearances

First club album appearance: *Calciatori 1985–86* (Italy) (154)
First World Cup album appearance: *Italia '90* (46)

Selected Panini Appearances

Calciatori 1985–86 (Italy) (154); *Calciatori 1986–87* (Italy) (184); *Calciatori 1987–88* (Italy) (156); *Euro 88* (Italy) (87); *Calciatori 1988–89* (Italy) (205); *Calciatori 1989–90* (Italy) (234); *Italia '90* (46); *Calciatori 1990–91* (Italy) (215); *Calciatori 1991–92* (Italy) (212); *Euro '92* (240); *Calciatori 1992–93* (Italy) (24, 214); *USA '94* (307); *Calciatori 1993–94* (Italy) (177); *Calciatori 1994–95* (Italy) (205); *Calciatori 1995–96* (Italy) (160); *European Football Championship England '96* (242); *Calciatori 1996–97* (Italy) (176); *Calciatori 1997–98* (Italy) (215); *France 98* (92); *Calciatori 1998–99* (Italy) (190, 424); *Calciatori 2000* (Italy) (200); *Champions League 1999/2000* (293); *Euro 2000* (170); *Calciatori 2000–2001* (Italy) (224); *Calciatori 2001–2002* (Italy) (222); *Korea/Japan 2002* (460); *Calciatori 2002–2003* (Italy) (234); *Calciatori 2003–2004* (Italy) (223); *Calciatori 2004–2005* (Italy) (296); *Calciatori 2005–06* (Italy) (272); *Calciatori 2006–07* (Italy) (248); *Champions League 2006–2007* (109); *Calciatori 07–08* (Italy) (246, T3) *Calciatori 2008–09* (Italy) (267); *Paolo Maldini* (2009) (1–24)

PAOLO MALDINI
ITALIA

Euro 88

ITALIA
PAOLO MALDINI

Italia '90

ITALIA

PAOLO MALDINI

2002 FIFA WORLD CUP

Korea/Japan 2002

MICHEL PLATINI

NANCY

MICHEL PLATINI

Football 76

NANCY

MICHEL PLATINI

Football 78

The talisman of great sides at both club and international level, Michel Platini evolved into arguably the best player in the world during the first half of the 1980s – as evidenced by his appearances in around 40 Panini albums and his starring roles in *Euro 84* and two World Cup albums of the '80s. As well as winning the Ballon d'Or three times in a row between 1983 and 1985, the playmaker famously captained France to victory at Euro 84 and led his country to the semi-finals of both the Spain 82 and Mexico 86 World Cups.

Platini's club career began with lengthy spells in his homeland at Nancy, for whom he made his Panini bow in *Football 76* and with whom he won the 1978 French Cup, and at Saint-Étienne, where he won the French League title. He appeared in seven consecutive French league Panini albums. However, it was his move to Italy with Juventus, making his first *Calciatori* appearance in black and white stripes as part of the 1982–83 album, that catapulted him to even greater heights. He featured in another four *Calciatori* albums – and in an era when goals were at a premium in the Italian domestic game, the attacking midfielder scored a phenomenal 54 times in 88 Serie A appearances over the course of his first three seasons at Juventus.

Platini made his Panini debut in *Football 76* playing for Nancy, with whom he won the French Cup.

MICHEL PLATINI
NANCY

Football 79

SAINT·ETIENNE

ASSE

MICHEL
PLATINI

Football 80

SAINT-ETIENNE

ASSE

MICHEL
PLATINI

Football 81

MICHEL
PLATINI
FRA

Euro 84

Platini captained France to their first major trophy. He scored nine goals in five games, to lead his side to the Euro 84 title.

MICHEL
PLATINI
FRA

Europa 80

ARGENTINA 78

MICHEL
PLATINI

Argentina 78

Although he retired from playing in 1987, it wasn't the end of Platini's Panini career: he featured in the *Euro '92* collection as France's manager.

Espaňa 82

Mexico 86

Football 82

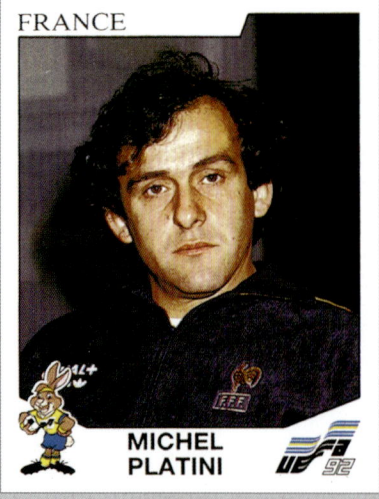

Euro 92

Calciatori 1983-84

Calciatori 1984-85

His crowning glory, though, came back on home soil, when he scored an incredible nine goals in five games, including one in the final against Spain, to lead his side to the Euro 84 title. Although he retired from playing in 1987, it wasn't the end of his Panini career: he featured in the *Euro '92* album as France's manager, having got them to that tournament on the back of a 19-game unbeaten run.

Calciatori 1985-86

Calciatori 1986-87

Playing Career
Nancy (1972–1979); Saint-Etienne (1979–1982); Juventus (1982–1987) and France (1976–1987)

Panini Album Rookie Appearances
First club album appearance: Football 76 (France) (172)
First World Cup album appearance: *Argentina 78* (90)

Selected Panini Appearances
Football 76 (France) (172); *Football 77* (France) (171); *Euro Football (1976–77)* (106) *Football 78* (France) (155, 227); *Euro Football 78* (101 A); *Argentina 1978* (90); *Football 79* (France) (183); *Euro Football 79* (232); *Calciatori 1979–80* (Italy) (314); *Football 80* (France) (283); *Europa 80* (207); *Football 81* (France) (265); *Liga 80–81* (Colecciones ESTE) (Spain) (AA17); *Football 82* (France) (252, 488); *España 82* (286); *Calciatori 1982–83* (Italy) (161); *Football 83* (Switzerland) (436); *Calciatori 1983–84* (Italy) (117); *Football 84* (France) (1, 363 –370); *Euro 84* (48) *Calciatori 1984–85* (Italy) (146); *Football 85* (France) (203, 215, 221 and other action shots); *Football 85* (UK) (248); *Calciatori 1985–86* (Italy) (120); *Supercalcio 1985–86* (Italy) (127); *Mexico 86* (175); *Calciatori 1986–87* (Italy) (169); *Fussball 87* (Germany) (384); *Euro 88* (18); *Euro '92* (43 – as manager); *European Football Championship England '96* (13); *Champions 98* (France) (67, 151)

BRASIL

BEBETO

Italia '90

BEBETO R. C. Dptvo. La Coruña

Liga 93-94 (Colecciones ESTE)

BRASIL

BEBETO

USA '94

BEBETO

BRASIL

France 98

BEBETO

Born José Roberto Gama de Oliveira, Bebeto played a starring role as Brazil reached the final of successive World Cups during the 1990s. The striker from Bahia made his Brazil debut in 1985, but then spent a long period in the international wilderness, before advancing his claims when forming a fearsome strikeforce with Romário in the 1988 Olympics.

After being the top scorer in Brazil's 1989 Copa América victory, Bebeto earned the first of three consecutive Panini World Cup stickers in the *Italia '90* album. His only run-out came from the bench in Italy, but the Bebeto-Romário front pair were back in tandem by the time of USA 94, when the duo shared eight goals along the way to Brazil, defeating Italy on penalties in the World Cup final. Another three goals came at France 98. By this stage he was partnering Ronaldo up front and everything went smoothly until the 3-0 final defeat by the hosts.

Bebeto had already enjoyed a lengthy club career in his homeland with Flamengo and Vasco da Gama before he moved to Europe at 28 with Deportivo La Coruña in 1992. Top La Liga goalscorer in his first season at the club in 1992–93, he was again among the goals as Deportivo came within a whisker of beating the Barcelona 'Dream Team' to the title the following season.

His final season in La Coruña, 1995–96, proved to be Bebeto's most prolific, with 32 goals in all competitions. He then appeared in Panini's *Campeonato Brasileiro* albums with four different clubs in the space of six years, and also briefly returned to Spain with Sevilla. He closed his career in Mexico, Japan and Saudi Arabia.

Playing Career
Vitória (1982); Flamengo (1983–1989); Vasco da Gama (1989–1992); Deportivo La Coruña (1992–1996); Flamengo (1996); Sevilla (1996–1997); Vitória (1997); Cruzeiro (1997); Botafogo (1998–1999); Toros Neza (1999); Kashima Antlers (2000); Vitória (2000); Vasco da Gama (2001); Al-Ittihad (2002) and Brazil (1985–1988)

Panini Album Rookie Appearances
First club album appearance: Liga 92–93 (Colecciones ESTE) (Spain) (139)
First World Cup album appearance: *Italia '90* (206)

Selected Panini Appearances
Italia '90 (206); *Liga 92–93 (Colecciones ESTE)* (Spain) (139); *Liga 93-94* (Colecciones ESTE) (88); *USA '94* (106); *Supercalcio 94–95* (Italy) (202); *Liga 94–95* (Colecciones ESTE) (Spain) (153); *Liga 95–96* (Colecciones ESTE) (Spain) (171); *Campeonato Brasileiro 1996* (110 – Flamengo); *Los Mejores Equipos de Europa 1997* (259 – Sevilla); *Campeonato Brasileiro 1997* (294, 398 – Vitória); *Campeonato Brasileiro 1998* (193 – Botafogo); *France 98* (30); *Campeonato Brasileiro 2001* (43 – Vasco); *R.C. Deportivo 2011–2012* (190, 200)

FABIEN BARTHEZ

FABIEN BARTHEZ

Foot 1994

Fabien Barthez
MONACO

Foot 96

Goalkeeper Fabien Barthez was the formidable last line of a solid defence, which enabled France's attacking talents to work their magic towards World Cup and Euro glory. The Lavelanet-born stopper's professional debut came for Toulouse early in the 1991–92 season and he established himself over the rest of that campaign.

So impressive were his performances that he was signed by reigning champions Marseille the following summer – and by the end of the season Barthez was a Champions League winner, keeping a clean sheet in the final against AC Milan. He was awarded a belated first Panini sticker in *Foot 1994*, but Marseille were subsequently demoted to the second division for match-fixing and, after helping the club back to the top flight, he then joined Monaco.

Having made his international debut in 1994, Barthez finally made the 'keeper spot his own in 1997, which was perfect timing ahead of the following year's World Cup in his home country. By now he was sporting a shaven head and Laurent Blanc, his teammate, famously kissed Barthez's pate before every game on France's march to glory. He conceded only two goals in seven matches – along with a penalty save in the quarter-final shoot-out win over Italy – as France won the trophy for the first time.

A second Ligue 1 title with Monaco in 2000 was followed that summer by Euro victory with his country, with Barthez once again earning a space in the Team of the Tournament. A move to Manchester United came soon after and he won the Premier League in his first and third seasons at Old Trafford.

Monaco
FABIEN BARTHEZ

Foot 97

MONACO

FABIEN BARTHEZ

Foot 2000

FABIEN BARTHEZ

Euro 2004

EURO 2000

FABIEN BARTHEZ

FRA

Euro 2000

Playing Career
Toulouse (1990–1992); Marseille (1992–1995); Monaco (1995–2000); Manchester United (2000–2004); Marseille (loan) (2003–2004); Marseille (2004–2006); Nantes (2006–2007) and France (1994–2006)

Panini Album Rookie Appearances
First club album appearance: *Foot 1994* (France) (134)
First World Cup album appearance: *France 98* (158)

Selected Panini Appearances
Foot 1994 (France) (134); *Foot 1995* (France) (302); *Foot 96* (France) (213); *Foot 97* (France) (183); *Foot 98* (France) (213); *Superfoot 1997–1998* (France) (19); *France 98* (158); *Champions 98* (France) (49, 50, 51;) *Foot 99* (France) (193); *Superfoot 1998/99* (France) (19, 177); *Super Football 99* (A, 10); *Superfoot 99–2000* (France) (20, 119); *Foot 2000* (France) (172); *Euro 2000* (339); *Champions League 2000/01* (249); *Champions League 2001/02* (173); *Korea/Japan 2002* (27); *Foot 2003* (France) (343); *Euro 2004* (94); *Foot 2005* (France) (185); *Superfoot 2004–05* (France) (21–23 and 64); *Foot 2006* (France) (189, 541); *Superfoot 2005–06* (France) (152, 165, 189); *Champions of Europe 1955–2005* (231); *Germany 2006* (456)

At France 98 Barthez conceded only two goals in seven matches as France won the trophy for the first time.

Barthez remained in goal for the Germany 2006 World Cup, an appearance that turned out to be his final Panini sticker as an active player. After disappointing tournaments at Korea/Japan 2002 and Euro 2004, France – and Barthez – were back to their irresistible best, denied by Italy only on penalties in the final.

FRANCE 98

FABIEN BARTHEZ
FRANCE

France 98

LIONEL MESSI

Lionel Messi is arguably the world's greatest ever footballer. He has accumulated a record eight Ballon d'Or awards and won every possible trophy for club and country. Many of his Panini stickers and cards command huge sums: a special 'one of one' sticker for the USA version of the 2022 World Cup album sold for £115,000 in 2023, while others, including his 2004–2005 Barcelona Colecciones ESTE (classed as a Panini sticker) rookie and Germany 2006 World Cup Panini sticker are also highly sought after, especially in mint condition.

LIONEL ANDRES MESSI

Germany 2006

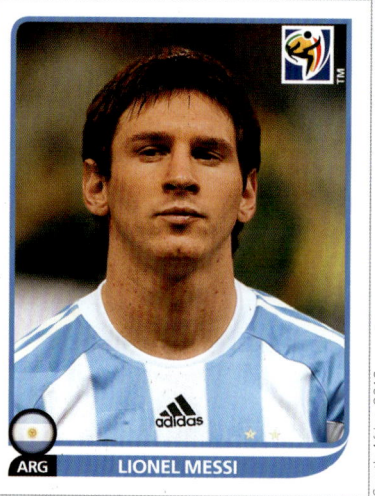

LIONEL MESSI

South Africa 2010

Lionel
MESSI

24-6-1987 1,69 m 67 kg

Barcelona (ESP) ARG

Copa America Argentina 2011

Qatar 2022 'One of One' (US album)

After unsuccessful attempts in 2006, 2010, 2014 and 2018, Messi led Argentina to the 2022 World Cup, having scored in every round.

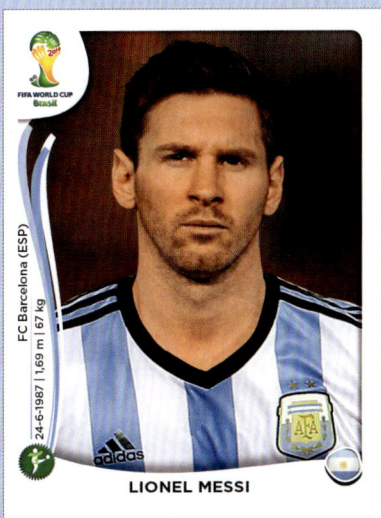

Brasil 2014

Copa America Centenario USA 2016

Russia 2018

Messi has won a record eight Ballon d'Or awards and was named the world's best player for a record eight times by FIFA.

LIONEL ANDRES MESSI

BARCELONA

Champions League 2006–2007

FC Barcelona

Lionel MESSI

FIFA 365 2017

Lionel Messi

FIFA 365 2018

Messi made his Barcelona debut aged 17 in 2004 and by 2008–09 was helping the club achieve the first ever treble of Champions League, La Liga and Copa del Rey in Spanish football. He spent nearly two decades as part of the first team squad, displaying levels of skill, control and passing unmatched in the modern game. Among the many trophies were 10 La Liga titles and four Champions League trophies, scoring memorable goals from solo runs, free kicks and even towering headers. In 2021, Messi left Spain for Paris Saint-Germain and then joined Inter Miami of the MLS in 2023.

He made his debut for the Argentina national team in 2005 and was named captain in 2011. However, despite becoming the nation's all-time leading goal-scorer in 2016, Messi endured defeat in the 2014 World Cup final and in three Copa America finals. He finally achieved Copa America success in 2021 and then in 2022 lifted the World Cup, having scored in every round.

LIONEL MESSI

ATT

Foot 2022

Liga 2004–2005 (Colecciones ESTE)

Liga 2011–12 (Colecciones ESTE)

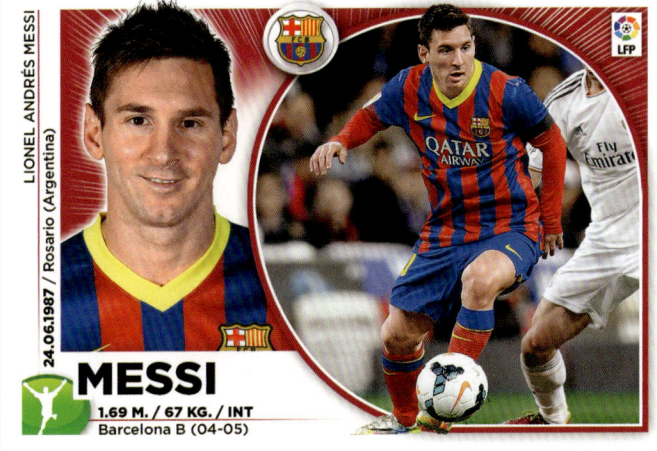

Liga 2014–15 (Colecciones ESTE)

Playing Career

Barcelona (2004–2021); Paris Saint-Germain (2021–2023); Inter Miami (2023–) and Argentina (2005–)

Panini Album
Rookie Appearances

First club album appearance:
Liga 2004–2005 (Colecciones ESTE) (Spain) (91)
First World Cup album appearance:
Germany 2006 (185)

Selected
Panini Appearances

Liga 2004–2005 (Colecciones ESTE) (Spain) (91); Liga 2005–2006 (Colecciones ESTE) (Spain) (90); Champions of Europe 1955–2005 (74); Germany 2006 (185); Liga 2006–2007 (Colecciones ESTE) (Spain) (82); Copa America Venezuela 2007 (200) Liga 07–08 (Colecciones ESTE) (Spain) (111); Liga 08–09 (Colecciones ESTE) (Spain) (92); 09–10 (Colecciones ESTE) (Spain) (112, 712); South Africa 2010 (122 plus Tournament Tracker – C); Liga 2010–2011 (Colecciones ESTE) (Spain) (112); Copa America Argentina 2011 (40, 345); Liga 2011–12 (Colecciones ESTE) (Spain) (82); Liga 2012–13 (Colecciones ESTE) (Spain) (80); Liga 2013–14 (Colecciones ESTE) (Spain) (141, 763); Brasil 2014 (430 plus V9 – Ecuadorian version); Liga 2014–15 (Colecciones ESTE) (Spain) (107, 114, 115); Copa América Chile 2015 (132, 341); Liga 2015–16 (Colecciones ESTE) (Spain) (77); Copa América Centenario USA 2016 (325, 398); Liga 2016–17 (Colecciones ESTE) (Spain) (146, 651); Liga 2017–18 (Colecciones ESTE) (Spain) (146, 655); Russia 2018 (288); Liga 2018–19 (Colecciones ESTE) (Spain) (146, 655, 787); CONMEBOL Copa América Brasil 2019 (144 and 222); Liga 2019–20 (Colecciones ESTE) (Spain) (147, 645, I4); Liga 2020–21 (Colecciones ESTE) (Spain) (117, 626, T4); CONMEBOL Copa América Argentina 2021 (ARG20, Gol 3, M1/M1a); Liga 2021–22 (Colecciones ESTE) (Spain) (103, 119); Foot 2022 (France) (357); Qatar 2022 (ARG19 and LM – Extra Sticker); Foot 2023 (France) (239 – AC, NC, BC – and 340); CONMEBOL Copa América USA 2024 (ARG19, LEG6, LM)

THIERRY HENRY

Champions League 1999/2000

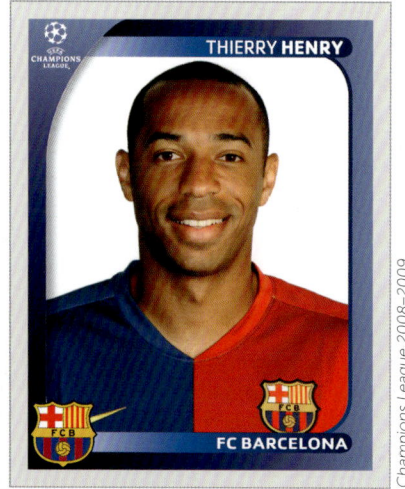

Champions League 2008–2009

Rated by many as the greatest player of the English Premier League era, Thierry Henry is one of a number of French stars to have developed his young talents at the Clairefontaine football academy. Born in the Les Ulis suburb of Paris, Henry was snapped up by Monaco at the age of 13 and made his professional debut two weeks after turning 17. The striker's first Panini sticker appearance came in *Foot 97* and his rapid rise also earned him a place in the *France 98* World Cup album.

Despite not playing in the World Cup final, Henry's three goals in the tournament caught the eye of Juventus, who signed him in January 1999. He was rescued from an unhappy spell in Turin by compatriot Arsène Wenger at Arsenal, who shifted him to a more central starting position... to deadly effect.

By the time Henry left for Barcelona in 2007 he had broken the Gunners' goalscoring record with 226 goals (adding two more in a brief further spell in early 2012). Among a glut of honours during his time in north London were two Premier League titles, two FA Cups and four Golden Boots. More silverware followed in Spain, including the Champions League and two La Liga titles. Henry then took his talents to the MLS with New York Red Bulls, to bring down the curtain on a glittering career and put an end to sleepless nights for countless defenders who lay in his wake.

Foot 97

Thierry Henry appeared in four consecutive Panini World Cup albums.

France 98

Germany 2006

Playing Career
Monaco (1994–1999); Juventus (1999); Arsenal (1999–2007); Barcelona (2007–2010); New York Red Bulls (2010–2014); Arsenal (loan) (2012) and France (1997–2010)

Panini Album Rookie Appearances
First club album appearance: *Foot 97* (France) (195)
First World Cup album appearance: *France 98* (172)

Selected Panini Appearances
Foot 97 (France) (195); *Los Mejores Equipos de Europa* (1996–97) (182); *Foot 98* (France) (222); *Los Mejores Equipos de Europa* (1997–98) (180); *France 98* (172); *Champions 98* (France) (39 and 79); *Superfoot 1998–99* (France) (40, 41, 145, 194) *Foot 99* (France) (206); *Champions League 99/2000* (33); *SuperFoot 1999–2000* (France) (110); *Champions League 2000/2001* (113); *Champions League 2001/2002* (75); *Road to the FIFA World Cup 2002* (114); *Korea/Japan 2002* (41); *Foot 2003* (France) (318); *Superfoot 2003–04* (France) (45 to 47 and T) *Euro 2004* (111); *SuperFoot 2004–05* (France) (54 to 56); *Superfoot 2005–06* (France) (166, 179); *Foot 2006* (France) (548); *Champions of Europe 1955–2005* (57); *Germany 2006* (469); *Champions League 2006–2007* (88); *Liga 07–08* (Colecciones ESTE) (Spain) (633); *Champions League 2007–2008* (57); *Euro 2008* (355 and 515); *Liga 08–09* (Colecciones ESTE) (Spain) (95); *Champions League 2008–2009* (108) *Liga 09–10* (Colecciones ESTE) (111); *Champions League 2009–2010* (361); *South Africa 2010* (103); *Los 100 Cracks del Jugon 2005–2014* (Spain) (39); *Premier League 2022* (England) (333)

ANDRÉS INIESTA

Euro 2008

Few players have made the game of football look as effortless as Spain and Barcelona midfielder Andrés Iniesta. A product of Barça's La Masia youth academy, he went on to win four Champions Leagues, three FIFA Club World Cups, nine La Liga titles and six Copa del Reys during his time at the club. Add in a World Cup plus two Euros for Spain and Iniesta can rightly claim to have completed football.

He was part of the Spain squad that won the UEFA European U-16 Championship in 2001 and the UEFA European U-19 Championship the following year, so it was clear from early on that a rare talent was in the country's midst. Panini spotted that quality by giving him a rookie sticker in the *Cracks del Futuro* (Future Stars) section of their *Superliga de Estrellas 2002–2003* collection. A first Panini sticker for his national side came in Euro 2008.

Euro 2012

Brasil 2014

Russia 2018

Liga 2003–2004 (Colecciones ESTE)

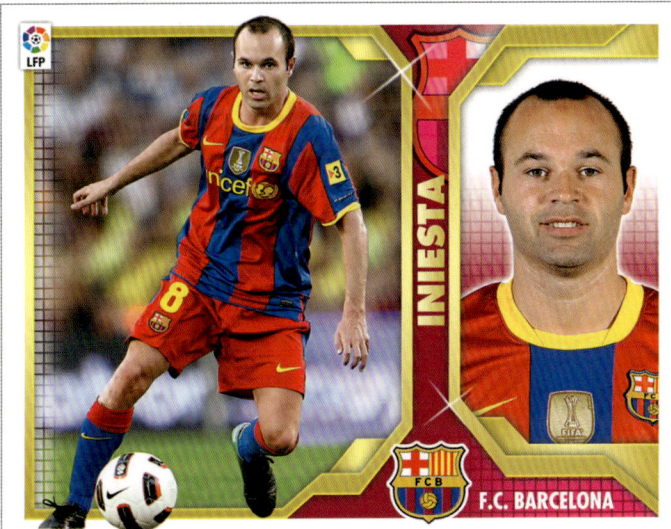

Liga 2011–12 (Colecciones ESTE)

Playing Career
Barcelona (2002–2018);
Vissel Kobe (2018–2023);
Emirates (2023–) and Spain
(2006–2018)

**Panini Album
Rookie Appearances**
First club album appearance:
Panini Superliga de Estrellas
2002–2003 (Spain) (392)
First World Cup album
appearance: *South Africa 2010*
(577)

**Selected Panini
Appearances**
*Panini Superliga de Estrellas
2002–2003* (Spain) (392); *Liga
2003–2004* (Colecciones ESTE)
(Spain) (102); *Liga 2004–2005*
(Colecciones ESTE) (Spain) (93);
Liga 2005–2006 (Colecciones
ESTE) (Spain) (89); *Champions
of Europe 1955–2005*; *Liga
2006–2007* (Colecciones
ESTE) (Spain) (77); *Liga 07–08*
(Colecciones ESTE) (Spain) (104);
Euro 2008 (428); *Liga 08–09*
(Colecciones ESTE) (Spain) (91);
Liga 09–10 (Colecciones ESTE)
(Spain) (108, 711); *South Africa
2010* (577); *Liga 2010–2011*
(Colecciones ESTE) (Spain) (105);
Liga 2011–12 (Colecciones ESTE)
(Spain) (78); *Euro 2012* (299,
309, CC–C Coca Cola); *Liga
2012–13* (Colecciones ESTE)
(Spain) (76, 606); *Liga 2013–14*
(Colecciones ESTE) (Spain)
(136); *Brasil 2014* (119, P11); *Liga
2014–15* (Colecciones ESTE)
(Spain) (102); *Liga 2015–16*
(Colecciones ESTE) (Spain)
(74); *Euro 2016* (363, 373); *Liga
2016–17* (Colecciones ESTE)
(Spain) (143, 648); *Liga 2017–18*
(Colecciones ESTE) (Spain) (143,
651); *Russia 2018* (146); *Liga
2021–22* (Colecciones ESTE)
(Spain) (624)

With the Xavi-Iniesta midfield axis in full flow, and Lionel Messi performing miracles a little further forward, Barcelona were unstoppable the next season, winning the Champions League final against Manchester United. Iniesta would go on to win another two Champions League titles with Barcelona.

Injury restricted him in 2009–10, but he was ready for Spain's victorious World Cup in South Africa (scoring the winner in the final), the first of his three Panini stickers for the tournament. And, at the peak of his powers, he added a Player of the Tournament award to his accolades in Spain's Euro 2012 win. Spain's period of dominance eventually came to an end, though, and their master craftsman retired from international duty after the 2018 World Cup, 131 caps and 14 goals to his name. After 15 successive Colecciones ESTE Liga album appearances, Iniesta then enjoyed a five-year stay in Japan with Vissel Kobe, adding more silverware to an already enviable haul.

DENNIS BERGKAMP

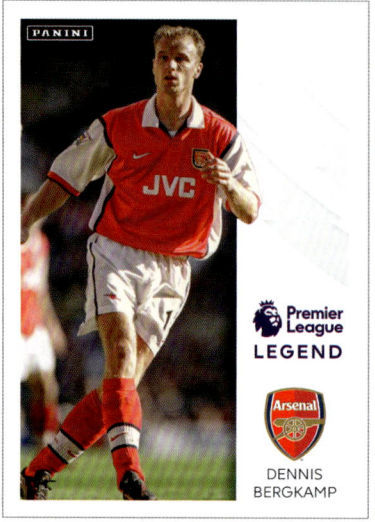

Premier League 2023

DENNIS BERGKAMP

Voetbal '91

For anyone too young to have watched Dennis Bergkamp, a compilation video of his greatest assists is even more sublime than a 'best goals' montage – and that is saying something for a player with his repertoire of memorable finishes. The Amsterdam-born number 10 could spot a pass like few others in the history of the game. He honed his skills at the exalted Ajax academy and another Dutch master, Johan Cruyff, gave Bergkamp his senior debut at 17, in 1986, although he didn't make his rookie sticker appearance until Panini's *Voetbal '91*.

That 1990–91 season was also when he made his senior debut for the Netherlands, earning a first Panini international sticker in *Euro '92*. It was clear Bergkamp's skills were destined to be tested outside his homeland, resulting in a move to Italy with Internazionale in 1993. A UEFA Cup triumph followed in his first campaign, but those two years in Milan were deemed largely underwhelming.

That was not a complaint that could be levelled at his subsequent 11 years with Arsenal, during which time he won three league titles and four FA Cups. The forward's aesthetics made him one of the most breathtaking players of the English Premier League era, goals against Leicester (1997) and Newcastle (2002) bringing his subtleties to the fore.

While during his career the Netherlands were frequently thwarted at the semi-final stage of major tournaments, Bergkamp's 37 international strikes were similarly easy on the eye – his goal against Argentina in France 98 one for the ages. The Dutchman has appeared in more than 25 Panini collections.

France 98

DENNIS BERGKAMP
NEDERLAND

Playing Career
Ajax (1986–1993); Internazionale (1993–1995); Arsenal (1995–2006) and Netherlands (1990–2000)

Panini Album Rookie Appearances
First club album appearance: *Voetbal '91* (Netherlands) (14) First World Cup album appearance: *USA '94* (431)

Selected Panini Appearances
Voetbal '91 (Netherlands) (14); *Voetbal '92* (Netherlands) (12 and 269); *Euro '92* (133); *Estrellas de la Liga Futbol 1992–1993* (Spain) (185); *Voetbal '93* (Netherlands) (32 and 255); *Calciatori 1993–94* (Italy) (108); *USA '94* (431); *Calciatori 1994–95* (154); *European Football Championship England '96* (89); *Superplayers '96* (England) (14); The *Official PFA Collection '97* (England) (26); *Superplayers 98* (England) (28 and P4); *France 98* (314); *Champions League 1999/2000* (30); *Oranje Kampioen!* (2000) (Netherlands) (74 to 78); *Euro 2000* (287); *Champions League 2000/2001* (110); *Champions League 2001/2002* (72); *Champions of Europe 1955–2005* (56); *Euro 2012* (Dutch special edition) (75, 133, 188); *Premier League 2023* (England) (333)

Euro 2000

DENNIS BERGKAMP
HOL

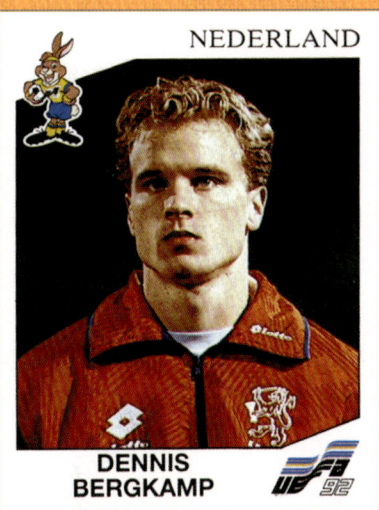

NEDERLAND

Euro '92

DENNIS BERGKAMP

Calciatori 1993–94

DENNIS BERGKAMP
INTER

WAYNE ROONEY

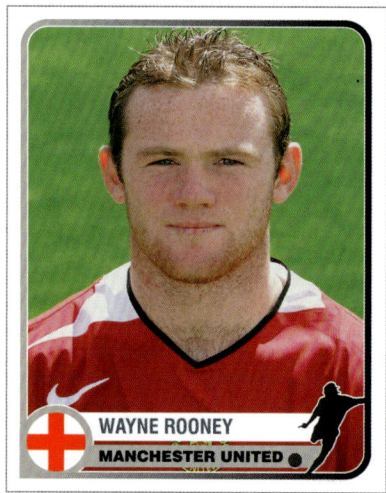

Champions of Europe 1955–2005

Champions League 2006–2007

If Wayne Rooney wanted to announce himself to the football world at large, scoring from a long-range shot five days short of his 17th birthday against reigning champions Arsenal was as good a way as any. Life would never be the same for Rooney after that October 2002 strike for the Toffees and, tipped for stardom from an early age, it took little more than 18 months between that opening Premier League strike and his first England appearance in a Panini sticker album.

Rooney played for his boyhood idols Everton up to the end of the 2003–04 season, before completing a big-money move to Manchester United. That summer also saw the tenacious attacker make his international tournament bow and an appearance in the *Euro 2004* Panini album, having first pulled on an England shirt in February 2003, when he was only 17 years and 111 days old.

In his time at Old Trafford, Rooney won five Premier League titles and among nine consecutive Panini Champions League album appearances included the 2007–08 season, when United beat Chelsea on penalties to win the trophy. His later career took in a return to Everton, a spell at Derby County, including as manager, plus a couple of years in the MLS at DC United in between.

At international level, Rooney scored 53 goals – then a record, now surpassed by Harry Kane – and his longevity as an England player saw him appear in three Panini World Cup and three Panini Euro albums in all.

UEFA Champions League

WAYNE ROONEY

MANCHESTER UNITED FC

10

1

24-10-1985 ENG
1,78 m
80 kg

66   26

Champions League 2012–2013

WAYNE **ROONEY**

MANCHESTER UNITED FC

Champions League 2008–2009

WAYNE ROONEY

10

MANCHESTER UNITED FC

Champions League 2009–2010

Playing Career
Everton (2002–2004); Manchester United (2004–2017); Everton (2017–2018); D.C. United (2018–2019); Derby County (2020–2021) and England (2003–2018)

Panini Album Rookie Appearances
First club album appearance: *Champions of Europe 1955–2005* (229)
First World Cup album appearance: *Germany 2006* (111)

Selected Panini Appearances
Euro 2004 (131); *Champions of Europe 1955–2005* (229); *Germany 2006* (111); *Champions League 2006–2007* (70); *Campeonato Brasileiro 2007* (489); *Champions League 2007–2008* (244); *Champions League 2008–2009* (24); *Champions League 2009–2010* (89); *South Africa 2010* (198); *Champions League 2010–2011* (157); (351); *Champions League 2011–2012* (157); *Euro 2012* (509, 512); *Champions League 2012–2013* (531 and 533); *Champions League 2013–2014* (16); *Brasil 2014* (316); *FIFA 365 2015–16* (329, 340); *Euro 2016* (145 and 149); *Football 2017* (UK) (37 and 51); *Road to FIFA World Cup Russia 2018* (61); *Premier League 2022* (England) (335); *One England* (2023) (192)

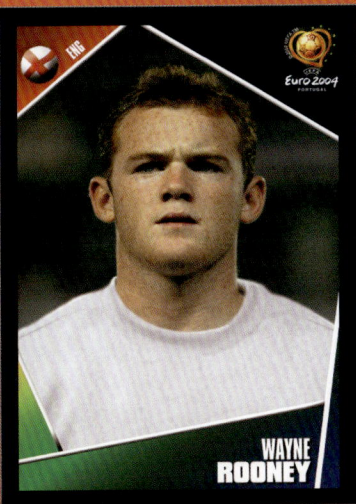

WAYNE ROONEY

EURO 2004

Euro 2004

ENG

WAYNE ROONEY

FIFA WORLD CUP GERMANY 2006

Germany 2006

ENG   WAYNE ROONEY

South Africa 2010

FRANCESCO TOTTI

Calciatori 1994–95

FRANCESCO TOTTI

Calciatori 1996–97

As one-club players go, few rank alongside Roma's Francesco Totti. The playmaker with few peers remained loyal to his club through thick and thin when opportunities to win more silverware existed away from the Italian capital. Totti's run of 23 Panini *Calciatori* appearances in a row is even more remarkable for an attacking player who had to resist the attentions of rugged defenders throughout his career. Only Paolo Maldini surpassed that consecutive run, with 24, though Gianluigi Buffon equalled it soon after.

Totti's first team debut came as a 16-year-old during the 1992–93 campaign. He was given a few more outings the following season, but it was in 1994–95 that the versatile attacker really made his presence felt, scoring his first Serie A goals and gaining a Panini rookie sticker. The Serie A Young Footballer of the Year accolade followed in 1998–99 and in 2001 Roma won the league and the subsequent Supercoppa Italiana.

It was around this point that Totti established himself in the national side. His first Panini international tournament appearance came for Euro 2000. After struggling for form in the 2002 World Cup and Euro 2004, he went into Germany 2006 on the back of an injury-hit season. It didn't show, however, as he played in all seven of Italy's matches during their triumphant campaign.

Totti never represented Italy again after 2006, officially retiring from the international set-up the following year. He continued to play for Roma for another decade, though, and Panini were able to devote several stickers to Totti in his retirement season's *Calciatori 2016–2017*.

ROMA

FRANCESCO TOTTI

Calciatori 1997-98

FRANCESCO TOTTI
ROMA

Calciatori 2001-2002

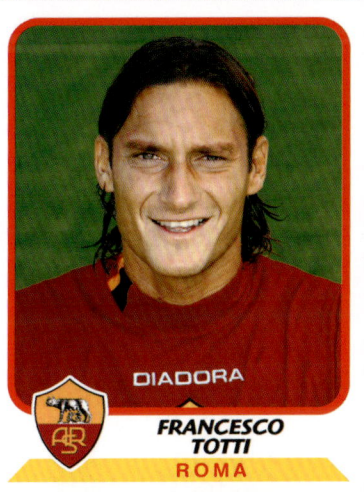

FRANCESCO TOTTI
ROMA

Calciatori 2003-2004

ROMA

FRANCESCO TOTTI
Roma
27.9.1976 | 1,82 | 80 | ITA

Calciatori 2012-2013

EURO 2000

FRANCESCO TOTTI

Euro 2000

ITALIA

FRANCESCO TOTTI

Korea/Japan 2002

ITA

FRANCESCO TOTTI

Germany 2006

Playing Career
Roma (1993–2017) and Italy (1998–2006)

Panini Album
Rookie Appearances
First club album appearance: Calciatori 1994–95 (Italy) (320)
First World Cup album appearance: Korea/Japan 2002 (470)

Selected Panini Appearances
Calciatori 1994–95 (Italy) (320); Calciatori 1995–96 (Italy) (264); Calciatori 1996–97 (Italy) (300); Calciatori 1997–98 (Italy) (314); Calciatori 1998–99 (Italy) (295); Calciatori 2000 (Italy) (334); Euro 2000 (181); Calciatori 2000–2001 (Italy) (356); Calciatori 2001–2002 (Italy) (332); Champions League 2001/2002 (34); Korea/Japan 2002 (470); Calciatori 2002–2003 (Italy) (399); Calciatori 2003–2004 (358); Euro 2004 (237); Calciatori 2004–2005 (Italy) (407); Calciatori 2005–06 (Italy) (383, 775); Germany 2006 (338); World Champions 2006 (Italy) (4, 140, 141); Calciatori 2006–07 (Italy) (334, 350); Calciatori 07–08 (Italy) (381); Calciatori 2008-09 (Italy) (382); Calciatori 2009–10 (Italy) (405, v5); Calciatori 2010–11 (Italy) (429); Calciatori 2011–2012 (Italy) (432, P4, P16); Calciatori 2012–2013 (Italy) (V7, 389); Calciatori 2013–2014 (Italy) (473, D6); Calciatori 2014–2015 (Italy) (414, V1); Calciatori 2015–2016 (Italy) (466); Calciatori 2016–2017 (Italy) (446, 569, 580, C16); Calciatori 2021 (Italy) (X19 – Top Team Panini 60)

ANTOINE GRIEZMANN

Qatar 2022

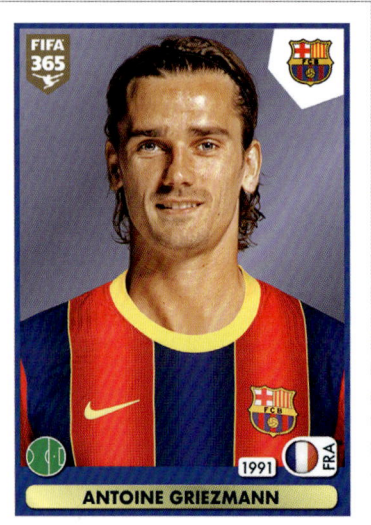

FIFA 365 2021

Deployed right across the attacking line over the years, Antoine Griezmann is both a prolific maker and a taker of chances. Even though he was born and grew up in Mâcon, in France, Griezmann had spent his senior club career entirely in Spain up to the 2023–24 season. Spotted by Real Sociedad as a 14-year-old, he joined their youth set-up before rising to the first-team squad four years later. After helping the club win promotion to La Liga in his debut season, 2009–10, he earned his first Panini sticker in Colecciones ESTE *Liga 2010–2011*.

A move to established Champions League competitors Atlético Madrid followed in the summer of 2014, but not before Griezmann had made his France debut. As that was in early March there was no place for the newcomer in Panini's *Brasil 2014* album, but he did receive a sticker in the update set further down the line. Manager Didier Deschamps trusted the novice with three starts, including in the quarter-final defeat to Germany.

Griezmann has been a mainstay for Les Bleus ever since, winning his 100th cap in 2021. A first Euro sticker came for the 2016 event hosted in France. His nation ultimately lost the final to Portugal, but their rising star did not have long to wait for redemption: France proved unstoppable in the Russia-held 2018 World Cup. Griezmann contributed four goals and several assists on the way to the French triumph.

On the domestic front, Griezmann won the Europa League and UEFA Super Cup with Atleti either side of his World Cup success and, after a brief spell at Barcelona, he returned to Madrid. Further international success came in the 2021 UEFA Nations League before another World Cup final was

Liga 2010–2011 (Colecciones ESTE)

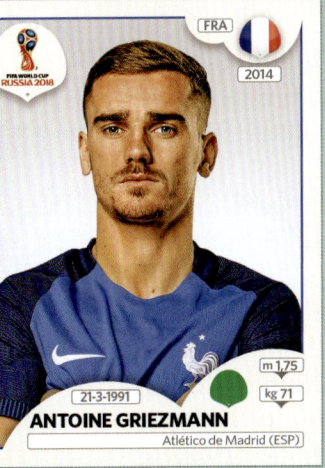

Russia 2018

Euro 2020 Preview Edition

Playing Career
Real Sociedad (2009–2014); Atlético Madrid (2014–2019); Barcelona (2019–2022); Atlético Madrid (loan) (2021–2022); Atlético Madrid (2022–) and France (2014–)

Panini Album Rookie Appearances
First club album appearance: Liga 2010–2011 (Colecciones ESTE) (Spain) (436)
First World Cup album appearance: Brasil 2014 (Update set – 389x)

Selected Panini Appearances
Liga 2010–2011 (Colecciones ESTE) (Spain) (436); Liga 2011–12 (Colecciones ESTE) (Spain) (439); Liga 2012–13 (Colecciones ESTE) (Spain) (470); Liga 2013–14 (Colecciones ESTE) (Spain) (498); Brasil 2014 (Update Set – 389x); Liga 2014–15 (Colecciones ESTE) (Spain) (495, 658); Liga 2015–16 (Colecciones ESTE) (Spain) (49); Euro 2016 (32, 42, FR–7 France Coca Cola sticker); Liga 2016–17 (Colecciones ESTE) (Spain) (117, 647); Spanish Liga 2017–18 (Colecciones ESTE) (Spain); Russia 2018 (207); Liga 2018–19 (Colecciones ESTE) (Spain) (117, 649); FIFA 365 2019 (78, 423, 425, 431); Liga 2019–20 (Colecciones ESTE) (Spain) (712); Euro 2020 Preview Edition (FRA–23, C5); Liga 2020–21 (Colecciones ESTE) (Spain) (120, 616); Euro 2020 Tournament Edition (589, 597); Liga 2021–22 (Spain) (Colecciones ESTE) (121, 713); Liga 2022–23 (Colecciones ESTE) (Spain) (91, 632, T3); Qatar 2022 (FRA–18); Liga 2023–24 (Colecciones ESTE) (Spain) (119, 615, 730, MP4)

reached in Qatar 2022, this time ending in defeat. Although he was substituted in the final by the time Mbappé set about overhauling Argentina's lead, Griezmann had enjoyed another fine tournament.

Liga 2018–19 (Colecciones ESTE)

JEAN-PIERRE PAPIN

JEAN-PIERRE PAPIN
MARSEILLE

Football 87

JEAN-PIERRE PAPIN

Foot 90

Jean-Pierre Papin was one of the star strikers of European domestic football for around a decade. Beginning his senior career in division three with INF Vichy, the young Frenchman made his first Panini appearance in *Foot 85* after moving to second division Valenciennes. The forward's mobility and eye for goal soon caught the attention of one of the leading sides in Belgium: Club Brugge. Papin was a huge hit during his only season, scoring 33 goals in all competitions to help win the Belgian Cup in 1986.

As well as receiving a first individual Panini sticker in the Belgian *Football 86*, Papin was accorded a Legend space 30 years later in the *Pro League 2016* collection. Papin's rise saw him given a first cap for France in February 1986, too late to feature in Panini's *Mexico 86* album, but in time to make the squad, scoring twice as France finished third.

A return to his homeland followed later that summer, where he enjoyed huge success with Marseille, as well as finishing top scorer in Ligue 1 five seasons in a row, from 1987–88 to 1991–92. Papin was also joint top-scorer in the 1990–91 European Cup to aid Marseille's journey to the final. While their star forward scored in the penalty shoot-out versus Red Star Belgrade, the French side went down 5-3 after a goalless draw. Despite that disappointment, Papin's contribution to club and country earned him the Ballon d'Or at the end of 1991.

A move to AC Milan then brought two *Calciatori* album appearances, including an eye-catching caricature in which he was depicted as Napoleon Bonaparte in the second of those collections. Papin's first season at the San Siro in 1992–93 was his most prolific. Those goals helped AC Milan win Serie A and reach the final of the Champions League.

Foot 91

Calciatori 1993–94

Foot 89

Fussball '95

Playing Career
INF Vichy (1981–1984); Valenciennes (1984–1985); Club Brugge (1985–1986); Marseille (1986–1992); AC Milan (1992–1994); Bayern Munich (1994–1996); Bordeaux (1996–1998); Guingamp (1998–1999); JS Saint-Pierroise (1999–2001); US Lège-Cap-Ferret (2001–2004) and France (1986–1995)

Panini Album Rookie Appearances
First club album appearance: Football 85 (France) (405)
First World Cup album appearance: N/A

Selected Panini Appearances
Football 85 (France) (405); Football 86 (Belgium) (107); Football 87 (France) (125); Football 88 (France) (158); Foot 89 (France) (140); Foot 90 (France) (140); Foot 91 (France) (101); Foot 92 (France) (1–6, 115); Euro '92 (62); Calciatori 1992–93 (Italy) (227); Foot 93 (France) (H); Calciatori 1993–94 (Italy) (183, 372); Fussball '95 (Germany) (18); Fussball 96 (Germany) (156); Foot 97 (France) (43); Foot 98 (France) (57); Champions 98 (France) (153); Foot 2008 (France) (108 – as manager); Olympique de Marseille 2010–2011 (151, P10); Pro League 2016 (Belgium) (53); Club Brugge – 125 years/jaar (2017) (19, 154)

Jean-Pierre Papin's rise in 1986 saw him receive a first cap for France and make his first individual Panini appearance in the Belgian *Football 86*.

Late heartbreak occurred in World Cup qualifying for USA 94, meaning France failed to qualify and injuries meant this was his last major tournament. Spells with Bayern Munich and Bordeaux, and appearances in their respective Panini albums followed, before Papin's career wound down in the French lower leagues.

Calciatori 1992–93

GIANFRANCO ZOLA

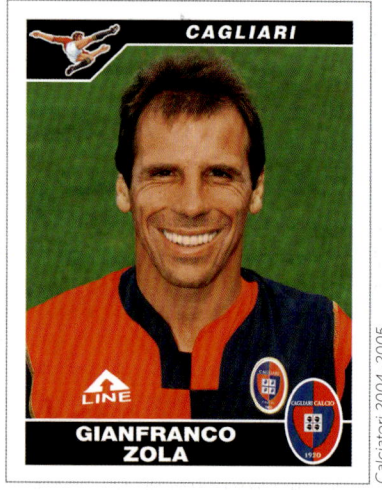

CAGLIARI

GIANFRANCO ZOLA

Calciatori 2004–2005

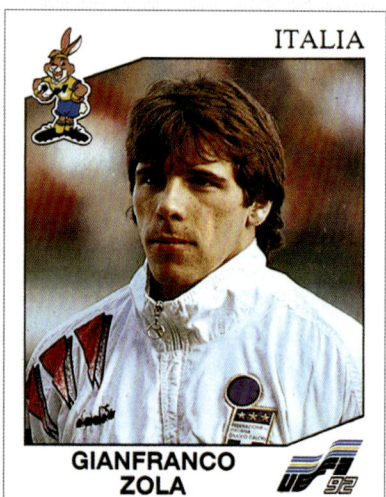

ITALIA

GIANFRANCO ZOLA

Euro '92

Gianfranco Zola experienced a long apprenticeship in the lower leagues before finally making his Serie A debut at the age of 23 with Napoli, in 1989–90. He received a first Panini *Calciatori* sticker that season, serving as Diego Mardadona's understudy as Napoli won the league. But once Maradona left he became the side's creative hub. The diminutive playmaker then joined Parma during the greatest period in its history, having won domestic and European honours in the two seasons before he arrived. Zola contributed to a European Super Cup win in 1993 and in 1994–95 a UEFA Cup final win over Juventus.

A move to Chelsea beckoned and the Oliena-born player's first four seasons at Stamford Bridge brought silverware in abundance, including two FA Cups and the 1998 Cup Winners' Cup, where he scored the winner immediately after coming off the bench.

He returned to Italy with Cagliari in 2003–04, steering them to promotion and then establishing them in Serie A before retirement in 2005. Zola earned his final playing sticker for the Sardinians, as well as his only Panini sticker as manager during a brief spell in charge of the club in 2014–15.

He appeared in Panini's *Euro '92* album, but not in the tournament, as Italy were only on standby.

Zola played all three of Italy's matches at Euro 96 and was also part of Italy's USA 94 World Cup squad (although he missed out on a Panini sticker), while, conversely, he made the *France 98* sticker album yet was not selected, a decision that persuaded him into international retirement.

NAPOLI

GIANFRANCO ZOLA

Calciatori 1989–90

NAPOLI

GIANFRANCO ZOLA

Calciatori 1991–92

GIANFRANCO ZOLA

NAPOLI

Calciatori 1992–93

GIANFRANCO ZOLA

PARMA

Calciatori 1993–94

Playing Career

Nuorese (1983–1986); Torres (1986–1989); Napoli (1989–1993); Parma (1993–1996); Chelsea (1996–2003); Cagliari (2003–2005) and Italy (1991–1997)

Panini Album Rookie Appearances

First club album appearance: *Calciatori 1989–90* (Italy) (266)
First World Cup album appearance: *France 98* (101)

Selected Panini Appearances

Calciatori 1989–90 (Italy) (266); *Calciatori 1991–92* (Italy) (239, 382); *Euro '92* (250); *Calciatori 1992–93* (Italy) (40, 238); *Calciatori 1993–94* (Italy) (222); *Calciatori 1994–95* (Italy) (274); *Supercalcio 1994–95* (Italy) (173, P21); *Calciatori 1995–96* (Italy) (224); *Supercalcio 95–96* (Italy) (148); *European Football Championship England '96* (250); *Supercalcio 96–97* (Italy) (168); *Futebol 1996–1997* (Portugal) (350); *Superplayers 98* (England) (SS, TT, P24, 360); *European Football Stars 1998* (120); *France 98* (101); *Champions League 1999/2000* (288); *Azzurro Mondiale 1910–2002* (Italy) (94); *Calciatori 2004–2005* (Italy) (95); *Calciatori in Sardegna 2004–2005* (10); *Obiettivo Campionato 2004–2005* (Italy) (11); *Calciatori 2014–2015* (Italy) (A2 – as manager); *Premier League 2022* (England) (334)

PARMA

GIANFRANCO ZOLA

Calciatori 1994–95

GIANFRANCO ZOLA

PARMA

Calciatori 1995–96

ITALIA

GIANFRANCO ZOLA

European Football Championship England '96

ZINEDINE ZIDANE

Foot 92

An elegant midfielder whose technique, vision, close control and passing were unsurpassed, Zinedine Zidane was a three-time FIFA World Player of the Year and was awarded the Ballon d'Or in 1998. After he had retired as a player, he coached Real Madrid to an array of honours, including two La Liga and three Champions League trophies.

'Zizou' began his career at Cannes and his rookie Panini club sticker appeared in *Foot 92*. Later that year he moved to Bordeaux and in 1994 earned a place in the national team, with his rookie international Panini sticker appearing in the *European Football Championship England '96* album. He moved to Juventus that same summer of 1996, where he helped them win Serie A in successive years and twice reach the Champions League final.

Foot 93

Foot 1995

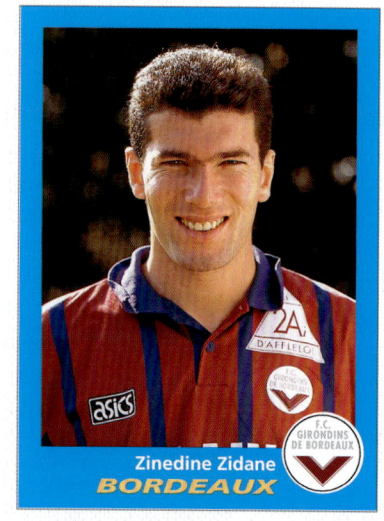

Foot 96

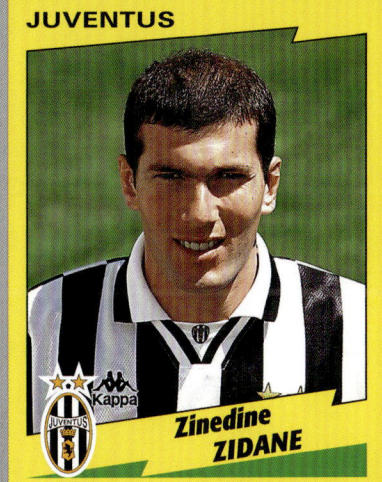

Calciatori 1996-97

France 98

Zinedine Zidane was named FIFA World Player of the Year in 1998, 2000 and 2003, and won the 1998 Ballon d'Or.

Calciatori 1997-98

Calciatori 1998-99

Calciatori 2000

Calciatori 2000-2001

After he had retired as a player, Zidane coached Real Madrid to an array of honours, including two La Liga and three Champions League trophies.

Liga 2004–2005 (Colecciones ESTE)

Champions League 2001/2002

Liga 2005–2006 (Colecciones ESTE)

European Football Championship England '96

Euro 2000

Euro 2004

Korea/Japan 2002

Germany 2006

Playing Career

Cannes (1989–92); Bordeaux (1992–96); Juventus (1996–2001); Real Madrid (2001–2006) and France (1994–2006)

Panini Album Rookie Appearances

First club album appearance: *Foot 92 (France) (43)*
First World Cup album appearance: *France 98 (164)*

Selected Panini Appearances

Foot 92 (France) (43); *Foot 93* (France) (24); *Foot 1994* (France) (34); *Foot 1995* (France) (75); *Foot 96* (France) (62); *European Football Championship England '96* (187); *Calciatori 1996–97* (Italy) (144); *Calciatori 1997–98* (Italy) (164); *France 98* (164) *Calciatori 1998–99* (Italy) (156); *Calciatori 2000* (Italy) (139); *Euro 2000* (352); *Calciatori 2000–2001* (Italy) (162); *Champions League 2000/2001* (186); *Liga 2001–2002* (Colecciones ESTE) (Spain) (207); *Champions League 2001/2002* (11); *Korea/ Japan 2002* (38); *Liga 02–03* (Colecciones ESTE) (Spain) (209); *Liga 2003–2004* (Colecciones ESTE) (Spain) (222); *Portugal 2004* (107); *Liga 2004–2005* (Colecciones ESTE) (Spain) (241); *Liga 2005–2006* (Colecciones ESTE) (Spain) (260); *Germany 2006* (467); *Foot 2007* (France) (561–570); *Calciatori 2010–11* (Italy) (Top Team Panini 50) (X7); *Liga 2015–16* (Colecciones ESTE) (Spain) (731 – shared with Eusebio Sacristán, Real Sociedad) (as manager); *Liga 2016–17* (Colecciones ESTE) (Spain) (26 – as manager); *Liga 2017–18* (Colecciones ESTE) (Spain) (30 – as manager); *Calciatori 2021* (Italy) (Top Team Panini 60) (X15); *FIFA 365 2024* (437)

Zidane then became one of Real Madrid's Galácticos, signing for a world record fee of £46.6 million in 2001. A stunning volley won his side the Champions League final against Bayer Leverkusen in his first season and the team went on to win La Liga the following year.

The midfield orchestrator scored two goals as France won the World Cup final in 1998 and was Player of the Tournament when they won Euro 2000. He also played in the 2002 World Cup, Euro 2004 and the 2006 World Cup, his appearance in the final of the latter ending his playing career.

FRANZ BECKENBAUER

FRANZ BECKENBAUER

Calciatori 1966–67

Grandi club · BAYERN M. · Germania Ov
FRANZ BECKENBAUER
nato a Monaco di Bav. il 12-8-1945

Calciatori 1967–68

Franz Beckenbauer, also known as *Der Kaiser* (The Emperor) for his refined style, dominance and leadership on the field, is one of the greatest players the game of football has known. He is credited with developing a new aspect to the *libero* (sweeper) role, thanks to his ability to bring the ball out of defence, and has appeared in more than 30 Panini albums.

Beckenbauer made his club debut with Bayern Munich in 1964 and went on to win numerous honours, including captaining the side to three successive European Cups between 1974 and 1976. At international level, he played an important role in helping the West German team reach the World Cup final in 1966 and a third-place finish in 1970. He then led the squad to victory as captain in the 1972 European Championship and, after winning the 1974 World Cup, West Germany became the first European national team to hold both titles simultaneously.

In 1977 Beckenbauer headed to the other side of the Atlantic, where he spent four seasons with New York Cosmos until 1980. He returned in 1983 and in between had a spell back on home turf with Hamburger SV, helping them to win another Bundesliga.

Beckenbauer's first Panini appearances came in 1966–67, following his eye-catching 1966 World Cup tournament, and he was honoured with a special section in the German *Fussball 85* album, for which he wrote the introduction and was afforded a large selection of his stickers. After playing retirement he also appeared in a Panini album as West Germany's manager – *Euro 88* – in between steering his nation to both the Mexico 86 and Italia 90 World Cup finals, winning the latter.

FRANZ
BECKENBAUER

BRD

WM 74

München 74

Playing Career

Bayern Munich (1964–1977);
New York Cosmos (1977–1980);
Hamburger SV (1980–1982); New
York Cosmos (1983) and West
Germany (1965–1977)

Panini Album
Rookie Appearances

First club album appearance:
Calciatori 1966–67 (Italy) (449)
First World Cup album appearance:
Mexico 70 (278)

Selected Panini
Appearances

Calciatori 1966–67 (Italy) (449);
Campioni dello Sport 1966–67
(Italy) (172); *Calciatori 1967–68* (Italy)
(601); *Calciatori 1968–69* (Italy)
(595); *Mexico 70* (278); *Fotboll 72*
(Sweden) (Williams Förlags/Panini)
(156); *Football 1972–73* (Belgium)
(323); *Football 73* (UK) (Top Sellers/
Panini) (198); *Fotboll 73* (Sweden)
(Williams Förlags/Panini) (234); *OK
VIP (1973)* (Italy) (162); *Campioni dello
Sport 1973–74* (Italy) (110); *München
74* (89); *Calciatori 1975–76* (Italy)
(619); *Football 76* (France) (353); *Euro
Football (1976–77)* (46); *Argentina 78*
(31); *Football 80* (France) (572 to 575);
Europa 80 (16); *Fussball 85* (Germany)
(344–356); *Football 87* (UK) (293 – as
manager); *Euro 88* (51 – as manager);
Fussball 91 (Germany) (405 – as
manager); *Panini Supergol 2000*
(Israel) (393); *Champions of Europe
1955–2005* (10)

STORIA DELLE COPPE — BAYERN M.

FRANZ BECKENBAUER

Calciatori 1968–69

DEUTSCHLAND

FRANZ
BECKENBAUER

1970

Mexico 70

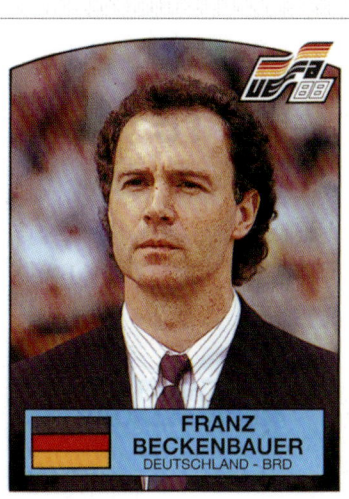

FRANZ
BECKENBAUER
DEUTSCHLAND - BRD

Euro 88

GIANLUCA VIALLI

Euro 88

Calciatori 1981–82

Gianluca Vialli's Panini career spanned his playing days, from the early 1980s to the late 1990s. His rookie sticker, shared with Mario Nicolini, appeared in *Calciatori 1981–82*, when he was playing for newly promoted Serie B side Cremonese. In 1983–84, the Italian forward scored 10 league goals to help secure another promotion for the club, but as one of his country's most exciting prospects he then moved to Sampdoria.

The new signing made himself an instant favourite in his first campaign there by scoring six goals in the 1985 Coppa Italia – including the third in a 3-1 aggregate final win over AC Milan – as Sampdoria won the trophy for the first time. Just a few years' later Vialli was a regular of the national team set-up, earning him a place as the main cover star on *Calciatori 1987–88* – he was shown leaving West Germany's Pierre Littbarski on the floor in an April 1987 friendly clash.

Then in 1990, his seven goals – including the two in extra-time to defeat Anderlecht in the final – led Sampdoria to Cup Winners' Cup victory and the knockout specialists proved their mettle over the long haul in 1990–91 when they carried off the Serie A title in fine style, with Vialli's 19 goals making him the league's top scorer. He was again instrumental as Sampdoria reached the following season's European Cup final, scoring six goals along the way to the Wembley meeting with Barcelona. There would be no fairytale ending in his last game for the club, however, when he was substituted not long before Ronald Koeman's free-kick winner for the Spanish side.

Calciatori 1984–85

Calciatori 1985–86

Calciatori 1993–94

Calciatori 1995–96

Playing Career
Cremonese (1980–1984); Sampdoria (1984–1992); Juventus (1992–1996); Chelsea (1996–1999) and Italy (1985–1992)

Panini Album Rookie Appearances
First club album appearance:
Calciatori 1981–82 (Italy) (367)
First World Cup album appearance:
Italia '90 (54)

Selected Panini Appearances
Calciatori 1981–82 (Italy) (367); Calciatori 1982–83 (Italy) (442); Calciatori 1983–84 (Italy) (429); Calciatori 1984–85 (Italy) (247); Calciatori 1985–86 (Italy) (236); Supercalcio 1985–86 (Italy) (175) Calciatori 1986–87 (Italy) (254); Calciatori 1987–88 (Italy) (259); Euro 88 (97); Calciatori 1988–89 (Italy) (311); Foot 89 (France) (387); Calciatori 1989–90 (Italy) (297); Italia '90 (54); Calciatori 1990–91 (Italy) (316); Calciatori 1991–92 (Italy) (296, 378); Euro '92 (252); Calciatori 1992–93 (Italy) (37, 186); Calciatori 1993–94 (Italy) (133); Calciatori 1994–95 (Italy) (173); Calciatori 1995–96 (Italy) (130); Supercalcio 1995–96 (Italy) (134); The Official PFA Collection '97 (England) (258); Superplayers 98 (England) (330); Juventus 2000 (130); Azzurro Mondiale 1910–2002 (Italy) (77, N4)

Vialli appeared playing for Italy on the cover of the *Calciatori 1987–88* album.

Following his move to Juventus, five major honours were won over the course of four seasons, including an elusive Champions League in his final campaign of 1995–96. By then 32, there was still time for a playing swansong in England at Chelsea, where he featured in Panini collections for the 1996–97 and 1997–98 seasons. He also appeared in Panini's *Euro 88* album, was selected for UEFA's Team of the Tournament for that competition, and made the *Italia '90* World Cup album, too.

Euro '92

HONOURABLE MENTIONS

If I get a Panini sticker every time I am asked: 'Why isn't [insert name of all-time great footballer] in this book?', I suspect that in no time at all I will have enough to complete an album. Selecting the players for this anthology was a pleasurable process, yet also full of regrets over those who missed the cut. When it comes to explaining their omissions, those lamented absentees fall into several categories.

As Panini's output in the 1960s was restricted to Italian releases, legends whose careers were largely played before the wider output from the 1970s lack sticker coverage: Alfredo Di Stéfano, Ferenc Puskás, Garrincha, Jimmy Greaves, Sir Stanley Matthews, Denis Law, Lev Yashin, Eusébio – to name but a few.

In terms of women's football, any player whose career was over by the time of the first Panini World Cup album in 2011 had no chance of featuring on a sticker: Mia Hamm, Michelle Akers, Kristine Lilly, Hege Riise and Sun Wen among the most celebrated. England's Kelly Smith could have made the 2011 World Cup collection, but a licensing issue forced her to miss out and then by the time of Canada 2015 she had retired from international duty. Conversely, Abby Wambach, Nadine Angerer and Caroline Seger did get to play during the Panini era and are a trio of the more recent big names unlucky to miss out.

British-based players for whom most, if not all, of their career was played between 1993–94 and 2018–19 suffered from a lack of Panini stickers as the Modena-founded company didn't have the Premier League licence during that period – Steven Gerrard, Paul Scholes, Ryan Giggs, Ashley Cole, Rio Ferdinand, Sol Campbell and John Terry are just a few of the leading lights over that period.

Some of today's rising stars are likely to stake an undeniable claim for inclusion over the years ahead should a second volume be published. Vinícius Júnior, Jude Bellingham and Bukayo Saka all earned rookie Panini World Cup stickers in 2022 and will hope to make an even bigger impact at the 2026 World Cup. Similarly, Aitana Bonmatí, Salma Paralluelo and Mary Earps starred in the 2023 Women's World Cup and have a lot more to offer in the years to come.

There's a surfeit of Barcelona and Real Madrid luminaries in the book (nearly 30 players have represented one or the other, sometimes even both), so all-timers such as Xavi, Gerard Piqué, Iker Casillas and Emilio Butragueño missed out... but who of those representing those clubs should have been dropped to make way for them? Similarly, Brazilians feature regularly, so compatriots Kaká, Cafu, Sócrates, Rivaldo et al have lost out.

Pre- or early-Panini World Cup stars like Just Fontaine, Sir Geoff Hurst and Jairzinho would also have had strong claims if they had a few more stickers to their names. So to fans and family members of all those players: apologies, and be in no doubt that they – and many others – would have greatly enriched *Panini Legends*.

MARIO ALBERTO KEMPES

Argentina 78

VASILIJ RATS

Mexico 86

IAN RUSH

Calciatori 1987–88

XHERDAN SHAQIRI

Brasil 2014

GERD MÜLLER

München 74

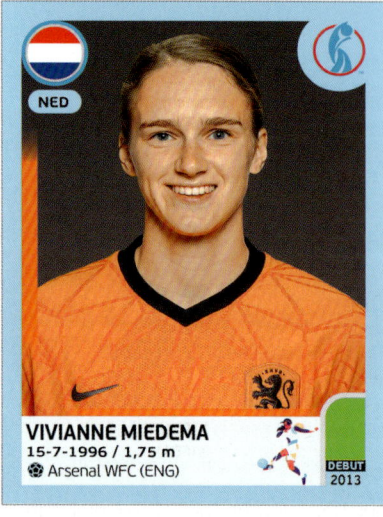

VIVIANNE MIEDEMA
15-7-1996 / 1,75 m
Arsenal WFC (ENG)
DEBUT 2013

Euro 2022

ALI DAEI

Germany 2006

LUCY BRONZE
Manchester City WFC (ENG)
1,72 m   28-10-1991
DEBUT 2013

Euro 2017

BETH MEAD

One England (2023)

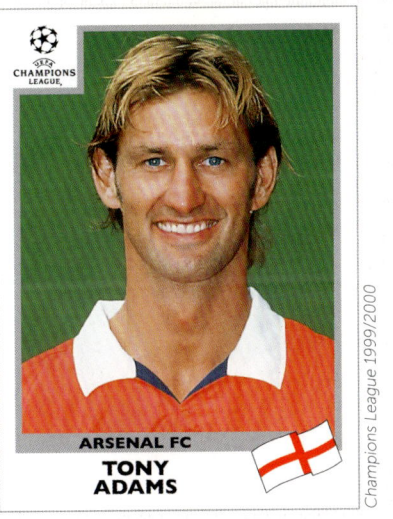

Champions League 1999/2000

ARSENAL FC
TONY ADAMS

Panini's World Cup sticker collection is sold in more than 100 countries worldwide. Panini's album for the 2026 tournament will be its 15th World Cup sticker album release.

NOR
ADA STOLSMO HEGERBERG
Olympique Lyonnais (FRA)
1,76 m 10-7-1995 DEBUT 2011

Euro 2017

Birgit Prinz
Deutschland

Germany 2011

ARSENAL
DAVID O'LEARY

Football 78

USA

LANDON DONOVAN

Germany 2006

Carli Lloyd
USA

Germany 2011

MEXICO **HUGO SANCHEZ**

USA '94

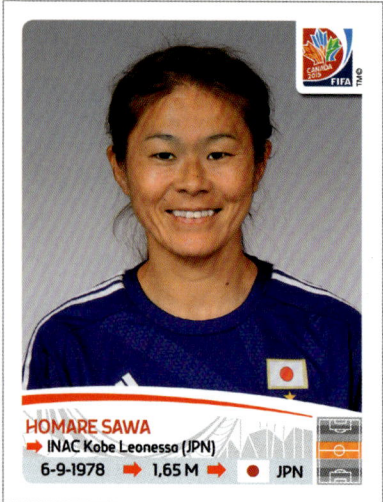

HOMARE SAWA
➡ INAC Kobe Leonessa (JPN)
6-9-1978 ➡ 1,65 M ➡ ● JPN

Canada 2015

Hope Solo

USA

Germany 2011

ALAN SHEARER
BLACKBURN ROVERS

Football '93

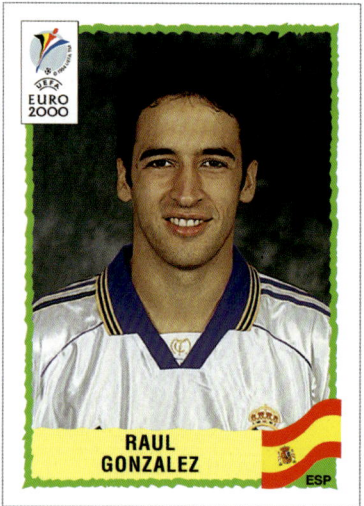

RAUL GONZALEZ
ESP

Euro 2000

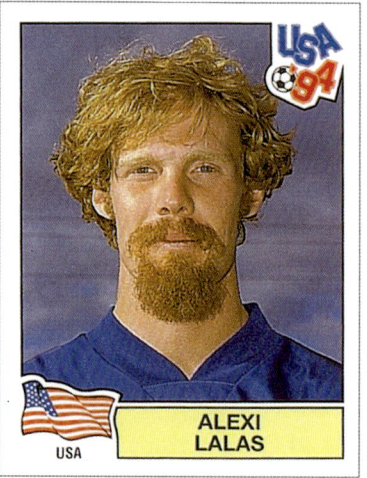

ALEXI LALAS
USA

USA '94

ZBIGNIEW BONIEK
POLSKA

España 82

DAVID SEAMAN

European Football Championship England '96

ROMELU LUKAKU
Manchester United FC (ENG)
13-5-1993 · m 1,90 · kg 93

Russia 2018

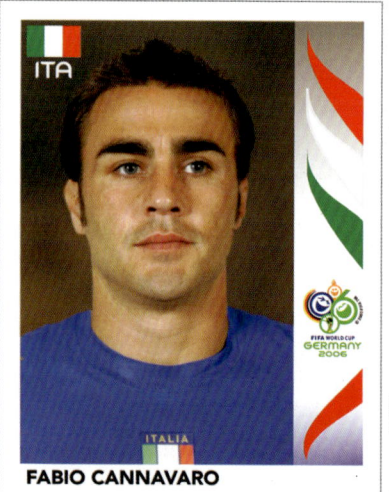

FABIO CANNAVARO

Germany 2006

Sam Kerr
Australia

Germany 2011

ESPAÑA 82

**MARCO
TARDELLI**
ITALIA

España 82

URU
2008

EDINSON CAVANI
Paris Saint-Germain (FRA)

14-2-1987   m 1,84   kg 71

Russia 2018

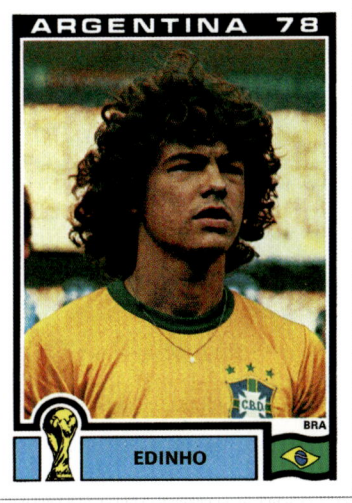

ARGENTINA 78

EDINHO
BRA

Argentina 78

BRASIL

ROBERTO CARLOS

2002 FIFA WORLD CUP

Korea/Japan 2002

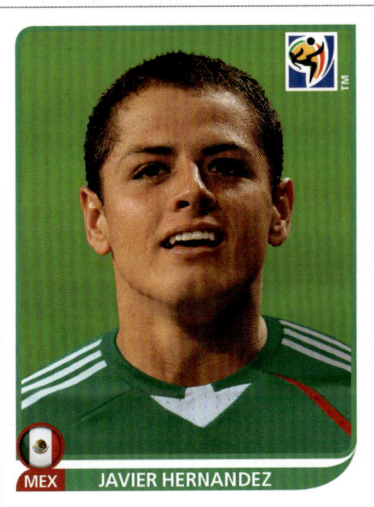

MEX   JAVIER HERNANDEZ

South Africa 2010

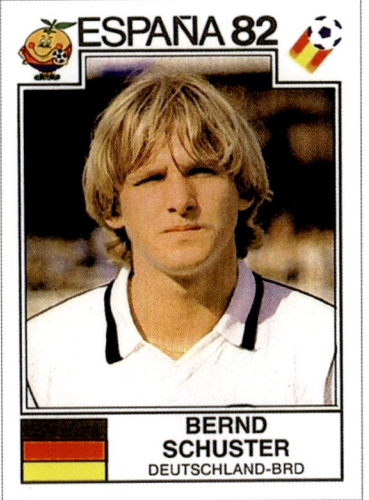

ESPAÑA 82

**BERND
SCHUSTER**
DEUTSCHLAND-BRD

España 82

The Panini logo is a knight because Giuseppe Panini (one of the four brothers who ran the business) loved riddles and puzzles and invented his own crosswords under the pseudonym 'The Knight'.

FRA FRANCK RIBERY

South Africa 2010

ÖSTERREICH

ANTON POLSTER

Italia '90

POR

DECO

Germany 2006

GER

MICHAEL BALLACK

Germany 2006

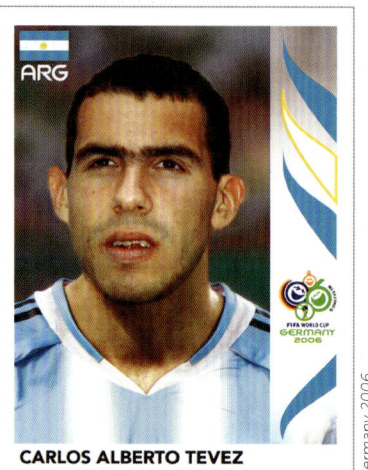

ARG

CARLOS ALBERTO TEVEZ

Germany 2006

ESPAÑA 82

ZICO
BRASIL

España 82

Panini's Calciatori **album, covering Italian domestic football, is the longest-running football collection in the world, celebrating its 63rd consecutive edition during the 2023—24 season.**

ESP DAVID SILVA

South Africa 2010

ANDREAS BREHME

DEUTSCHLAND-BRD

Italia '90

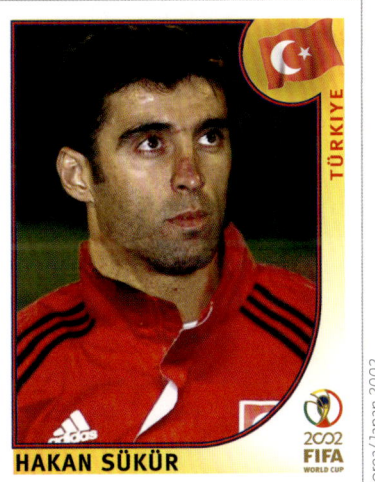

TÜRKIYE

HAKAN SÜKÜR

Korea/Japan 2002

JAPAN

JUNICHI INAMOTO

Korea/Japan 2002

NORTHERN IRELAND

NORMAN WHITESIDE

Mexico 86

USA

TONY MEOLA

Italia '90

NED — NIGEL DE JONG

South Africa 2010

ESPAÑA 82

OSVALDO CARLOS ARDILES

ARGENTINA

España 82

ENGLAND

CHRIS WADDLE

Italia '90

ARGENTINA 78

ARCHIE GEMMILL

SCO

Argentina 78

The first player represented on a Panini card (as they were at the outset) was Italy and Internazionale midfielder Bruno Bolchi, printed on 27 August 1961.

JAMES RODRÍGUEZ

Brasil 2014

MICHAEL OWEN

Korea/Japan 2002

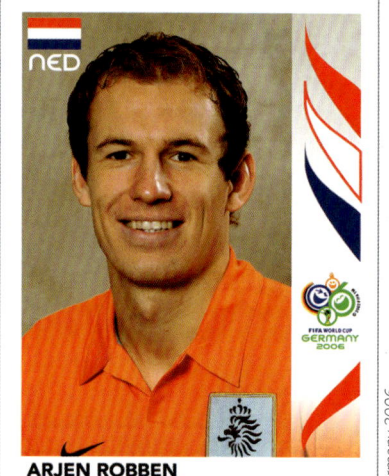

ARJEN ROBBEN

Germany 2006

USA
ERIC WYNALDA

Italia '90

HRISTO STOICHKOV
BULGARIA

USA '94

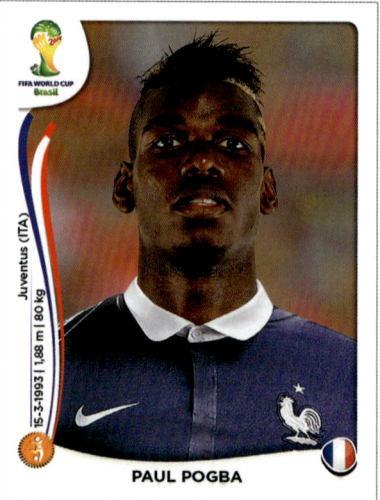

PAUL POGBA

Brasil 2014

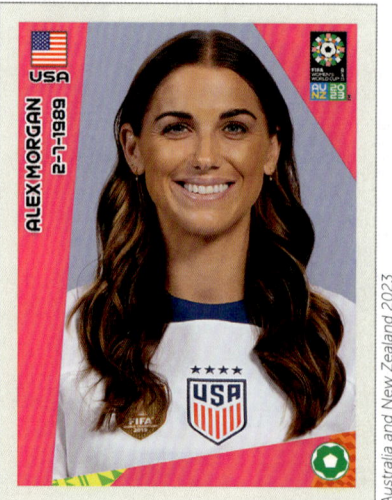

ALEX MORGAN

Australia and New Zealand 2023

ITALIA

BRUNO CONTI

Italia '90

BRA
2010

PHILIPPE COUTINHO

12-6-1992

m 1,71

kg 68

FC Barcelona (ESP)

Russia 2018

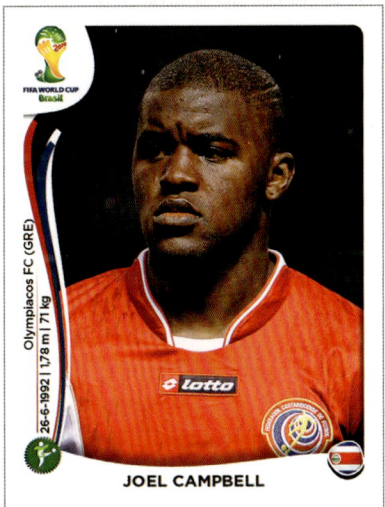

Olympiacos FC (GRE)

26-6-1992 | 1,78 m | 71 kg

JOEL CAMPBELL

Brasil 2014

SWE

FREDRIK LJUNGBERG

Germany 2006

BELGIQUE-BELGIË

JAN CEULEMANS

Mexico 86

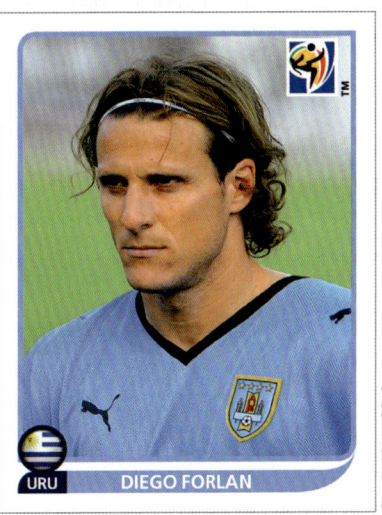

URU

DIEGO FORLAN

South Africa 2010

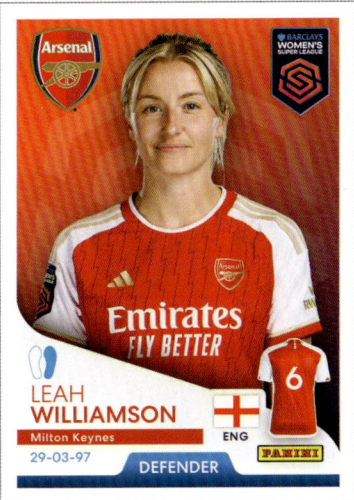

LEAH WILLIAMSON

Milton Keynes

ENG
6

29-03-97

DEFENDER

PANINI

Women's Super League 2024

ROMANIA

GHEORGHE HAGI

Italia '90

COLOMBIA

CARLOS ALBERTO VALDERRAMA

Italia '90